The Church Beyond The Congregation

The Church Beyond
The Congregation

James Thwaites

paternoster
press

Copyright © 1999

First published in 1999 by Paternoster Press
Revised edition published in 2000, reprinted 2001

07 06 05 04 03 02 01   8 7 6 5 4 3 2

Paternoster Press is an imprint of Paternoster Publishing,
P.O. Box 300, Carlisle, Cumbria, CA3 0QS, UK

Website – www.paternoster-publishing.com

The right of James Thwaites to be identified as the Author of this
Work has been asserted by him in accordance with the Copyright,
Designs and Patents Act 1988.

British Library Cataloguing in Publication Data
A catalogue record for this book is available from the British Library

ISBN 1-84227-040-0

Unless otherwise stated, Scripture quotations are taken from the
New American Standard Bible
© The Lockman Foundation

Cover Design by Campsie
Typeset by WestKey Ltd., Falmouth, Cornwall
Printed in Great Britain by
Cox and Wyman Ltd., Reading, Berkshire

Contents

James Thwaites, is the Director of the Biblical Studies Faculty of Hillsong, Australia, and lectures regularly at colleges and conferences. He has been in pastoral ministry for over 20 years and is currently co-leading a joint congregation in Sydney, which is a partnership between Assemblies of God and Methodist (Uniting) congregations. James also works with business and health networks, equipping Christians in those spheres with a theology of work derived from the Hebrew worldview. He also trains ministry gifts of Christ to resource and release the saints to engage and impact their cities through working life.

Since the first publication in 1999 many church and workplace leaders have taken up this book with great enthusiasm. James Thwaites makes a dynamic contribution to the current discussion on the nature and purpose of the church in the 21st century by encompassing creation into his theology of life and work.

His vision of the church is of one that is a very part of marriage, family life and work and not just confined to a building. He explores strategies for societal engagement and provides an in-depth exposition of the Hebrew worldview, raising many issues that need to be pursued if we are going to be an effective body of God's people in his world today.

Preface

A few years after giving my life to Christ in 1976 I began to hear about the Hebrew worldview. The little I gleaned at that time convinced me that it contained the remedy to the version of Greek dualism I had been struggling with as a Pentecostal Christian. I pursued the study of the Hebrew vision a little at that time, but soon the demands of pastoring a church overtook that search and so its treasure for me remained mostly buried.

Many years, trends and multiple conferences later, I began to look with increasing frustration at the shortcomings of the Sunday event and the growing competition between churches. In particular I realised that in both my own and other church settings the incredible allocation of resources was not producing many saints able to impact their world. In times of reflection I would often think, 'I did not sign up for this'. God had called me to bring the saints to maturity, but increasingly I wondered if a lot of what I was doing and saying might in fact be having the opposite effect. The 'gift' of desperation – that which moves many to discover things which otherwise they would never have looked for – was mine!

During this time it was the new Christians who began to call my name and ask me to stand with them to equip them for their work. Their observations and questions were telling and I was in the mood to listen. They asked me why the local church demanded so much of their time and energy and in return gave so little back to them. They wanted to know why the work of the local church was deemed to be more important than their everyday life and work. With a heart now tuned by that gift of desperation, I responded. I was ready to concede that these brave new saints, as irreverent and insensitive in relation to ecclesiastical realities as they might appear to be, had a point!

I began to spend more time ministering and resourcing them in the context of their working life. It was great to be a novice again, learning to serve and build up the saints in, what were for me, unfamiliar fields. The results, in terms of maturity and substance (in both my own and their lives), surprised and drew me further down that track. Also at that time books written by John Dawson (*Taking Our Cities for God*) and Ed Silvoso (*That None Should Perish*) called me onward and gave me a larger vision of the church. These men stirred my heart to know that something more life-encompassing was in the traumatic winds of change coming over society and the church.

It was then that I began to hunger for more of the Hebrew vision. I knew that methods were good, principles were great and truths were essential, but all of these held together in accordance with the way the individual saw their world. The best I could do for people in equipping them to live and work with impact was to give them the worldview given by God. So I began to research and then apply the Hebrew vision in a thorough way to my understanding of Scripture. As discoveries were made I allowed them to influence both the gatherings of the saints and our ministry to those in work settings. Those years were far from ideal; there was trauma for many in the changes that came, but these changes for me and for others were bearing the kind of fruit that I had signed up for!

With so many things colliding to create and destroy at this time, it is good to be travelling an ancient and God-given road into the future. The further I have travelled down that road, the more I have become convinced that the Hebrew vision of reality is a necessary ally for the body of Christ at this time. Over time the questions and frustrations that moved me to commence researching and writing have continued to increase in the church at large. My prayer and my confidence is that the vision of the heavens and the earth that God spent thousands of years developing in the hearts and minds of his chosen people will, at this time, find a place in believers made by his hands and indwelt by his Spirit.

Before I sign off here and reintroduce myself as a writer, a brief outline of the book is in order.

The book is divided into four sections. The first section looks at where our current thinking and church structure come from. It details the history and development of the Christian and Western mind and the influence of the Greek worldview on this. It then looks at the large creation context God put in place for the church and contrasts it with the congregation-focused pattern we currently hold to. Finally it examines the postmodern world and the opportunities it gives us to re-evaluate our understanding of the way in which God comes to, and exists in, the world (divine revelation).

The second section looks in detail at the Hebrew worldview and then applies its vision to the creation reality, the Fall, divine revelation and the incarnation. This is somewhat of a theological and philosophical section and may in places be difficult to wade through. That being said, the Hebrew worldview is far from unintelligible. For those who press on to gain an understanding of it the rewards are many and great! For those who find over-much philosophy and theology not to be their cup of tea, there is a brief summary of the Hebrew worldview at the end of this section.

The third section looks at the application of the Hebrew worldview to Christian life and church strategy. We travel to the church of the New Testament era and see how Spirit-filled Hebrew saints like Paul followed the plan set out by Jesus. There we see the way in which the body of Christ emerged to substantially transform and reach its immediate world within three centuries of the resurrection. This section includes a chapter on the nature of the church gathering and a chapter that looks at the place of revival in the light of the divine strategy.

The fourth section takes up the Hebrew worldview and through its vision of creation looks at the nature and purpose of the saints' paid and unpaid work. The daily work of the saints, relatively overlooked by the church at present, will, I believe, become the front line of our engagement of the postmodern society. In these chapters we will see the Hebrew vision open up the powerful and strategic place of all work in the eternal purpose of God.

A note in relation to the communication style of the book. I have used gender-inclusive language wherever possible but there are occasions where, for the sake of good English style, this has not been appropriate. My approach is to gradually paint a portrait of the Hebrew worldview, putting down several layers (historical, biblical, philosophical, anecdotal) to bring it up to full-colour presentation. Once the painting is on the canvas and the creation context in place, I then draw out principles from Scripture and history relating to New Testament church strategy and the saints' working life. The Hebrew worldview is seen before it is understood. To put it in another way – when reading this book it is more important initially to get the picture than it is to get the point. This is the case with most things in life. It is certainly the case in a postmodern media-oriented era – not to mention the fact that it is also the main way in which the Bible communicates truth.

This book is predominantly about the saints as individuals, in relationship with others, engaging life and work in a postmodern time. As we know, the saints are the church. God is at work to raise up and empower them to forge and form a church able to speak into and impact a postmodern world. For this reason the saints are not only the focus of this book, they are the hope of all glory!

James Thwaites
February 1999

THE LANDSCAPE

PART I

Chapter 1

The Church Landscape

The society that Christians live and work in has in recent times taken on a new description. It's being called 'postmodern'. In a postmodern world the very foundations of Western thinking are crumbling and a new way of constructing reality is emerging. People no longer put their faith in the promises of science. They are turning away from absolutes and searching out their own spiritual, social and emotional paths in life. For many of these seekers of truth the church holds no answers, only old creeds and dogmas. How can the saints relate to, let alone reach, these people with the message of the kingdom? Apart from such concerns believers also face a fast-moving, stress-filled, market-oriented world. So many things in their life and faith are changing. Is it any wonder they question where they and their church can make a stand in this postmodern age of unreason?

Mike Regele, the American church commentator, describes the challenge facing us in this way:

> Again we find ourselves not knowing how to be the church, because we don't quite know how we are supposed to live in the world. As of now a new paradigm (of church) has not emerged with clarity. It may not occur in our lifetime. But we

know that what has been will be no longer. (*Death of the Church*, p. 195f.)

When we survey the landscape we see a dying process at work in many streams of the church. We also, thankfully, see new life and renewal emerging. In this renewal many are reaching for something more than what they have seen and done in the past 30 years. Rather than just looking for some new management structure or marketing strategy they are looking for something deeper, more far-reaching, to emerge. Certain church leaders believe that even when revival comes it will be different from that experienced by Wesley, Whitefield and Finney. They believe that the present work of the Spirit in renewal and revival is meant to accomplish much more than simply filling meetings with people.

One young megachurch leader expressed it this way:

> In my spirit I am hearing a sound that I know is calling for a radical change to the way we do church. I cannot yet work out what it's calling for, but I do know that what we will be doing and saying in the future will not be the same as what we said and did in the past. Much of this change will happen for us outside of the walls of our church and our one-and-a-half hour Sunday meetings.

What kind of church and what kind of Christian will emerge for a postmodern time? At this point in time we may not know all there is to know about the church of the future, but I believe we can begin to envisage what it might look like. In many ways we are already crossing the border into a new expression of the church. Whether we plan it or not, whether we like it or not, we are being moved by divine providence and cultural necessity into a new landscape. This is what the dying is for and this is what the renewal is about.

Postmodern Premise

The reason we can engage in such a process at this time brings us to the major premise of this book. My conviction is that the postmodern period gives the Christian and the church the ability to come out from under centuries of Greek influence and take hold of the worldview God intended us to have all along. That worldview is the one given by God to the Hebrew people. It is the vision of life carried forward by Jesus and Paul and it formed the foundation and set the context for all that they said and did.

The Greek worldview divided the spiritual realm from the created realm; the Hebrew worldview unites them. The Greek vision of reality has made the church something separate from much of the saints' life and work; the Hebrew worldview brings these back together under one divine strategy and eternal purpose. The Greek paradigm has confused our understanding of the way in which God comes to, and exists in, our world; the Hebrew vision clears a way through that will enable the revelation of God to engage every facet and dimension of our life in creation. The Hebrew vision of life has the ability to accomplish this. It has the clear vision we need if we are to see change come at this critical time.

This transition, if it is to be successful, will involve us in a re-evaluation of our present congregation-focused approach to church life. This, I believe, is long overdue. In spite of all the changes we have seen in our society in the past 30 to 40 years we, as saints, still remain focused on the building, the meetings and the programmes we call 'church'. If the saints are to strongly engage and light up their world then our containment in the local church (or local cell) must be reviewed. In this I don't want to undermine the powerful place of the gathering. Rather I want to explore and discover the strategic place it might begin to occupy at this time in history.

Saints in every nation are being challenged to be reconciled to the original inhabitants of their lands. In this process there is a growing restoration of the body of Christ to the land or, to use another term, to the creation. Romans 8 says that the creation cries out for the sons to come. To this day the cry from deep within every thing and every heart is sounding out to the body of Christ to give its answer. We are being called back from rationalism and a spirituality that is set over and against much of life to strongly engage the creation that is our inheritance.

The Hebrew worldview resides at the very core of our heritage as the body of Christ. It is the over-reaching and indigenous nature of its vision of life and creation that can ignite and fulfil the created purpose within every tribe and nation. Its sight and its sound will enable the body of Christ to see into and call forth the blessing of every land in answer to the cry of a waiting creation. It can make a way for the already emerging church to fully live and work with impact in a postmodern era.

Before we proceed, I want to introduce you to George, the church elder.

> ### GEORGE THE ELDER (1)
> #### The trouble with George

Reluctantly George flicked off the last light switch. He stood for a moment in the darkened church. Everything was in order; there was no reason to stay any longer. He was about to walk out, but something in the back of his mind told him there was more that needed attention before he could go. Pale beams of moonlight filtered through the stained glass windows onto a photo hanging over the welcome table. It was of Pastor Steve. The photo was leaning slightly to the right. George walked over and straightened it, pleased that he could adjust one more thing. He stood staring at the friendly face for some time. The twinge of some unidentified emotion held him there looking at the smile. He frowned, felt a little puzzled and then the feeling passed.

George walked out the front door and closed it hard behind him. Then he stopped and stood, looking up and down the empty street. He decided to take a quick look down the side of the building. Nothing was there that needed his attention. The car park, except for the one car, was empty. George thought to himself 'All is as it ought to be' and wondered briefly what that meant. The truth was that George didn't want to leave. 'But I'd better go,' he told himself as he began to walk across the almost empty lot. He got into his car, turned on his mobile through force of habit and placed the key in the ignition. Turn, fire, accelerate – the sound of the engine pushed aside his reflections as he headed out into the night. Four streetlights later, the phone rang.

'George here,' he said in a slightly anointed but business-like tone.

'Where are you darling?'

In the background George could hear the wail of his newborn. 'Hi, sweetheart. I'm, uh, just leaving church.'

'Will you be long?'

'Long?' said George, stalling for time. There was no reply. 'No sweetness, I'll be home soon. Is everything OK?'

'Baby's just fine, and I'm having a wonderful time,' his wife answered with an edge to her voice that George knew well.

'I'll be there soon; want me to get anything?'

'Milk, bread and you would be great.'

'Fine honey, see you soon.'

'Great,' he thought, 'now I'm on a countdown, the clock's ticking, Rebecca's waiting and it'll be my turn for

the baby. I'll have no time to work out . . .' George reached
for the next words and finally came up with, *'the plan. The
plan! God, will you give me a plan? Give me some direction
here.'* George had searched all day for the answer. He had
looked for it in the first service, in every song and sentence
in the sermon. He looked for it in the exhortation before the
evening offering, even in the prayers of the King James
crew. But he had found nothing. It was Sunday night. He
was expected home for baby duty but there was still no plan
for Monday morning.

He addressed himself firmly. *'OK George, let's get a handle on this one.'* He began with some up-beat self talk. *'I
sure drew that line! Right there in front of those Divisional
Managers. It was God, Elijah, Daniel and me on one side
and mammon, Ahab, corporate lions and them on the
other. I can still see their faces, angry, confused, jealous. But
hey, what could I do? I had to draw the line.'*

He was sounding good and feeling better, but George's
attention had wandered too far. A corner came up that he
wasn't ready for and he hit the brakes so hard the car almost
ground to a halt. The positive flow stagnated and George's
heart plummeted down like a runaway elevator. It was then
that the dread really hit him. *'Monday, what will I say, what
will I do?'* George got scared, really scared. His life was
moving along that road towards one of those few defining
moments. Everything – job, money, family, church – his
whole future was on the line and he had no answer, no plan
and no word from anyone or anywhere.

His thoughts raced around in his brain, searching for any
kind of positive confession to rescue him. An image of the
pulpit raced in. It was Pastor Steve, preaching strong,
decided and anointed. George latched on to the pulpit in an
attempt to make his way out of the dread. He pressed down
on the accelerator pedal and the car began to pick up speed.
'Talk about drawing the line, now wasn't that Word on-line

tonight? The one about the rhino and the pin. Out of the cave into the harvest. Pastor sure knows how to turn a phrase and make it stick.'

From this vision of the pulpit George turned to face the congregation. As soon as he saw the crowd, the Elder in him began the Elder's commentary. 'Good strong night, a reasonable offering, musicians finally got the balance right. One recommitment, no one saved. Peter and Felicity weren't there again and neither was Roger. That's three weeks and I haven't seen or heard anything from them.' From here George's report began to trail off and down. The pulpit was anointed and strong but the rest of the church was far too fragile to build a base from which to launch Monday's battle. George snapped his mind to attention and demanded some focus. The problem was, there was nothing to focus on. So after a few moments his mind rebelled and turned on the imagination screen. George followed, inquisitive, wondering if the plan might emerge from there.

In his imagination he could see Rob, his CEO, in the back row of the church. He could hear him yelling out in the middle of the sermon. 'We've gotta pull together on this one boys. It'll only be for a few months. By that time the China push will pay off and we'll be out of the woods.' Pastor Steve didn't seem to hear him, nor could anyone else, just George. Time to take up the offering. The bag was getting closer to Rob. George knew how much money he had in his wallet. But when it arrived all Rob did was gaze down into the scarlet-red sock. He did this for so long that the offering song had to be sung again. Suddenly Rob looked up and yelled, 'Market share is diminishing. Asia is the region of growth. Get on with it or get out.' No one paid any attention. He passed the sock to George and said, 'Wear it'. George was about to count the money, but he knew nothing was there. At this point George turned off the 9:20 pm day-

dream. His imagination may have had a vision but he didn't have a clue what it meant.

'I can't go home yet,' George said to himself as he pulled into a service station to buy the bread and milk. 'Rebecca doesn't even know about this. I couldn't tell her,' George said to the car as he got back in. He then extended the conversation to include his conscience. 'Don't want to worry her before I've got a plan.' Conscience replied, as conscience does, 'She's expecting you soon.' So George rehearsed his homecoming. 'It took so long to find a shop on a Sunday night that sold milk, honey.' The simile of the Promised Land to cover his white lie amused him, but he doubted Rebecca would think it was funny. 'Won't be long darling,' he said to Rebecca, 'this is for both of us.' Then he turned to the dashboard for support and said, 'Let's go to the lookout – get a plan.'

George pulled into the lookout. There was only one light in the parking lot working, making it look twice the lonely place it was this time of night. George stopped the car and looked out at the city lights. The outside air was cold so he kept the engine running for warmth and company. He sat there waiting for inspiration. The only sign he saw was 'Lookout', so he responded by glancing up at the moon. His imagination switched in again – 'Man in the moon. The cheese and the mice and the cow, right over that spoon.' George was a 'pictures' man – Steve called him a 'big picture man'.

George broke into the rhyme. 'I should have asked Steve's advice you know.' The truth was that he was scared that Steve would 'strongly encourage' him to pursue the hard option, while distancing himself, of course, from any consequences arising from George's actions. He could hear Steve say, 'It's your choice George, you know you gotta put the kingdom first and then all these things . . .' Now of course he may not have said anything like that, but the fear *that he might had kept George well clear. George also knew how much he was needed to keep things going at church. It's not that George didn't trust Steve to give a straight answer. It was just that George knew that the pastor side of Steve was under great pressure to keep everybody focused on the vision, to convey the message that everything was going all right. 'I would have spoken to him tonight,' George said to his conscience, 'but before every service the sermon is written all over him and afterwards the visitors are in his sights.' George finally laid his conscience to rest on this one by saying, 'I'll ring Pastor if I get fired.'*

Suddenly the correction popped into his mind. 'The dish ran away with the spoon and the cow relates to the moon.' George thanked the cells that had been quietly foraging away in the archives for that revelation. And back to the moon he went to make the necessary adjustments. Then, as a further contribution, his imagination transformed the moon into a fat, round and enigmatic Winston Churchill. George played along by placing a hat on him and giving him a cigar. Something about the comforting familiar face and, in particular, the cigar, made George want to tell Winston about his new baby. But, before he could speak, the wartime Prime Minister of the moon lifted his hands for silence and began to sing what sounded like a well-known church chorus. 'Never, never, never, never, never give up.' George was transfixed. The words were like a battle cry galvanising him to fight. Even when the vision faded like a cigar puff, George could hear the call to arms resounding in his soul.

We will tune back into George's frequency later. For now we need to open the church history books. They will help us understand a great deal about why George is where he is tonight, and why George, under that starry sky, thinks the way he thinks about his job, his church and his life.

Chapter 2

Where Have We Come From?

All kinds of questions we might ask about this time and about the future can only be assessed in the light of our heritage. You have no doubt heard the saying that those who do not know their history are bound to repeat it. That is why we begin to look into the possible and potential future by looking at the past. In particular we want to look here at the way in which the Christian and Western mind has developed through the centuries. In this we are seeking to understand the way in which history has established the patterns of church/Christian life we have and hold to this day. The more we understand these things the better we will be able to respond to the challenges and changes this age demands of us.

You may be among those who don't get overly excited when the after-dinner conversation turns to history. I will try to be brief. My purpose here is only to establish a context for our discussion throughout the book. So, let's spend a little time wading through the archives.

Who Split the Universe?

An immense shift took place in human history in and around the sixth century BC. It arose in both Eastern and Western thought and has profoundly influenced the course of human thinking since that time. From the record in Scripture we know that after the Fall idolatry became the predominant religious expression of mankind. The revelation of the one true God was there, but it became increasingly submerged by the dark mist of idolatry. Abraham was called out of idolatry to worship the one true God and from him came the nation of Israel. This chosen nation, although progressively given the revelation and vision of the one God, never totally broke free of the idol. Their worship of the creature rather than the creator continued until the judgement of God fell and Judah was exiled into Babylon in the year 586 BC. After 70 years of captivity a remnant returned and never again would the chosen nation descend into the worship of the idol.

What is amazing is that soon after this time two men arose in two different nations whose teaching moved away from an idolatrous worldview to a more philosophical and abstract approach to life and reality. One took the West, the other the East. Their teaching held many parallels to what had occurred in Israel's religious life at the time of the exile. However, its impact has worked against, rather than for, the eternal purposes of the one true God. It is essential that we understand the philosophical changes that were made at that time if we are to grasp the where and why of our present worldview two-and-a-half thousand years later.

The first man arose in India. His name or title was Buddha (563–483 BC). He broke with the idolatry of Hinduism and put forward a philosophy that denied most of life, both the good and the bad, in an attempt to find enlightenment and an ultimate dissolution of the soul in an eternal spirit realm. The second man arose in Greece and his name was Plato (427–347 BC). He broke from (or, more accurately, disregarded) the worship of the Greek Pantheon and, like Buddha, moved the focus away from the present life towards a removed spirit realm. Plato said that the created world we see around us was not actually the real world. Rather it was one of dark shadows and imperfect forms that only served to represent a perfect realm that was forever removed from life. This ideal dimension was found in the eternal realm, detached from the temporal, known only vaguely through concepts and possibly available after death. The teaching and influence of Buddha and Plato philosophically divided the universe in two.

Plato the Western hero

As we know, the early church commenced in a Hebrew setting and soon became predominantly Gentile in its make-up. The Gentile worldview of the time drew heavily from the Greek philosophical system of Plato and also from the age-old pagan attachment to the idol. It was this worldview, rather than the Hebrew worldview of those who penned the Old and New Testaments, that over time came to dominate the thinking of the church. Plato and the Greeks conquered the church and through the church they came to dominate the Western mind. How did this happen?

After the second century AD the early church fathers were mostly Gentile converts, steeped in Greek thinking and philosophy. Plato was by far their favourite. In defending Christianity against charges by pagan Greek philosophers that it was a ludicrous Hebrew invention, the Christian apologists of the third century relied heavily on Plato and his view of the cosmos. As is the tendency when a war is fought (whichever side wins), it is the technology and weapons used in that war that will dominate the arena from then on. Christianity overcame its pagan adversaries but, from the fourth century on, the church became much more Greek than Hebrew in its worldview. Thus Plato, enshrined by Neoplatonism, became a patron saint of the early church.

He was likened to a kind of philosophical Trojan horse that God had sent to bring down the pagan Greeks before the Christ. Colin Brown says, in relation to Plato's influence on Christian thought, that it 'continued scarcely unabated down the centuries' (*Philosophy*, p. 16). This victory over and against the pagans came at quite a price for the Christians.

The Church – Gateway to the Spiritual Realm

The church's triumphant defeat of itself is clearly in evidence in the Roman Catholic Church of the sixth century. Plato's leaven had by then moved through the church to substantially form the theological lump of Catholic structure and thought. At this time the average Christian believed in a spiritual realm that was very much separated from his everyday or 'common' life. Hope of heaven was centred on the church and in turn dependent on the priest who represented this removed realm. The Eucharist and the priest were the key mediators between God and humanity and the only gateway to salvation. The Christian lived in a wispy land of shadows that was not much more than a temporary testing ground before the reality of the next world arrived. This world denial meant that things like human sexuality and everyday life were considered to be in opposition to higher spiritual pursuits. Marriage, family and secular work were devalued, giving way to otherworldly things like celibacy, sacraments and obsessive moralism.

The Neoplatonic spiritual realm, standing in opposition to the real world and available only through the church, increasingly became the *status quo*. It was this brand of Christianity that spread across Europe, extinguished the lamp of Celtic Christianity in Ireland and Britain and found its way into the Holy Roman Empire. This marriage of

Rome and Empire launched the crusades, saved Europe from Islam, kept the masses confused by Latin and made nations and rulers subservient to the Pope under threat of excommunication. With the help of Plato we won the battle but lost the war. The Dark Ages descended to blanket the Christian church in Platonic mist and empire-building arrogance.

The medieval church

The next move came from the renowned Catholic theologian Aquinas. In the thirteenth century he put together a theological system that is still the basis of much Roman Catholic doctrine. He, like many of his time, was steeped in Platonic thought, but was also deeply influenced by the recently rediscovered teachings of another Greek, Aristotle. Aquinas kept very much to the split-universe approach but began, with Aristotle's help, to adjust the terms used to access the bottom half. Aristotle did not see truth or perfection as being up and out there in some spiritual or eternal realm; rather he saw reality as being found in the things of earth and life (in the thing itself). Aquinas' dual attachment to Plato and Aristotle caused him to propose what might be called a 'philosophical two-step'.

Following Aristotle, Aquinas said that human reason and observation would enable us to understand the world around us. This he called 'natural theology'. He then said, in keeping with the old Platonic system, that the Bible and the traditions of the church enabled us to understand and access the spiritual realm. This he called 'revealed theology'. This apparently simple emphasis on reason applied to the lower storey of the universe had a profound effect. In particular, it sowed the seeds of the renaissance of art and literature that followed in the fourteenth century. The reason for this renaissance was that the two-step process freed humanity to use its reason to discover the world, independent of the church. The church was preoccupied with the 'upper storey' that was taken care of by the priest, the mass and the sacraments. The 'bottom storey', with artisans and intellectuals now empowered by reason, broke free of the church and, along with much of the populace they influenced, never really came back. Colin Brown summarises this period by saying that, 'Medieval thought was a curious mixture of Christian faith and pagan philosophy' (*Philosophy*, p. 19).

The Reformation

The Renaissance brought about a revival in the study and appreciation of Greek culture and learning. It was at this time that the Bible became more widely available in the original Greek, enabling people to discover its truths and begin to question the hold of Rome over Christendom. The Protestant Reformation of the sixteenth century was just around the corner. When Luther nailed his objections against Rome to the church door in 1517, Europe was ready for change and change it got! The Reformers put the Word of God back at the centre of the Christian church. They took hold of Biblical revelation and established the Protestant church firmly on that rock of God's revealed will.

Drawing from their Renaissance ally, reason, the Reformers adopted what might be called a 'biblical rationalism'. Their emphasis was on systematic theology drawn from Scripture. The conclusions reached in this study of the Word came to define Reformed church life and spirituality mostly in terms of assent and obedience to orthodox creeds and confessions. To be a Christian was to believe the right truths, live morally, attend church and hear these truths preached faithfully. This was an important start; however, it was not enough to carry the sunrise of the Reformation into a new day. Within a century much of the Reformed church had descended into a cold and dogmatic formalism.

The Enlightenment

What happened to bring about such an early collapse of this promising restoration? To answer this question we need to look at a movement called 'the Enlightenment' that swept in a century after the Reformation began. This dramatic surge in human thinking and philosophy owed its origins to Renaissance thought and the new-found political and social freedoms gained by the Reformation.

The French philosopher Descartes (1596–1650) has been called the 'Father of the Enlightenment'. He strongly inscribed the split universe into the core of Enlightenment thinking, ensuring it became the very foundation of the Western mind we think with to this day. Descartes used basically the same approach as Aquinas, drawing the line between faith and reason, spirit and world, revelation truth and scientific truth. He did argue for the existence of God. However, his treatise was based not on revelation but on human reason; he began his argument not from faith, but from doubt. Descartes said, 'I doubt, therefore I think, therefore I am, therefore . . .' and on to 'therefore, God.' In the Age of Reason the upper storey of the universe was no longer the dwelling place of the God of the Lord Jesus Christ; it was now home to the 'god of the philosophers'. This very tame and silent god acted mostly as an absent landlord, a kind of backstop or ultimate guarantor of the systems of truth man worked out via his reason. Pascal tried to say to the gamblers and humanists of his day that 'the heart has reasons that the mind knows not of', but no one saw any sense in such intangibles. Pascal died young; Descartes 'lived' for centuries.

Losing Reformation Ground

Even though the Reformation leaders were strong in doctrine and understood a great deal about the direction the church should take, they quickly became isolated. The Reformers, as mentioned, had taken their stand on reason applied to the Word of God. This was good initial ground. However, it was soon mostly eroded away by the fast-flowing currents of the Enlightenment. The Age of Reason, joining with and taking hold of the European mind, rushed in to lay claim to the rest of the world. With science and technology, with new lands discovered and with revolutions fought, secular humanity gained its independence from religious dogma and became the centre of its world. Reason was its servant and only reasonable religion need apply.

Deism became the flavour of the century until the English philosopher David Hume dispatched it with obvious glee. Hume's scepticism awoke the great German intellectual Emmanuel Kant from his dogmatic and Enlightenment-induced slumber. But, rather than derailing the 'Age of Reason', Kant simply serviced the Cartesian philosophical trolley, changed a few parts and names, steadied it and sent it on its way to the modern world. Kant removed whatever understanding the Western mind thought it might have had of the eternal God of heaven and earth. Kant said that God did exist but then told us that we could never know him – thanks a lot, Emmanuel!

Meanwhile, back a few centuries to the Reformation, the Roman Church had lined up Ignatius Loyola to go head-to-head with John Calvin. A counter-Reformation was launched which mired many nations in Europe in political intrigue and war. Another battlefront on which the Reformers had to fight was in the hearts of the people who ended up living in Protestant nations. To substantiate their rational and Biblical turf the Reformers had to distance themselves from that Catholic upper storey associated with sacramental, mystical or experiential spirituality. In many cases this meant that the kind of Christianity to which most of the populace was accustomed was replaced overnight by Reformed preaching and pulpits.

The challenge here was that the peoples of northern Europe and their ancestors had lived through centuries of medieval Catholic and Renaissance thought. So they did not wake up on the morning of the Reformation with Reformation minds. Most of them woke up that morning with the same mind they went to bed with the night before. Yes, the Reformers did dispatch much of the Catholic preoccupation with visible forms and holy relics, but it is not hard to see its survival in the reverence attached to the sacred book in the hands of the holy man behind the lectern.

The Reformers did well, all things considered. The Renaissance was still very much in the people's minds, the Catholics were stirring up trouble from the south and the Enlightenment was pretty well everywhere! Is it any wonder that after a century of this so many were left clinging to their creeds, their buildings and their state funding?

☞ The Reformation only briefly postponed the growth of that thick dark line drawn in the heavens above the systems of man. These heavens continued to move away into the nether region that Plato had long ago consigned them to. So it was that the line from Plato, through Aquinas, to Descartes and into the modern period was etched deep and drawn straight.

The Light of the Great Awakening

This is not to say that the Reformation had little impact. The landscape of Europe was greatly changed by its influence. These changes were as much political as they were religious and established an environment for both the Enlightenment and for Bible-based and heartfelt Christian movements. God was at work to keep the light from the Reformation burning and, in time, this would ignite a fire in many nations.

Oliver Cromwell's Puritans arose in England around 1560, aligning their emphasis on the Word with an agenda to separate church from state. They ultimately failed in their attempt to rid England of the monarchy and, though many good reforms were instituted, they nonetheless created a backlash against Puritanism that is felt to this day. Those who sailed on the Mayflower were, however, able to strongly influence the new colony of America. The Pietists arose in the mid-1600s in reaction to the cold formalism of the Reformed and Lutheran churches. They emphasised 'heart' Christianity and acts of compassion along with a love for the gospel. These streams met in the English evangelists Whitefield and Wesley, who burst onto the scene in the early 1720s and under God ushered in the 'Great Awakening'. This revivalist movement came in several waves throughout the next two centuries and had a strong impact on many nations, particularly America.

Throughout this period the church was basically afloat in a sea of Enlightenment and modern thought, with the tide of Humanism and Naturalism rising. Science was filling the gaps and squeezing out the Enlightenment 'god' who lived in them. By the time Darwin declared all life to have evolved and scientific laws rode atop of the industrial machine now in charge of the West, the 'little flock' was swamped. It was all too much. Many denominations in the nineteenth and twentieth centuries gave in to Humanism, with the remaining 'superstitious' elements in their Christianity being tamed into Liberalism. Their social justice was commendable but it was mostly commandeered by, and subsumed into, the popular Humanism of the day.

Early in the twentieth century the Fundamentalists reacted by returning to the first base of the Word, and the Pentecostals, against all odds, took off to make their mark. The Evangelicals kept preaching the gospel and, as the liberals' influence waned, their message not only held on but gained ground through the '40s and '50s, particularly in countries like America, with its long and strong history of revivalism. The '60s were anybody's guess but, in the latter part of that wild decade and into the early '70s, the Pentecostal heritage met the Evangelical stream and the charismatic move began. Meanwhile, some of the Evangelical/Puritan streams in America, gaining in strength, called to mind and scrubbed up the 'good old days' and began to rally, once again making moral moves on the political scene.

From Modern to Postmodern

Secular humanity came of age in the modern period of the nineteenth century. Many philosophers declared that God was dead or, at best, no longer needed to verify Humanism's truth or fill the gaps remaining in scientific understanding. There was no need to pretend any longer that there was in fact any upper storey in the universe. Secular humanity, it seemed, was finally in charge of its destiny. The truth was almost in its grasp and a humanist utopia was just around the corner. The twentieth century dawned fair, bright and British. With it came two world wars, the great depression, communism, the Jewish holocaust and the atomic bomb –

not to mention Einstein, who opened up a whole new universe while closing down (except at slow speeds) Newton's shop of fixtures, fittings and timepieces. All of this and more put paid to the short-lived modern optimism. A ticket arrived, in the form of drugs, rock and roll and eastern mysticism, inviting a new generation to a postmodern age. The quest for a single truth gave way to relativism, people's faith in science's ability to supply the answer faded and the once bright hope for a humanist paradise took flight.

Postmodernism has, for the greater part, shattered the modern worldview into pieces, but is yet to bring in any comprehensive definition of reality. It is in fact this very lack of cohesion and uniformity that is the most cohesive and uniform thing about postmodernism. Stanley Grenz, in his excellent book on the subject, says that postmodernism represents an overthrow of the very foundations of Western thought. The grand project to find universal and absolute truth via rationalism has failed. Reason and science have not delivered and now an uncertain and fragmented future is arriving. In this postmodern period, reason has to take its place alongside emotion, experience and intuition in the journey of discovery and life. People in a postmodern time are not rational knowers of things outside and separate to themselves. They are seen as one with the process of knowing and knowledge, interacting with reality and, in effect, creating it by their own language, experience and cultural context. Grenz says of the postmodernist that for them 'knowledge cannot be merely objective . . . because the universe is not mechanistic and dualistic but rather historical, relational and personal' (*Postmodernism*, p. 7).

In this postmodern era a vast mosaic of ideas, tribes and stories are clothed in the historical remnants of the past times we have examined. Christianity has never really been a dominant force. It was pervasive in nations like America, but in the Western world in general, and even in America, the Bible served the Enlightenment rather than the other way around. Of course, the saints made much positive impact. Many new nations were reached with the gospel and those willing to stand up and be counted accomplished societal changes. Christianity has undoubtedly bequeathed many good things to the West and to the world. There are, however, 'the best of times and the worst of times' that flow from its heritage and its influence.

The postmodern mosaic

Everyone born into the Western world, Christian or not, inherits the mindset or worldview we have been looking at. This mindset has been developing for thousands of years and, even in the scattered postmodern era, pieces of past broken worlds still determine most of the way we think, act and feel. To this day we hear:

'I live in the real world, not some spiritual realm in the clouds.'
'I believe only science has the ability to discover the truth.'
'I am into spirit channelling, I know it's not rationally provable, but that's a sure sign to me it's true.'
'I have experienced it, so it must be valid.'
'All we need is the Bible, it's the truth and that is that.'

We arrive as the church in an emerging postmodern era with all of this in our philosophical suitcase. It is this history that has set out the design specs and patterns within which we, as Western Christians, think and plan. The church has inherited a vision of the universe (creation) that has been split in two by Plato, Aquinas and Descartes. The Catholic, the holiness and the Pentecostal streams for the most part pursue the upper storey, tending to move away from an emphasis on everyday life towards experiences of, or encounters with, the 'spiritual realm'. To gain access to the upper storey the Catholics hold to the sacraments and the priest, the holiness stream stresses moral purity as the key and the Pentecostals focus on worship and the anointing.

The Reformed and fundamentalist streams are predominantly engaged in the lower storey where the rational dimension is pursued. Here belief, understanding of truth and obedience form the major focus of Christian life. For them the eternal realm is certainly there but not accessible until the next life comes with its transcendent reward. Both streams use the Word of God to validate their approach and there is, of course, a degree of overlap and interaction between them, as evidenced in the broader evangelical stream. Individual saints will not precisely fit this or that category. Life is complex. We are all a mixed philosophical bag, often believing one thing because of our creed but doing another because of our need.

Split-level church

Our heritage has ensured that, to this day, the church has great difficulty defining the nature of the spiritual and created realms apart from the grid of Greek thinking. We continue to struggle, trying to balance on the line drawn through our vision of life. For the most part we continue to fall either side of the faith/reason, spiritual/material or upper/lower divide. This is the history that has worked to establish our patterns of church life and structure. This is the philosophical/theological baggage we carry with us to church on any given Sunday. As history turns another chapter into a postmodern era, the church is being left behind. Most of our way of church life as Protestant Christians was formulated in the late Enlightenment and early modern period. This time is gone. The pace of change means that we have to play more than catch up; we have to engage in radical change. That change will involve a thorough reappraisal of our heritage.

Before we ask the question – How can the church speak so as to be heard in a postmodern world? – we need to settle the issues relating to a more fundamental question: what, who and where is the church that seeks to make such a sound? There was a teacher of Israel in the time of Jesus who, no doubt, had very similar questions. He was, it seems, feeling somewhat hemmed in by synagogue, Sabbath and Law and, having heard the claims and seen the power of Jesus, decided to pay him a visit. He came by night and the answer he received was, to say the least, telling!

GEORGE THE ELDER (2)
'God, is there a sound from you?'

George was about to drive home on the strength of Winston's words when he noticed that the moon wasn't as full as he had first imagined. He took a breath, exhaled and realised that he was still not ready for home or for Monday. He turned off the ignition and the sound of the engine died or slept (he could never decide which). The lookout became a very quiet, dim-lit place.

'I won't ever give up, I'm going to fight all the way,' George began in response to Winston's chorus. 'The problem I'm having is working out who the enemy is. If only I knew who to fight, then I could work out how to win.' To sort out possible contenders for the ring, George, putting on his Divisional Manager's hat, began to survey the field of action.

'Yes the company is in trouble. The local scene is tight and getting tighter, far too many competitors in the market. The Americans arrived last year with their usual ploy – cut the prices on the big-selling items by half, starve the competition

out of existence and then, when their market share is strong, gradually lever up the prices and hope no one remembers. It's definitely bunker-down survival time. We've even joined forces with some of our old enemies to ward off the invasion.' George loved this kind of talk. If he lost his job it would be this game of survival in the jungle he would miss the most.

'With costs going skyward we did have to cut back. I know how much it hurt Rob to have to send so many fine people home for good. There was so much pressure coming from the board. To think that was over a year ago and the spilt blood has yet to dry. It's sent the place into a permanent panic. Everybody's working with fewer staff trying to meet higher quotas to justify their employed existence. They call it economic and rational, I call it cruel and stupid. You can't talk to anyone these days without them lying about how great they're doing – beating it up for the next round of appraisals due in May.'

This was George's language. Like the Pastor's theology this was George's way of seeing the market, seeing the world and seeing himself in it. He pressed on with the language he knew so well.

'It was during that downsizing that I realised how much Rob believed in me. He stood by me even when some of the other managers thought my performance was lagging. He knew it was fear that drove them to try and shift the heat away from their division. Rob's a good man, not a Christian, but good in the secular sense. I feel I know him and can trust him to be straight with me. I knew it was on when Rob called a snap meeting of Divisional Managers last thing Friday. I'll bet he had a strong nudge from someone on the board and decided to act.' George paused, smiled and said out loud – 'in the shareholder's interest of course.'

George sighed deeply, hesitated and then pushed himself to go on. 'So there we were. Rob finished his thing about the state of the nation and then wrapped it up with the usual rally call – "So, we expect a big effort from all the Divisional Managers. You guys, and of course Helen, need to set the benchmarks if you want others to follow. It will only be for a four- to six-month period. With some extra effort and focus on the game we'll get through this tight spot. I won't support any rise in salaries, I think you're all doing well as it is, but there is a large bonus in it if we pull through." '

'I still don't quite know what came over me. I don't know what time it was, but I know the time had come. And so I said it, every word of it.'

George shook his head in amazement at what came next. ' "I won't do it. I've got a family, a church and a life to live." I don't know why I started, but I couldn't stop. It was like I was finally preaching at work, I think I felt anointed. "Rob, extra effort just means more time, more blood, more than any one man . . . or Helen . . . should have to give to their job. You keep telling us, just a few months and we'll be out of the woods. You said that in the late '80s after the crash. You said it during the early '90's recession. Even when things picked up you got us twice as busy, telling us we had to make up for lost time. You said that when your razor gang slashed its way through this place the year before last. You said that when we first pushed our way into China. The 'get busy' cycles are getting closer and faster. You keep saying things will change if we get stuck into it, but frankly, I don't believe it any more." '

'Then I drew that thick black line – "I can't keep giving you 60-plus hours a week. I won't do it. Like I said Rob, a family, a church, a life! You get in what you need. Get some consultants. Get back some of those people who used to work here, the ones you fired the year before last, leaving us with all this extra work." '

George had felt the initial rush of solidarity from the other managers. But it was only a brief alignment of fellow slaves that fell apart as George's self-made precipice got larger. He soon realised he was alone, standing on the edge of a chasm with Rob and his gang facing him on the other side. That lonely feeling made him suddenly aware of what he was doing. With that came the first wave of panic. The last sentence George spoke he didn't remember. His final few words limped away into the grim silence that now stood between himself and his company. That was it; it was said.

Like the strong but straight CEO he was, Rob measured out his response in managerial tones. 'George. All of you, you know the score. You're old hands. You've been round long enough to know . . . the score.' His use of 'score' twice ruined his momentum and got him a little angry which made him somewhat flustered. George noticed and for a brief moment felt like he was winning. But it was too soon for anybody to tell.

Instead of getting angry, like he wanted to, Rob retreated to his GM persona. 'No one was expecting the Americans to come in with such force. And moving into China while trying to stay ahead in the local market has been hard. None of us expected the Chinese to drag things out – the red tape, the cultural stuff and the currency fluctuations. But the factory is up and running, the managers are in place, the papers are signed, the government's paid up. We've got to keep this side of things going until the Asian returns start coming in. I know the currency's been hit and demand is down, but it will sort itself out, given time. The Americans are in our sights now, it's time to keep focused on the game.'

He was on a roll, back in control. If any of the other managers had any doubts, all it took was a bit of this kind of 'team talking' to get them well back on side – the side their bread was buttered on. Rob was now winning and as such he could afford to offer George some help. 'George, you've done some great things in Supply. Delivery times are the best they've been and you've driven costs well below

*budget. If we could all match your effort I know we'll pull
through, I just know it.'*

*By this time George had drawn several breaths. He was
more startled at what he had said than resolute in relation to
his manifesto. As such he was unable to take the lifeline now
being offered to him. In effect he was frozen, his eyes were
fixed; he dared not look down. Now Rob's anger began to
surface. 'It's late, let's go home. We'll meet first thing
Monday. I want your ideas about expenditure cuts for the
Project Managers and some budget estimates on the Ultimo
job. And George, we appreciate your beliefs, but we don't
run a charity here.' Then twisting the knife he added, 'If our
opposition ever lets us start one you'll be first in line for the
job George. But until then, I'll give you 'til Monday. I want
to know if you're on the team or out.'*

*Slowly George swam up to the surface of his memory and
looked around. He reassured his conscience with 'I should
be going home'. But instead of leaving he sat there looking
at the meandering safety fence silhouetted along the edge of
the lookout. His mind spluttered into gear with some short
sharp questions. 'Where do I stand here? Who am I com-
mitted to?' He looked at the bread and thought of Rebecca.
'Is it her and the kids? The company? Rob?' The Bible rest-
ing on a large pile of papers on the passenger seat caught his
attention. 'Church? God? Steve?'*

*He had left something out. He went back over the list
then let out a long sigh. With a sarcastic tinge in his voice he
said out loud, 'Me. What about me? Yeah, what about me?'
George had made a discovery. He had tapped into a deep
well called himself and the waters were troubled and angry.
With his new-found focus he looked around for possible
targets. Rebecca came to mind. 'No. The kids? No. The
shareholders? Too invisible to detect. Rob? No.' Then the
picture in the church foyer came into view. George reached
out to adjust it again and said, 'Steve'. George swung the car*

door open; it bounced back and hit him, causing him to hit it back. Feeling angry and stupid he stepped out to find the space he needed to pace this one through.

Addressing the picture in the church foyer, George began. 'Steve, listen to me . . . I've worked hard at church. I've worked . . .' George had to guard himself against using the wrong word too early in the piece here. So he tried it again. 'I've worked jolly hard to see the church come from nothing to just over two hundred on the books. But every time we arrive at our goal, get somewhere and get it right, we move on to the next build-up phase, to the next vision thing.' George paused to calculate. 'Fourteen years of my life Steve, eaten up in building programmes, ministry projects, fund-raising for seats, rooms, ministries, books and carpets. Not to mention the never-ending string of conferences you go to. You have got to stop going to those things. You come back either disappointed at how well everybody else is doing or over the moon about some new growth formula. Whichever way – it amounts to more work for you and all of us.'

George stopped for a moment and waited to feel bad. But the spring-cleaning had been good for his soul. So carefully he went back to it. 'It all amounts to more of my money and more of my time. And for what? An endless parade of people who come for this reason and go for that one? It all adds up to life – my life!'

George walked to the lookout, jumped over the safety fence and sat on the edge, holding onto the sign that said don't do what he had just done. Feeling like a naughty kid, George waited for more anger to come. But that was it; there was nothing there. All was quiet until George heard himself thinking. 'I know he's got a calling; he's got the vision thing. I know he's tried hard over the years to keep the whole thing happening. He's a good man, works hard, preaches well. He sure is looking tired lately. One too many *elders' meetings, one too many problem people. I told him months back that we couldn't afford that youth pastor. The budget's stretched enough as it is. But he still went ahead, steamrolled the board and hired him anyway.'* Anger flared briefly and then subsided. *'But I know what's really rocked him. It's the six families that left last month to join the megachurch up the road. Funny, the only reason he got that youth pastor in was because of the pressure from those parents. So he responds, against our advice, and they leave anyway. It was a real body blow to his confidence and the leadership thing means that he can't back down now. Effectively it ruined whatever momentum that last build-up phase had created.'*

The last wisps of George's anger had now evaporated into the night. *'Thing I like about Steve is he knows God and he knows people and he loves them both. I wouldn't put up with what he puts up with. I don't know how he does it year in year out. Always on call – everyone expecting him to fix the unfixable. If it works, God gets the glory, if it doesn't then Steve cops the flack. But every time you think he's down for the count, he bobs up like a cork and keeps on going. You can't fault the guy. He's got a job to do, an eternal one.'* So Steve was off the hook. But the trouble was there was still no enemy in sight. Like the shareholders of his company, the real owners of his problem remained well out of sight.

It was the sound of the word 'job' that brought George back to the cold hard fact that it was late Sunday night and Monday was almost upon him. *'My job? Well unlike Steve's it's definitely finite. In fact it could well be finished this time tomorrow.'* He leaned forward and peered into the blackness beneath his feet. *'It could be over the cliff and heading for the rocks.'* The thought struck George hard, so much so that he carefully pulled himself back over the fence. Once safely back on the path to his car, he resumed his remake of Pastor Steve.

'I know that most of the stuff Steve talks about doesn't happen like he says it should. I know that what isn't happening in our church is the most important thing in life, not to mention eternity. So if it's good enough for Steve to hang in there and trust God, then it's good enough for me to hang in there with him. The renewal is going well, it's really helped Sunday night attendance. I know God is up to something. I just wish he would tell us! One thing's for sure, I believe in God a whole lot more than I believe in life at the moment. I won't let go. I just have to hold on. Steve and I, we'll pay off that building and we will fill it!' George didn't know quite what he meant by all this, but he felt good saying it.

'That's it then, no plan and I'm due home for baby duty. I've come all this way and still have nothing to take to work on Monday.' George was about to get angry with God but he knew it was too late in the day for that. All he could do was to make an attempt at a summary. Clearing his throat to clear his mind, George said to anybody willing to listen, 'A man's got to draw the line sometime in his life – church first and then family. No, that's wrong. Family. Yes, family first. Job third. Or is it kingdom first and then all these things? Whatever! I can't do what you want Rob. I've got commitments. Three nights a week down at church, most all of Sundays and then there are people to see, new contacts to follow up. Then there's family. The third child was much more than we bargained for. It's the kingdom call. I know you can't hear it, but Rob, listen to me. You and I only have one life and it's forever, I have got to make it count forever Rob.' It was a strange and open-ended kind of summary, but at this stage it would have to do.

George picked up a dead branch, swung it hard around his head and released it to sail over the cliff. He then looked up into the night sky. Such obvious confusion at this late stage brought a strange smile to his lips that turned to smile

*at God. It was then that the Churchill moon hit a cloud
and hid, causing the stars to bounce out a little brighter.
George's childhood came up to him. 'You know God, I was
a boy who loved stars. I remember the poem I wrote when I
was eight, "I know the starhouse closes at breakfast. So
I travel to meet you all. Tell me all of your names there on
the edge of night-time, look at me and speak one by one." '
He forgot the next lines of the poem but carried on talking
to the stars. 'Your lights first captured me, they called me to
the creator and when I was sixteen, I found out his first
name. There was so much of life then, everything was possible.'*

*George looked up at the stars one last time and cried,
'God, is there a sound to bring all of this together? Is there
something that could turn all this noise from work, all this
wanting, all these things into, like, music?' He laughed out
loud at himself. 'No, not some chorus to sing but something
stronger, something that resonates, something that touches
those stars and names them one by one.'*

*No words came in answer, only a stronger desire for
more of life before it was over. So George, with no particular plan in mind, got back into his slumbering car. It woke
at the turn of the command key. He pressed his foot on the
power, turned the wheel and headed home. The stars
blinked as George the Elder moved towards the line.*

Chapter 3

Three Cries and The New Creation

My sister had been a Christian for only six months when she came up to me with one of those questions that new Christians tend to ask. She said to me, 'Do Christians do anything else but meet?' It was not that she did not enjoy worshipping God and hearing the Word preached. Rather she was beginning to realise that being a Christian meant that for the rest of her days on earth the local church was meant to be the focus of her life. There were certainly many other things she would engage in – marriage, friendships, family and work – but central to all of these was meant to be her local church.

As she contemplated the years ahead she began to feel somewhat hemmed in. Also she was wondering how she could possibly communicate to her many friends that local church life was in fact a viable alternative to their own world-oriented and diverse ways of life. Even at that stage of her Christian life and development the local church was becoming too small a place for her. The Jesus she had come to know was expansive and life-encompassing; the local church was turning out to be neither.

Where is That Church?

It was a lot easier for the New Testament saints not to locate the church in one particular building. Quite simply, they usually didn't have one. When Paul or others wrote to the saints, they addressed their letters to places like Rome. The setting for the life of the church was the entire city or the region. It encompassed all that life entailed – family, friends, homes, work and the market place. The saints lived and worked in the city, taking opportunity to gather during the week and on the Lord's day in different ways and settings both large and small. If you wanted to persecute the early church, like Saul of Tarsus, you would have to do so by going 'house to house'.

The fourth century changed all of this. Constantine saw a vision of the Cross in the sky, won the battle for Rome and, with a little help from his mother, changed all the religious rules. Suddenly Christianity was transformed from outlaw religion to flavour of the century. Soon the temples of old were being transformed into the churches of tomorrow. Increasingly the church no longer embraced all of life in the city; it now had a definite address. It was an address distinctly different from the saint's own home or business, one that was closely associated with the elemental religions of Rome's passing pagan era. From this time on, Christianity became located in a building and that building was called 'church'.

To this day we as saints are still focused on the building we call church, seeing it as the key to the ongoing discovery and expression of divine reality and Christian mission. It follows from this that, because the church gathered is considered to be central to the divine strategy, the saints' resources of time, finances and gifting are expected to flow in the direction of that expression of the church. The mission of the local church is considered to be eternal and its orientation spiritual, whereas the everyday life and work of the saints is thought to be temporal and hence transitory. The saints' everyday life and work are, yes, said to have an importance, but the believer must always give prime and line honours to the local church they should attend several times a week.

The strategy, of course, is that these churches will grow and multiply and in time reach the city. The facts, however, inform us that this plan of action is simply not working very well. The megachurches are presently being heralded as proof of the success of this strategy – a success that comes when the right man, management and marketing matrix is put in place. The reality is that, not only are much of the megachurches' clientele drawn from existing congregations, but also they only appear to be large in comparison to the smaller struggling churches around them. When measured against the cities they minister in, their numbers and their impact remain small. That is not to decry what they have achieved; rather it serves as a reality check on the advertising we receive.

In a postmodern time it is becoming more and more obvious that the Christian's split universe, mostly expressed in and from a building we have named church, is benefiting the saints less and less. It is not attracting the attention of the unchurched tribes heading into the diverse and desperate postmodern mosaic of the 21st century.

☞ I believe that our focus for divine meaning and mission on the church gathered is a major strategic error on the part of the Christian church. It must be overcome if we, as the body of Christ, are to enter into and impact a postmodern world. The Greek split has triumphed by detaching the church from most of the saints' life and work in creation. The reality we face at this time is that a kingdom divided cannot stand, a people divided cannot act, so a church divided cannot build.

How can we heal the divide the Greeks have created between church and life? How can we regain that unified vision of life and God the enemy has taken from us? In a postmodern time of apparent anarchy and growing confusion, I believe answers to these questions are closer than one might think. Before we proceed to search them out, let's consider what it might be like for an unchurched individual who one day decides to turn up at church.

The outside journey into church

I get up, dress, take my courage with me, go to my car and travel the distance. I've been thinking about it for weeks. It's been a year since my friend Susan died and left me that note saying she'd see me in heaven. I want to keep the appointment with her so I thought I'd make a booking, and what better place than church?

I don't play the radio, just keep quiet like you're supposed to, mostly just not thinking as I hum along the Sunday streets. Pulling into the parking lot I follow the flags and here I am, parked. I've gone too far now to go back,

so I get out and begin the walk to the door. There stands the first man, searching smile, hand pointed my way. Realising I am a woman, he doesn't know if he should smile or shake. I use the confusion to pick up the newsletter and move on my way. I am almost in but they send a woman to get me to surrender my name. She stops me, tells me her name and tries to politely trick me into giving her mine. All I can do is draw reference to the curtains and smile blankly at the form she gives me – hoping she will get my drift. She does and I breathe a silent prayer of relief. Stupid thing to say, 'Nice, those crimson curtains'; however, knowing the power of the list I would do anything to keep my name off none.

I walk in, forgetting about the door, as a much larger reality rises to meet me. I am aware that even though technically no one is thinking about me, everybody is thinking about me. So, eyes front and centre, I move to the aisle seat left and back, thanking God, in my first serious prayer, for the newsletter. I say hello to God in my second prayer and ask him to say hello to Susan. I'm really getting into the swing of things now. I look intently at the visitor's card, telling myself several times my name, address and age. I don't write anything but keep looking at the box for '35 and over'. I wonder what needs I might have that the reverend could help me

with and I think about a box I could tick for 'reservations in forever'.

Suddenly everyone rises to sing. I don't know the songs but pretend I do, thinking about comedy shows where people mumble along and sing the few words they know too loudly. I tell God I'm sorry (that's my third prayer) and sing with appropriate meaning the words 'strangely dim' from the overhead. The songs finish, the offering goes past and I put some money in quickly so nobody thinks I'm taking any out. The announcements about what amounts to a very busy week for someone are given by a man they call Deacon.

Then the next man, the pastor, rises from amidst the three on show at the front and says he is going to 'open the word'. He is nice, friendly, kind of chatty, with no one talking back, and he is very much aware of who is new. He keeps not looking, but looking at me all the time. Well do I know that feeling! Once or twice I have an overwhelming urge to stand up and shout my name, like in a confession or something, but I don't. A long time passes and then he signals the end is near, the final song has arrived and we here today can now stand to sing it. I make my booking quickly with God in what is my fourth prayer. 'God, I want to come to heaven, God, tell Susan I got her note, God, rest ye merry,' and then I stop myself short.

I sing the final song as if I've always known it, now planning my escape. There is a greater resolution in the voices around me. I am aware that they too know the end is near. Then, as all the heads suddenly bow and all eyes close, I make my move out into the aisle and past that door. I've done it. I've been to church and come out the other side. I now have my whole life ahead of me. No one's got my name and God's got my booking. I'll be back at Christmas to confirm it, but for now he knows I'm coming.

Then this sound erupts from the back of me. I hear the words 'Hello, lady, Msuzz'. They search me out and pin me down on the map. I think of Casablanca as I turn to face the fourth man with magazine, cassette and smile, speaking to me as if I now owed him something.

'Will we see you next Sunday?' I say, 'Maybe-yes-perhaps' as one word and he looks intently at me and says, 'And your name is?'

Relationships That Change Us

We begin our enquiry by asking another question: what context or setting did God intend to be the focus for the life and ministry of the saints? In answer, let's tune in to a discussion had long ago between a chief Rabbi in Israel and the Son of God. On that night all those years ago Jesus, speaking to Nicodemus, gave us his primary portrait of the new man in Christ. Jesus told of the amazing way in which the saint would relate to life and to God. In his words we are given the key to the identity and purpose of the new creation in Christ. This life-portrait, drawn by Jesus for the sons and daughters of God, reveals to us the focus of mission and meaning for the body of Christ.

Jesus said to Nicodemus, 'The wind blows where it wishes and you hear the sound of it, but do not know where it comes from and where it is going; so is every one who is born of the Spirit' (John 3:18). To a man accustomed to Law, Temple and Sabbath, this must have seemed a very strange definition. Imagine that – the key defining quality of the one born of the Spirit is that they hear a sound. Such an unusual phrase, so different from the structure of this man's religious thinking and experience – so fluid, so intangible, so relational.

God created the universe with a sound. The sound he makes must still be able to speak into the heart and purpose of all that he has made. What is this sound? What effect does it have on the hearers? Where do we go to hear it? If we want to follow this sound we need to take the journey to the summit of Romans, reached in chapter 8. There we hear of three distinct cries that are being made. These cries set the largest of contexts for our lives as sons and daughters of God. The sound of these cries is, I believe, the key to the nature and purpose of the new creation in Christ.

The cry of sonship

The first sound of Romans 8 is the cry of sonship the Holy
Spirit establishes in our hearts. It is the cry from deep within
our lives to our Abba Father. Galatians 4:6 resonates with
Romans 8:15 in saying, 'God has sent forth the Spirit of his
Son into our hearts, crying, "Abba, Father".' Isn't it amazing that our sonship is primarily defined by a sound, a cry
from our heart? A newborn baby can't do much, but it sure
can make itself heard! The ability to cry for food, for love,
for comfort, for a change of scene and clothes is all we need
to get off to a good start in life. The cry of a child does not
stop as it grows; it only gets more complex and sophisti-
cated. In every life God has placed the desire that cries out
for meaning and a sense of belonging. It stands to reason
that when we are born again we are given a new cry. A
desire from deep within, established by the Spirit, one with
the Son of God, emerging from our heart, given that we
might reach out into life and into God. Jesus told us that
'No one knows the Son except the Father, nor does anyone
know the Father except the Son' (Matt. 11:27). It is the cry
given to us in the Son that moves us into our identity and
carries us into our eternal purpose in the Father.

The cry of creation

Now Romans chapter 8 gets even more interesting. We
discover that there is another sound being made. We read
that 'The whole creation groans and suffers the pains of
childbirth together until now' (Rom. 8:22). The sound
of God that made and sustains creation after the Fall
became his very cry within all things. To whom is creation
making this sound? Verse 19 tells us that the longing for
freedom that sends forth creation's cry is directed towards
the sons. 'The anxious longing of the creation waits eagerly

for the revealing of the sons of God.' Right now the entire creation is calling us forth as sons and daughters of God. It may seem strange to our Western minds, but that is what Scripture reveals.

The cry of the Father

If the creation is crying out for the sons and daughters, how does God want us to answer it? In answer we tune in to the third and final cry spoken of in Romans 8. Scripture phrases the above question and then answers it in this way: 'In the same way the Spirit also helps our weakness; for we do not know how to pray as we should, but the Spirit Himself intercedes for us with groanings too deep for words' (Rom. 8:26). Because the sons and the creation are in view here, our understanding of the Spirit's 'groaning' must take these into account. 'Our weakness' must refer to the immense challenge we face in responding to creation's cry.

☞ What is being said here is that the Spirit, having searched out the depths of God, emerges with an answer for the sons and daughters to give to creation. The sound of the eternal God is sent into the sons and daughters to enable them to engage the entire created order and answer its cry for freedom.

The Creation and the Church

We will obviously be looking in more depth at the nature and purpose of these cries throughout the book. At present we need to simply draw attention to their existence. Three cries – the sons and daughters of God, the creation and the Father. Jesus said that the one born of the Spirit must hear the sound of the eternal creator God. Even though we will not always know logically where it is coming from or where it is going to, we must respond and be released by the sound God speaks into, through and over all of creation. We will of course not be able to rationally understand these three cries. They, thankfully, will always remain too deep for simple definitions to encase. The issue here, as was the case with Nicodemus, is not so much one of rational under-standing. Rather it is one of response. The record indicates that this teacher of Israel, this one so given to Sabbath, Law and synagogue, heard the sound and followed.

What is evident from the above consideration is that when we, with Paul, arrive at the summit of the book of Romans, it is not the gathering that comes into view. Instead it is the sons and the creation that occupy the field of apostolic vision. Rather than starting with the gathering and working out from there, God's primary reference points for our lives are to be found in the large and diverse setting and sound of creation. God intends that these establish the largest context for our life, relationships and work as saints. Not only does Romans emphasise this cre-ation context, but also, as we shall see, Ephesians, the book of the church, does the same. It is within this creation setting, given to the sons and daughters, that the church gathering must find its place, not, I believe, the other way around. The saints, who are the church, must get their bear-ings from the creation, rather than from the congregation.

The church made up of people like George, the church that pastors like Steve live for, will never know its true iden-tity and purpose unless they as individuals hear the sound being made by the created order and are called forth, equipped and released to answer the cry. Also the world will never know what the church really is unless it feels that the cry it makes is engaged and answered by the people of God. The saints have, for the greater part, been hidden away from much of the cry and travail of creation. We do not hear the cry of creation to anywhere near the extent we should. The result is that we cannot fully hear the sound of the Father coming through our lives in answer to its cry. Because of this our sonship/daughterhood does not engage the eternal purpose to the extent it should. This is why our sense of identity and relatedness to life as believers is in many cases so narrow and our impact so limited. We continue to listen mostly to our own voices echoing off the walls, defining and redefining us again and again. And we are left wondering why the people don't come.

We have located ourselves in the building, the meeting and the programme and we have not effectively engaged the creation that holds our inheritance. This has ensured that we have become predominantly defined and fixed within the congregational context. In that place of containment and definition we find we are not strong, we are not secure and, increasingly, we are not satisfied. We so need to hear the sound Jesus spoke of, that sound which daily intensifies, searching us out and calling us forth to engage and answer the heart's cry of the Father for his creation. 'Deep speaking unto deep at the sound of thy waters' (Ps. 42:7) has always been the design and purpose of our Father God for the image bearers. It is time to look again and locate the new people in Christ that make up the church. It is time to release them from their church containment set in place by the Greeks and send them into God's creation that, to this day, still knows and calls their name. Where then are these new people for whom the present creation so anxiously waits?

Chapter 4

Enter The New Creation

The end of history, as some have called this era, presents the church with a unique opportunity. Humankind has tried Paganism, Platonism, Rationalism and its child Humanism. None have delivered on their promises, none have produced the 'new man'. We have emerged from these into the postmodern time where the story, the experience and the tribes (within the global village) predominate. Paganism is again rushing in to fill that story, and the old dualism inherent in the New Age movement is grasping at its heels, trying to ride in on the new/old idols to stake its claim on the age. These past ways are retelling their story and reaching an audience who see no other narrative that appears to encompass the complexity and the evil all around them.

Yet the Bible speaks an eternal story: the story of the only true God who created, came, died and rose again. If this amazing reality is to light up this age it will have to shine out from the life of every saint. We can no longer depend primarily on reasoned, authoritative or anointed presentations of the message in church meetings to reach the unchurched. That time is past.

☞ The divine story will impact only to the extent to which the saints know how to live it in a postmodern age. In this stage of the story we need to empower the saints for much more than church life and its programmes. We need to equip them to *be* the divine and eternal story in all of life and work.

No matter what the present philosophical trends might or might not be, the underlying creation reality still cries out for the sons and daughters of God to come. If we, the body of Christ, are to travel into life and light the darkness, we will have to be given the right resources for the journey. If we are to engage with creation as God intends, then we must deal with the mindset formed by the Greek divide. To do this there needs to be a change in the way we see God as coming to, and being in, our world. We need a thorough overhaul of our doctrine (understanding) of divine revelation. This, I believe, is the starting point for the deep and thorough change we need. It stands to reason that the very area Plato infiltrated, the place where Aquinas redrew the dark line, the split that Descartes used to divide the Western mind, is the philosophical terrain to which we must return. That is where the battle lines were drawn and that is where we must return to recapture what was lost. It is from there that the change to the saints' understanding of, and relationship to, reality can and must emerge.

Old Questions in a New Time

Divine revelation is not a theological issue removed from everyday life: rather it has to do with the whole way we see and do life. To demonstrate this we only have to list the questions people, Christian or not, ask concerning divine revelation and human existence. 'Where is God to be found? If God is so big why can't we see him? Why doesn't he just appear and tell us who he is? How is God present in this world? How does God manifest himself to us? Does he live mostly in heaven and when does he visit the earth? If he is the Almighty God why does he seem so distant and removed? In what way is he present in nature? How much is he involved in everyday life and human suffering? How is he present in Bible truth?' The questions keep coming. What is common to them all is that each of them relates to the doctrines of God's transcendence and immanence:

- **Transcendence:** God's person as infinite and distinct from the creation.
- **Immanence:** God's person revealed in a finite way within creation.

Something else these questions have in common is that they have been asked in one form or another since time began. What is different is that they are now being asked at the end of history and in the time of the postmodern story.

Some might say, 'The church has dealt with all of these matters for millennia and so the report on the nature of divine revelation must be well in hand by now. Didn't Solomon say that there is nothing new under the sun?' In answer I would say that because Greek thinking has substantially framed that report, there are some things Solomon knew that we have forgotten. Others might ask, 'What makes today different from any other time in church history?' The difference is that, not only is the weather changing, the global climatic patterns are as well. As Grenz said, there is a radical change going on in the philosophical status quo. The postmodern season is setting in. This change is not a fad; it's the overthrow of a philosophical system that first appeared almost 2,500 years ago. I believe we are being given a unique and divine opportunity to change the way we as saints see into and engage reality. These times not only demand that change; they are calling it forth from us. With this in mind, let's look together at what must die and what will rise to greet a postmodern generation.

Climate Control and Favoured Crops

As we saw from our swoop through history, the culture of the times has always influenced the thinking and fortunes of the church. It is a clear lesson of history that theology arises from the historical setting in which it is formulated. When any of the above questions about divine revelation were asked through the centuries, the answer was predominantly derived from the prevailing cultural paradigm. Components of the answer may have been drawn, to a lesser or greater extent, from the Bible, but the pieces were always put together in accordance with the design specifications that ruled the particular age.

The Renaissance produced the climate for the Reformers who produced the biblical rationalism that gave birth to the Protestant church. Clear-cut predestination took shape in a world of clear-cut natural laws where time, matter and space were forever fixed. Christological election, popularised by Barth (we are the elect in Christ who is the elect one), found form around the same time that Einstein informed us that matter is created and destroyed, time contracts and space bends. Suddenly our vision of a static universe broke down and life became much more existential (experiential, encounter-oriented). End-time visions have changed in line with the fortunes of Western society. When things were looking good, the church was postmillennial. When things started to look shaky, people hedged their investments in amillennial options. When humanism began to crash, Scofield went public with his share offer and the premillennial futures' market took off, much to the dismay of the old-school investors.

The other side of the coin is that many theologies were formulated as a reaction to the times. This was the case with early twentieth-century Christian fundamentalism with its anti-social gospel and its anti-intellectualism. It is seen in Barth's reaction against the liberal emphasis on God as immanent in creation. He disregarded natural theology altogether and flew off into transcendence to make his stand and validate his statements. In an inverted way, reactionary movements carry much of the prevailing philosophical data of the day in their DNA. As much as we would like to think ourselves neutral and objective, we are creatures of our time.

☞ Once we know that our vision, as normal as it may appear to us, is not the only vision of life, we are in a better position to look at our present 'philosophical glasses' and consider ordering a new prescription. The first steps will be disorienting, but so it is with every great journey of discovery.

If then we are to learn to adapt to, and do business with, the emerging new world, it is crucial we learn about the thinking behind our thinking and understand the ongoing interaction between our worldview, our Bible and our theology. Rather than staying put, lamenting our losses and longing for those days of Enlightenment certainty, we should look up and gaze through the philosophical skylight being put in place at this time. I believe the postmodern paradigm, far from obscuring our vision by taking away rational certainty, will give us an opportunity for sight we have not had for thousands of years. A bold statement I know, but I believe it will be amply confirmed as we proceed. For the first time since Plato was invited to attend church and the building was set up to accommodate him, we are in a position to look differently into the nature of reality.

Laying old ideas to rest in hope of a resurrection

I understand the concerns many have with letting go of elements of their heritage in biblical rationalism. However, all will not be lost if rationalism dies a death. It can, indeed it must, be resurrected and find its place in life again. It is good for it to die so that reason might live to serve again. The church need not sustain the now dying rationalism with its meagre life-support systems. We must let it go. As the ruler of the Enlightenment and the modern period it was fascist. We gave it a leg up and it kicked us out of the arena of Western life. We do not owe it any favours.

☞ We must not let go of reason applied to the Word. But our approach to truth and knowing must take into account all the dimensions of life. Just as we have become accustomed in the West to going into the truth concept to experience truth, we need to give ourselves permission to go into every God-given facet of life to find the measure of divine reality therein.

It is only when we approach and apply the divine story revealed in Scripture in this way that we will be able to see the corresponding impact of all of its dimensions on every facet of our life. We can afford to let go of the rule of rationalism at this time: not to descend into the irrational; rather to go beyond rationalism and arrive at what Grenz calls the 'metanarrative' – the story behind, through and over every other story, one that is able to speak life into every facet of life in creation.

I am not advocating we give way to postmodernism. I don't want it to define us as the church. Rather the call is there for the church to name it. We have no choice really; we have to do business with the new paradigm. Some may like the name 'postmodern'; some may consider it overused. It may not be in vogue in a few years time, with the new catch phrase 'XYZ' replacing it. The issue is not so much the name; rather it is the cultural shift it describes. The modern world is over and a new mosaic is forming from its broken pieces. Many of our young people have already moved across to the postmodern way of life. They have been brought up in a world where this view of reality is increasingly taking prominence over all others. If we do not fathom and use it then, as in eras past, it will carry us along by default. We will find ourselves declaring we are being biblical and culturally sensitive and end up being neither.

The Divine Story

There is a time emerging in which we can begin to use a language for our theology that is no longer divided by the Greek mindset. We are being given cultural permission and context to go after something that was always there for us. Providence is moving away from the rational definition to the time of 'the story'. Time is turning the world around to an era where the portrait informs us more than the formula. A philosophical climate is emerging in which seeds that have lain dormant for many centuries can now spring up. The most striking way in which the postmodern paradigm can bring change will be in the area of divine revelation.

Our heritage, with its divided language, has muddled our vision of God's coming to, and being in, the world – so much so that our doctrines of transcendence and immanence are effectively incoherent. Take up many modern theological texts and turn to the pages that speak of general and special revelation and the related topic of transcendence and immanence. It is not hard, I believe, to see why Grenz and Olson say that, after an intensive twentieth century of debate by theologians, we are as much, if not more, in trouble than ever (*20th Century Theology*, p. 310f.). Recently I read a contemporary Protestant systematic theology text to refresh myself in this matter. There was certainly much good information, but the overall Enlightenment/modern paradigm in which the theologian operated was more than evident. The following summary may have some editorial leanings but this is the taste left in the mouth of many trying to swallow the Enlightenment buffet.

Immanence wrestling with transcendence

God lives in heaven and at special times he comes into the world to interact with people and do supernatural things. The culmination of this revelation of God to humanity is, of course, the incarnation of the Son of God as a man. The record of this revelation is the Bible. This Word is called special revelation. It is distinct from general revelation, which refers to God's activity in creation, conscience and general providence. In these three things the revelation of God is 'limited' and 'natural' and as such cannot really be considered to be divine or supernatural. This having been said, God is still present in these things. We don't really know quite how he is, but we know he must be there in some way. We go so far as to say that natural things and events give us pictures and help us form concepts of what God is like.

However, this natural way of revelation, besides being untrustworthy, is basically unnecessary now that we have the Bible in hand. Also, we tend to steer clear of this general revelation of God, because if we emphasise the divine activity or presence in natural things too much we may well fall into the error of pantheism. The tension between the natural and the divine must be kept in place at all times because it is one of the major rational tools we have to discern revelation. We must hold on to this polarity. If we don't, if we allow too much specific divine activity or presence in natural things, we will break down the wall we have spent millennia building between the natural created realm and the spiritually transcendent one. Hence the obvious need to keep to the line.

When we worship God we focus in on heaven where he lives. In the old days they used to think that heaven was 'up there somewhere in space', but now that we know the world is round we can no longer believe such a thing. Just where heaven exists is now uncertain, but it waits somewhere in the transcendent realm. In the meantime we can make use of metaphors like 'up', 'down', 'above', and 'below' in describing our spiritual life – as long as we don't take them literally or seriously. We are, of course, opposed to allegorical interpretation of any part of the Bible. However, this metaphorical approach to certain scriptures is our only option when dealing with pre-scientific language.

For the present, in this dark and fallen world, we can content ourselves by knowing that we are in a special relationship with God. To help us in that relationship we have the Word, the Spirit and the church. The kind of life we are called to live is very clear as long as it is described within certain parameters that, along with the big three mentioned above, have a whole lot to do with ethics, doctrine, witnessing and worship. Even though we don't know everything about how God relates to everyday life, we can be assured that he is with us in this spiritual life we live. One day this world will be over, or we will die, and then we will have a clear vision of the way things were actually meant to be.

We are aware that of late there has been some pressure on us as evangelicals to move away from what some say is our Platonic-induced dualism. Deep down we know that God must be more 'on the scene', or should we say 'in the scene', than we have led others to believe. Our response is to restate the ideas that more radical theologians have in this area and then criticise them for going too far. We appreciate their attempts to welcome God more positively into his creation, but, after all they have said and after all we have done, we occupy a sacred ground we cannot and will not surrender. In this happy medium we find that we can keep firmly to the orthodox centre and also be seen to wave knowingly and safely at the postmodern parade. It's like having your theologian and eating him too.

The real estate

Perhaps I have pressed against this text more than I should have! But the rendering I have given is not far removed from what is, to all intents and purposes, the standard position regarding transcendence, immanence and divine revelation. This Enlightenment code is then passed along to the frazzled pastor who is expected to present it to increasingly busy people who front up each Sunday trying to make sense of life. It is good that Grenz has blown the whistle loud and strong here. It gives us permission to come clean and admit there is a tremendous crack in our thinking.

☞ We have inherited philosophical terrain with a great fault line running through it. It is now coming under intense and increasing pressure. This is the real estate that we have sold to the saints. This is the terrain that they in turn have built their homes and lives upon. The tectonic plates are shifting, the cracks are visible and the time of reckoning is now.

Is it any wonder that so many are welcoming the post-modern paradigm? If there were an election to see it come to power I would vote for it any day over the old candidates. But there was no election. It came whether the church liked it or not; it arrived without our permission. Our greatest challenge will be in finding ourselves at a place where we believe we must again ask those old questions concerning divine revelation and reality. It is even more of a challenge for leaders to do that. For by calling, by profession and by expectation they are meant to have the vision and know the doctrine. But the times are forcing our hand and, hopefully, humbling our hearts. As Grenz says, it would be such a pity if the church held on as one of the 'last defenders of the now dying modernity' (*Postmodernism*, p. 10).

Place your visionary order

Grenz and Olson say that the doctrines relating to the transcendence and immanence of God have been at the centre of theological debate and consideration throughout the last century. They say that a clear perspective and balance between them will be the major challenge facing the twenty-first-century theologian. In the introduction to their book *20th Century Theology*, they state:

> The lessons of the theology of the era are becoming clear. A lopsided theological edifice – one that is built on an inherently unstable foundation, whether the foundation be a one-sided

emphasis on transcendence or on immanence – cannot be 'fixed' simply by renovation, by adding the missing element. On the contrary, the theological construction engineer must start again from the ground up. For when the foundation is improperly laid, no cosmetic changes will lead to a durable structure (p. 13).

How do we 'start again' in our understanding of divine revelation? Where can we find the right foundations on which we can build a 'durable structure'?

Welcome to the Hebrew Mind

The postmodern paradigm is able, I believe, to give us philosophical access to a foundational treasure buried for centuries under Greek constructs and modern edifices. With so many of these now crumbling or in out-and-out ruin, we have the ability, in this time of the story, to reach back into a creation story carried by a tribe called the Hebrews. This present age gives us the tools to dig down to the foundations of our Christian worldview, to return to the initial creation reality revealed by God to the Hebrew fathers and prophets. It is there that I believe we can build again – not from the Enlightenment, the modern or indeed the postmodern, but from the creation. Before the 'splitting of the universe' by Plato, before the idolatry that preceded it, before the Fall, there was the creation and there was God speaking and revealing his nature and purpose. If deep speaks unto deep then surely Hebrew must speak unto Hebrew in this crucial matter of our approach to the worldview the Bible reveals.

The paradigm shift Christians, and hence the church, so need to embrace in this postmodern time will come, I believe, by our laying hold of and entering into the creation story revealed to the Hebrew people. Over and against the

Greek or Enlightenment view of humanity and spirituality, the Hebrew worldview delivers for us what can only be our true spiritual heritage. I draw attention here to the teaching of Ephesians that says that God made the two, Jew and Gentile, into one new man in Christ. The Gentiles, who were once 'afar off', have now been brought near by the blood of Christ. We now share an inheritance made up of the Fathers, the covenants, the promises and all the blessings of Abraham. We are built as the household of God on this Hebrew bedrock. Our Christian worldview is to be established on 'the foundation of the apostles and prophets, Christ Jesus himself being the corner stone' (Eph. 2:20).

☞ As Gentiles we are grafted onto Hebrew stock, not Greek philosophy or mysticism. Our DNA is Hebrew, not pagan. Would God establish, over thousands of years, a culture and a people through whom the Messiah would come, just to see the church carried along in the stream of pagan and Greek philosophy? The answer is obvious. Never!

We need to return to this great foundation for the new creation in Christ. In that place we will receive a vision of the creation, we will gain insight into the nature of the spiritual realm and we will find the philosophical sight we need to reconcile the transcendence and immanence of God. It will be on the basis of these discoveries that we will be able to far better apprehend the strategy God has given to those who are in Christ to engage all of life and work in answer to creation's cry. As we dig, to our surprise we will find that the foundations we seek were in fact never very far from the land and the soil of the Word we cherish and the earth we live upon. It is time to welcome God decidedly into the creation he has made, into the creation in which we live – into the creation that knows our name and yearns for our arrival.

THE WORLDVIEW

PART II

Chapter 5

The Hebrew Vision

Before we dig down to discover the first foundation stone, I want to stress that I am not advocating the adoption of ancient or contemporary Jewish practice to our present way of being the church. Much of what God did in and through the Law – moral, ceremonial and civic – was but a preparation for the coming of the Son in the fullness of time. So let me allay at the outset any fears that might arise concerning Christian Reconstructionism. I do not have any latent nostalgic desire to usher in the rule of Christian kings! It was a social programme that God himself never wanted and ultimately rejected. I await with earnest interest and desire the rule of the King of Kings. When I refer to the Hebrew worldview, I am speaking of the way in which David, Isaiah, Jesus, Paul, Peter and Luke the Gentile saw and related to the universe around them.

I believe that the things God taught the Hebrews in relation to the structure and nature of creation were meant to make it across the cultural border and arrive in the Gentile church. Something as awesome and all-encompassing as the creation reality could not have been fulfilled and hence surpassed between the time of the Old Testament and that of the New. It is not a type or a symbol of something to come: rather it reveals a reality that encompasses all of life. The creation must continue to set the big picture for the divine purpose down through history. From the Garden, into the Fall, through to the time of incarnation and from there into the age of the church, this creation reality must stand. I believe that we jettison the foundation God spent all that time building in the Hebrew mind at our philosophical peril.

Creation and Heaven

The first major foundation stone of the Hebrew worldview (or cosmology) related to their understanding of the way in which the creation was made. We read in Genesis that in the beginning God created the heavens and the earth. God taught the Hebrews that creation was made up of three heavens (orders of creation) existing from the earth right through to the highest heaven. Man lived on the earth and inhabited the first heaven. The heaven above this was the dwelling place of angels, who visited the earth and inter-acted with humanity. The third or highest of the heavens was the place where the throne of God was established. The place of the dead was called Sheol. It was under the earth. Through this vision of creation the Hebrews came to understand that heaven (the heavens) and earth existed in space/time relationship with each other. Heaven's presence above the earth was, of course, unseen to the physical eye, but nonetheless was known and experienced by the Hebrews as a part of the unseen creation of God.

As is often the case, Scripture does not argue for such a worldview; rather it presupposes it, considering it as a given. Some non-canonical Jewish writings refer to seven heavens, some to ten and some to even more. In support of the threefold heavens being inherent to the cosmology of the New Testament writers, I enclose the following quote from Philip Hughes' commentary on Paul's second letter to the Corinthians:

The probability is that Paul had in mind the conception of the heavens as threefold. The first heaven was that of the clouds, that is, of the earth's atmosphere, the second that of the stars (cf. the appearance of 'the lights in the firmament of heaven' on the fourth day of creation, Gen. 1:14), and the third a heaven which is spiritual. (p. 433)

Paul said he was 'caught up to the third heaven' (2 Cor. 12:2). Daniel's prayer took twenty-one days to be answered because it had to make it through the angelic realm existing between the third and the first heaven. In relation to the correlation between the starry heavens and the angelic realm I note statements in Scripture like that which speaks of the Dragon who 'swept away a third of the stars of heaven, and threw them to earth' (Rev. 12: 4). Scripture, I believe, testifies to a threefold heaven existing over the earth. Once this spatial and interrelated vision of the heavens and the earth is acknowledged one can see the extent to which it is woven into the fabric of the entire Old and New Testament writings.

From such a vision of creation we can surmise that the throne of God in the third heaven is a finite representation of the infinite God. That is, it is an expression of the immanence of God rather than being something spiritually removed from or separate to the creation. From John's visit to this place we understand that the dimensions of space and time were clearly in evidence there. He saw the Son positioned spatially at the right hand of God and noted that 'there was silence in heaven for a half an hour' (Rev. 8:1).

The primary role of these heavens is to manifest the rule of the sovereign creator God over all creation. Heaven is not necessary to God as such: rather it exists for the sake of creation. To put it another way, if there were no creation, there would have been no need for God to establish the third heaven over it. These heavens give people the perspective they need to make sense of life in the creation. They

64   *The Church Beyond The Congregation*

speak of the origin, nature and goal of all finite existence. Through such a vision of the creation, the Hebrews were able to relate and respond daily to the person and rule of God in the heavens.

Shining down from heaven

God himself has placed all the heavens above within humanity's spatial and psychological experience of reality. To this day they are an integral part of human language. Throughout history people have expressed their identification with the stars above. We were created to look towards the night skies and ponder the issues of life and human destiny. Popular songs speak of 'reaching the stars', 'touching the sky', 'reaching higher'. Heaven, for most people, is still positioned 'up there beyond the sky'. It shines down on them from above. Growing up or going up spatially has always been considered the favourable option, whether it is children maturing or buildings scraping the sky.

This way of seeing reality is woven into the fabric of many cultures of the earth. The heavenly perspective was taken very seriously by those who long ago decided to build 'a tower whose top will reach into heaven' (Gen. 11:4) called Babel. The heavens above are a crucial component of the saints', and of all peoples', unseen creation reality. It is not a redundant Old Testament revelation now spiritualised in the New, nor is it an embarrassing cosmology needing to hide in shame from the discoveries of science. It is a gift of God!

☞ From the Hebrew worldview we learn that heaven is not something dislocated from life and available only after death; rather it is the culmination and ultimate destination for all of our present life in creation. Death is certainly a definitive event that ushers us into the next age and the heavens. But the next age flows on from this one. The heavens that you enter at that time are above you, within and through the space/time dimensions of the creation.

The Apostle's Heavenly Vision

Although the heavens were a definite part of the Old Testament Hebrew vision, they were not considered to be a place people could ascend to. It was only after Christ had ascended through the heavens, disarmed the principalities and powers and taken the captives held in Sheol along with him that these heavens became the destination for the new creation in Christ. Hence the stronger emphasis of the New Testament writers on heaven's relationship to earth. Paul bases much of the divine strategy for the church on this foundational Hebrew truth. He goes to some lengths in 1 Corinthians 15 to communicate the relationship between this present age and the one to come. He uses the clear-cut analogy of what is sown and its relationship to what is raised or reaped. Our lives begin here on the earth and reach for and grow towards the throne of God in the heavens. It follows from this that, if we view the spiritual realm as something removed from our present life on earth, we in fact sever the growing plant from its roots. If we do this we will not succeed in reaching out and up into the heavens. This is why Paul says, 'The spiritual is not first, but the natural; then the spiritual' (1 Cor. 15:46).

When Paul says that we are raised in a 'spiritual body', he is referring to the goal of our present life. In the age to come we will have a life that does not need the present intermediaries (such as marriage, family or other institutions) to encounter God. They will have fulfilled their purpose. At that time God will 'abolish all rule and all authority and power' (15:24). In that place and time we will have a more direct encounter with the person (spirit or essence) of God. For this purpose we will be given a new and glorified body, fitted out for eternity. When Jesus comes he will renew the heavens and the earth, filling them with righteousness. The New Jerusalem will come down from the third heaven and the earth will be one with the heavens forever.

A misplaced heaven

Our seeing into the third heaven may be like looking into a 'glass darkly'. It is, however, over and above the blindness that descends from the high places and lofty speculations inhabited by the Greeks. The Platonic version of reality put heaven outside of the immanence, off somewhere in the transcendent. It says that whenever God comes to earth from heaven he suddenly appears from some 'other' transcendent spiritual realm into our dim-lit natural world. The gulf this spiritual stronghold has created in our psychological/spiritual encounter and vision of God is immense. We cannot cross it. We were created to travel in real space and actual time into every facet of life. Only in this way can we carry the 'all things' of creation through all of our life's experiences towards the heavens existing over the earth.

Once this vision of the heavens and the earth is established we can reclaim many key Bible verses that have been supplanted by the Greek mindset and release their power into all of our life and work in the creation. Truths that call us to 'set our mind on the things above, not on the things that are on earth' (Col. 3:2) will no longer be taken as a denial of this present life. Rather we will read on and discover that it is only immorality, impurity and evil desire that Paul was speaking against. We are only called to deny that which keeps us under the elemental things of earth and prevents us growing up through life towards the heavens above. Earth is connected in a strategic relationship to heaven in real space and in actual time. It was that way in the beginning and, with some majestic changes, it will be that way forever.

Fixing the co-ordinates of the unseen

You might be asking at this point, are angels 500 metres above us and if so how high up is the third heaven? All unseen things exist in the dimensions of space and time, but their divine essence exists beyond space and time. God's infinity arrives in every point to create our space and God's eternity touches at every moment to make our time. Time is not infinity and space is not eternity. They both, however, contain and express, as Bonhoeffer said, the 'beyond in the midst of life'. To give an example closer to home – a friendship is an unseen experiential reality that happens in space and time. If your friend is two metres away and then walks ten metres away the friendship does not diminish. That is, unseen things exist in space and time but are not subject to, or measured by, their co-ordinates.

This natural observation applies to the heavens above. These unseen heavens are in space/time and they are over us. However, the total reality they convey is not bound or fixed by these dimensions. Rather heaven's reality comes into and penetrates our experience in a way that space and time cannot pinpoint or measure. So the heavens, and even the eternity beyond them, are above us (out there). We have no permission to place them anywhere else. If, though, you want to measure how far away they are, you had better start practising by measuring the love your spouse has for you with a compass and protractor! They, like heaven, are there, but to fix the co-ordinates of their affection will be a challenge you will never be equal to!

Let's keep digging for more foundation stones.

Chapter 6

God – In, Through and Over All Things

The second foundation stone of the Hebrew worldview has to do with the way they saw and encountered divine reality in their everyday life and work in creation. There is a verse strategically placed at the beginning of the great book of Romans. It is found in the largest section in the Word dealing with the way of God's revelation in and through the creation. The truth it speaks of is foundational to both the Hebrew worldview and to most of what Paul teaches throughout that letter. It is a most amazing revelation.

Verse 20 of Romans 1 says that in the beginning God made people, intending that they come into relationship with their creator through 'that which is made'. We see here that it is through every facet of our life in the creation that we finite beings were meant to come to an understanding of and encounter with the infinite God. This statement from Romans reveals the amazing extent of God's revelation of himself in and through the created order. Paul says that God's 'invisible attributes, his eternal power and divine nature' were to be 'clearly seen' through all the things he had made. As Paul said in Ephesians, God is not only 'over all (things) and through all (things)', his attributes, nature and power are in reality also 'in all (things)' (Eph. 4:6; 'things' is included in the original Greek). Scripture plainly teaches that God's unseen nature and presence exists in and is expressed from every created thing.

Bringing these two foundational Hebrew truths together we can conclude that God's revelation of himself emerges, or is manifest, from every created thing, from the earth through to the highest heavens above us.

☞ For the Hebrew the spiritual or unseen realm was one with the created realm. It did not exist in a separate or removed dimension; it was in union with all of life in creation. The spiritual dimension of life is the heart or essence of every created thing, both seen and unseen.

The way of this presence and manifestation has to be understood carefully, and that we will seek to do in a later chapter. For now, however, we need to acknowledge the unreserved extent to which the apostle places the divine person and presence in, through and over the all things of creation.

What we have generally called the 'spiritual realm' was, to the Hebrew mind, simply the unseen realm. The Greeks saw the spiritual realm as disconnected from the material and relational world. For them, it began in the angelic realm and moved away from there into a transcendent heaven removed from life. The Hebrews would never have tolerated such blurred vision. For them the spiritual encompassed all of life.

Faith sees

Paul encouraged us to 'look at the things which are unseen' (2 Cor. 4:18). This means that it must be possible to see the unseen. We do it all the time. Most of life is in fact unseen. Such realities as love, marriage, work, government and friendship are not visible in themselves but have immense impact in the world. We can see a married couple or the workings of government with our eyes, but we can't physically see the thing in itself. To gain 'insight' into these God-given things we need to enter into relationship with the people who express them. In that relationship we come to feel their impact in our lives and thereby come to understand and appreciate the essence or nature of God expressed in and through them. If we saw as the Hebrews saw we would understand that marriage exists in the unseen realm right now. It is visible to principalities and powers and angelic hosts. It permeates the very atmosphere around and above you, right through to the throne of God.

This human capacity to 'see' the unseen is called faith. Faith, as we know, is the evidence of things hoped for and the substance of things not seen. This relates to the future, yes, but a future that is in direct relationship to, and can only arise from, the present. Faith is able to see the evidence of what you are going into and feel the substance of what you are moving towards. It enables you to go into the finite things to search out and draw into your life the unseen essence or substance within them. Indeed, it is a mark of maturity for a person to be able to look past the form and grasp the essence of something or someone. God made things this way for a very good reason. For it is only as we go into the form (or the seen) and learn to relate to the unseen that it contains, that we are trained (matured) to be able to relate to God who is unseen.

In regards to this way of seeing into life I draw reference to God's call to Adam to rule over the birds of the heavens and the fish of the sea. Here, in the beginning, we see the way God began to orient humanity towards that unseen purpose to rule by relationally and visually connecting them to created things that moved in space and existed in time. As Adam saw, named and came into relationship with the birds flying around the heavens, he would have become increasingly oriented towards the divine reality the birds journeyed in and through. In this way he would have come to discover what these atmospheric heavens held in relation to his life and calling.

God in heaven and on earth

Our revelation of the highest heaven is meant to begin with our vision of the unseen attributes, nature and power of God in the visible heavens above. We look up, like the Hebrew Psalmist, and see God's glory in that place, hear his thunder in the storm, feel his power in the burning sun and touch his majesty in the night-starred sky. Even in the 'fallenness' we touch the divine sadness. In the decay we can see the good gone wrong. In the dislocation we can see a glorious world turned away from its eternal axis. These first heavens orientate us to the higher and highest heavens above them. From the seen emerges the unseen and from that unseen emerges the Son of God, the fullness of all things. This vision of the heavens, and of all things, is able to deeply influence our psychological and relational reality. Its power and its purpose is to carry us progressively into, through and up towards the unseen heavens existing in space/time relationship over and above all things created.

Neil and Matt

When Neil met with Matt for a time of prayer, Matt was pleased that Neil didn't launch straight into it. Matt had had a busy day as a mental health officer working with a number of boarding houses. He did the rounds, ensuring that the tenants were getting enough nutrition to stay healthy. It was a difficult job even at the best of times. But Matt was taking his ground, holding it and cultivating it. Neil's a plasterer; he too works hard and like Matt doesn't always feel 'spiritual' at the end of a day. Neil is an elder who has a very large office. It's the golf course and the surrounding parks down the road from his house – that's where he met with Matt. It was getting on towards twilight and the golfers were moving off the greens. It may have had something to do with the golf balls, it may have had something to do with the tiredness they felt from the day, who knows, but Neil and Matt first sat on and then lay down on the grass.

Looking up at the sky they began to talk about life, work, marriage, the struggles and the breakthroughs. As they spoke the first light appeared in the night sky. No doubt it was one of the planets to shine that brightly – Saturn or perhaps Venus. As they kept looking up, seeing the expanse of the universe, they began to feel the impact of its immensity. More and more stars filled the canopy of the skies and the glory of God began its speech from these heavens. Through the times of talk and the times of silence they listened to the heavens and each other's words and the fellowship and honesty travelling between them deepened. In, through and over all of this one of them started to pray. 'Father of the universe, bless you for my brother, thank you for our wives, lead us into your purpose' – and the other responded in kind, 'Thank you for my brother here, fulfil every heart's desire, strengthen his life in you and for you.' The night got darker and the stars got brighter and the kingdom of God got clearer, much clearer to Neil and Matt.

With these first two foundational truths in place, let's begin to look at what this vision of creation enabled the righteous Hebrew to see.

Seeing and Enjoying God in the Created Order

The Hebrews' understanding of the heavens and earth and the unseen dimension in, through and over all things naturally had a profound impact on the way they encountered God in all of life. They saw God move, speak and act in the created realm of nature and rejoiced in that vision. We read in the Psalms that, 'The earth shook and quaked and the foundations of the mountains were trembling and were shaken because he was angry . . . He bowed the heavens also, and came down with thick darkness under his feet . . . He sped upon the wings of the wind. He made darkness his hiding place, . . . darkness of water, thick clouds of the skies' (Ps. 18). We read that God 'casts forth his ice as fragments. Who can stand before his cold?' (Ps. 147:17). Here we see the extent and clarity of their view of the nature, attributes and power of God in creation.

There is no reservation or holding back in this regard in the Hebrew mind. Certainly the language is poetic, but this is much more than simply a colourful and expressive use of words. For the Hebrew, God *was* in and through and over all of the creation. The heavens were 'telling of the glory of God. And their expanse was declaring the work of his hands' (Ps. 19:1). They saw his law in these heavens and they knew his law in their hearts. These joined with his providence over the land to call them to himself. The righteous Hebrew knew that to refuse the sight of, and encounter with, God in creation would only invite the idol to fill the vacuum left in the heavens.

Berkouwer, the Dutch theologian, says that God's communication in nature is not primarily information about God; rather it must be considered to be the very speech and expression of God himself. Writing in his *Studies in Dogmatics* series, Berkouwer says:

> Israel does hear the voice of God in nature and in the thunder storm. Israel does see him when he covers himself with light as with a garment and rides on the clouds as his chariot, and walks on the wings of the wind (Ps. 104:2, 3). This under-standing, and seeing, and hearing, is possible only in the communion with him, in the enlightening of the eyes by the salvation of God, and by the Word of the Lord. But this seeing and hearing is not a projection of the believing subject, but an actual finding and seeing and hearing! (*General Revelation*, p.131 ff.)

Knowing God in the world of relationships

The sight and experience of God did not stop with the physical creation; it reached right into the day-to-day relationships God made for humanity in the beginning. The Word of God calls us to discover the person and presence of God in each other. To feel and know the friendship of God in the fellowship of a brother or sister. To enjoy the romance and love of God in the embrace of a wife or husband. To sense the tenderness of God in holding a child close. These are not pale analogies that point us in another direction to find the real God. As scary as it may sound, these are the experience of the nature, attributes and power of God himself.

The Word of God speaks of this truth many times. In 1 John 3:16 we read that if we want to know the love of God in an experiential way we need to give our life to others in the same way he gave his life for us. In Ephesians, Paul directs us to the reality of Christ's love found and expressed in the marriage bond. In many passages in the Old and New

Testaments we read of God's love being expressed in and through the fellowship of saints, through the father's love for the child or through the under-shepherds of Christ. The sense of this truth is expressed in the words of the character Eric Liddel in the film *Chariots of Fire*: 'When I run I feel his pleasure'. Finite beings like us are designed to know and feel the infinite and transcendent person of God through all that he has made for that very purpose.

Wisdom more than reason

This orientation towards the creation as the means of divine encounter had a profound influence on the way the Hebrews related to knowledge. Over and against the emphasis on rationalism by the Western mind, the Hebrew possessed a love for wisdom. This wisdom was not distinct from God: rather it was personified as being God himself. We see this in Proverbs 8 where we read that 'The Lord possessed me [wisdom] at the beginning of his way, before the works of old. From everlasting I was established. From the beginning, from the earliest times of the earth. When there were no depths I was brought forth' (Prov. 8:22, 23). This wisdom is generally acknowledged to be the very person of the Son of God. This Son, ever existing with God as God, became the author and essence of all of the creation, including the wisdom within it.

In line with this, we turn to an amazing truth written by another Hebrew to the saints at Colossae. The scripture from Colossians 1:9, 10 brings together the key elements of the Hebrew world vision we have looked at thus far. We will come back to it a number of times throughout the book. So, to tag it for future reference, I will call it the 'Colossians' truth'. It speaks of the journey God intends us to take from the Word of Truth through all of life in creation to encounter the person of God. Paul prays:

1. That you may be filled with the knowledge of his will,
2. ... in all spiritual wisdom and understanding,
3. ... so that you may walk in a manner worthy of the Lord,
4. ... bearing fruit in every good work,
5. ... and increasing in the knowledge of God.

It is good to put the Word of God into practice to gain the benefits and blessings of such a way of life. However, with Hebrew vision and the theological permission it gives, we can go much further than this. The written word of God is the starting point of revelation. The knowledge of his will must then travel, via our understanding, into the way that we live each day. This much is generally well acknowledged and encouraged from the pulpit. However, it is the next few steps that, with Hebrew vision, can take us into new territory. We discover that as we walk in a manner pleasing to the Lord we begin to bear fruit. These results or outcomes arise specifically from the work that we do in everyday life. What we discover is that the fruit of our good work, the outcomes from our works and initiatives, actually lead us into the knowledge of God himself.

☞ We were created to discover the very attributes, nature and power of God through all of life and work. Rather than relationships, recreation and work being the backdrop to our spiritual life, giving us conceptual pictures of what God is really like, these things are in fact the very way into the revelation of God himself. Via the Hebrew vision of creation, we come to understand that God waits in the good fruit of our everyday life and work to be discovered and encountered by us.

Hebrew Dividends

These perspectives on life and work are first among many dividends that flow from an excavation and application of the Hebrew world vision. The split universe of the Greek mindset or worldview so limits our ability to see, and thus enter into, everyday life. The Hebrew focus can remove that blurred vision, enabling us to clearly see the divine person and presence in, through and over all of our life in creation. The threefold heaven existing over the earth is not an ancient relic or medieval fairytale. It is a God-given creation reality established from the very beginning of space/time. It has the ability to bring our encounter with God into every facet of life and work in creation. The Hebrew worldview is able to powerfully unite 'all things' within our vision of and encounter with God, right through to the highest heavens. The all things of creation are not simply pictures pointing away to the God of elsewhere. They are the largest context God has given us for our discovery and appreciation of the divine person and eternal purpose.

Such a revelation has, I believe, the ability to profoundly change the worldview of any person trained in the ways of that Western mind derived from the Greeks. It can erase that dark line Satan has drawn in the heavens above us. That thick and heavy wound, made by the father of lies when he severed the fabric of creation, can be healed as the saints take up and live out this vision of the heavens and the earth. It can give saints ears to hear God's sound and sense to feel God's glory coming through the heavens into and over all of their life and into the creation. Certainly the creation reality these foundational Hebrew truths speak of was profoundly affected by the Fall, but it was not made redundant by the curse. Nor has the revelation of God in, through and over the creation become unnecessary because we have the Bible. It is that very Word that speaks of this way of revelation and its crucial place in the ongoing purposes of God.

For those shamed by modernism into disregarding the Hebrew cosmology or concerned that postmodernism will call it only one of the many stories on offer, the challenge is to come up with a better vision. For this is our story, the one given by God. It is more than strong enough to hold its own for all time. We need not cloak our embarrassment by hiding these heavens behind metaphors. We are so selective in our disdain for allegory. The Greek divide we embraced is a hopeless failure; it has led us astray. The humanist worldview, with its closed-in naturalism, leaves no scope for the soul to breathe the infinite. It leaves us born of chance to die in chaos in a world of matter and mistaken probabilities. Buddha may well speak of a nirvana but there is no consciousness there to know it is there. The efforts of so many theologians working with blunted Enlightenment instruments down through the centuries have not resolved the impasse the Greeks set up in our thinking concerning the transcendence and immanence of God. Perhaps the simple sight the Hebrews were given by God is the best fit after all. I think so. From here let's dig a little deeper to find the bedrock which undergirds all of this – that being the place the Son of God occupies in the all things of creation.

Chapter 7

The Son of God, The Father and The Creation

You might be wondering how George, while thinking about his life, could benefit from all this creation theology. It may appear to be even more removed from his situation than the church service he attended that Sunday night. However, when George looks out across the city, searching out his past, anxious about his future, wondering about his marriage, his children, the church and the crisis at work, what does he see? How does he look into and evaluate these things? On what basis does he assign meaning to each of them? What does he think about God's relationship to and presence within each of them? How will he correlate them in his experience so they can work together rather than compete with each other? And finally, just where does George think he is?

The way in which George sees God as coming to, and existing in, the creation will determine the whole way in which he will structure his reality. Truth is, it is impossible not to have a theology of creation. We either have one by design or by default – it is best we follow the argument from design.

If these key areas of George's life are separated into compartments, some called spiritual and others called secular, he is in trouble from the start. If, when he looks into his job, he sees mostly money, ethics and the need to act responsibly, his ability to penetrate the mist there will be minimal. When he considers his pastor's expectations and the church's programmes of ministry to be the primary expression of the kingdom on earth, then the way he thinks about everything else in life will be determined by that belief. If he sees marriage, family and work as the temporary backdrop to the real action that waits for the next life to arrive, then he will only half live in each of these spheres of creation. George needs to be able to see into all of the facets of his life. He can only do this to the extent he can see the nature, attributes and power of God in and through all of these things. The extent to which he does this will be the extent to which he will be able to think clearly. And the way he thinks in his heart will determine the way he will live, work, decide and prosper. George needs the Hebrew vision to see the creation reality God has made for him.

Father, Son and Creation

With that in mind we now turn to consider the strategic and pivotal place the Son of God occupies in relation to the Father and to the created order. Here I believe we come to the very heart of resolving that long-standing tension between the transcendence and the immanence of God. The reason why the Hebrew worldview can deliver so strongly here arises from its vision of reality. For, rather than holding to categorical definitions of transcendence and immanence, as the modern/enlightenment mind demanded, it enables us to see these expressions of God in the context of the relationship between the Father and the Son and the Son and the creation. So let us now locate ourselves within the eternal and glorious God of creation.

To lead into our consideration of the Son's place in

relationship to the Father and the creation we ask the question: where is this creation or universe situated? The answer is not hard to find. By definition it is impossible for anything to exist outside of an infinite God. God can never be separate from any point in time, space, matter or experience. As David the Psalmist asked, 'Where can I go from thy presence Lord?' The answer was a definite nowhere! Certainly we can be out of relational fellowship with God, but that is another matter altogether. From here the question is asked: what is the Son of God's place in, and relationship to, this universe?

We know from Scripture that before the creation was brought forth the Son of God existed eternally with and in the Father. Paul says in Colossians, the Son 'is before all things' (Col. 1:17). Also we know that the Son of God brought all things into being and is the ultimate purpose of all things. In this regard we read that, 'All things were created by him and for him'. The Son of God is the preeminent one *over* all of the created order. The next facet of the Son's relationship with the creation is a little more difficult to grasp. Paul says, following on from the above, that 'in him all things hold together' (1:17). What he is saying is that all of the creation exists in the Son of God. Paul told the Athenians the same thing when he said that it is 'in him we live and move and exist' (Acts 17:28). Thus the Son of God exists right through the created order, throughout our entire world – incorporating time, space, the atmosphere, matter, events, persons, everything in which we live and work.

Visions of the Son

If all of creation exists in the Son, then, from Paul's teaching in Colossians, we can conclude that the attributes, nature and power in all things must be those of the Son of God.

That is, the Son must in fact reside (in a particular or special way) in every created thing. He is the essence or substance (as in, 'the substance belongs to Christ', Col. 2:17) of all things in creation.

☞ The Son of God, ever radiating from the Father, brought the creation into being within his eternal person. He is before that creation, he is the purpose of that creation and he is in and through all of that creation. The Son of God is before all things, over all things, through all things and in all things. No wonder David had such difficulty trying to run from his presence!

In the jungle, the mighty jungle

To allay any fears about the above teaching being some form of pantheism (God is only all things), let me stress the fact that the Son of God is in no way bound within time, space or matter. He existed as God and in God in eternity before the creation and made space and time in himself as dimensions in which finite man could dwell. Time and space do not contain the Son, he contains them. As the Dutch theologian Bavinck says, God comes into and is present in every point in space and time (*The Doctrine of God*). Reformed and evangelical theologians certainly acknowledge the omnipresence of God. But broadly speaking we, as the church, have not gone very far with it for fear of where it might take us. We can bring ourselves to emphasise God as being 'through (and over) all things', somehow permeating the universe and beyond with his presence. Our difficulty arises when it comes to the way in which we define God as being or residing 'in all things'. It is one thing for God to exist throughout all things in a general and relatively undefined way, but when we try to locate him in specific created/natural things the resistance grows dramatically.

It is here that we stop, hitting that Greek wall that divides the temporal things of the present creation from the eternal realm. The building blocks of this Greek wall serve to define and safeguard us against the roar of animism, idolatry and their pantheistic associates that we hear moving around outside our philosophical compound. However, we are neither safe nor guarded in such a place. Rather we find ourselves in ongoing confusion about the way and nature of divine revelation. The safety we seek and the vision we need can only be found by acknowledging that the Son of God does in fact exist in all things. The safeguards we need will come as we learn to decidedly relate the way (and why) of the Son's presence in all things with the way (and why) of his presence through and over all things. Such an understanding of divine revelation will enable us to 'anchor' the divine nature *in* our experience of all of life in creation. From this location we can then 'connect' and correlate the experience of his divine nature through and over all things in creation. The *in* must be our starting point for revelation. Without its 'anchor' we remain adrift in Platonic mist.

Accepting that God's attributes, nature and power are indeed in all things will, I believe, keep us more than orthodox. It will serve to release us from our compound and enable us to name the creation as we should. It will banish the pantheistic stronghold that has rushed in to the vacuum we have made by not occupying the created space out there beyond the bunker. Before we expand further on this way of divine revelation, let's first look at the place of the eternal Father in relation to the Son and the creation.

The Creation in the Son in the Father

As we saw, the Son, ever radiating from the Father, created all things and fills all things. The eternal Father is *of himself* transcendent to the creation. He exists in unapproachable light, eternal without time and infinite without space. No one has seen him and no one can directly know him. Only the eternal Son does both. Only the Son can open the way through to the Father. (That being said, in the space/time dimensions of the third heaven the transcendent Father does 'appear' as one 'like a jasper stone and a sardius in appearance' [Rev. 4:3]. This finite manifestation of the Father God is given in this way to portray to finite man and angels the relationship between the transcendent Father and the Son, who is immanent to and in creation.)

It is the spirit of sonship that enables us to commune with and enter into relationship with Abba Father. Paul describes our relationship with the Father God in this way: he says that we 'have come to know God, or rather be known by God' (Gal. 4:9). The infinite God cannot be *directly* known or in any way encompassed by finite people. However, in the Son (the immanence of God) we are able to experience what it is to be known by God. That is, we cannot directly know the transcendent God, but we can in the immanence be known by him. This 'being known' is more than enough for anyone to cope with! To better conceive of this relationship, one might say that our life in the immanence of God the Son is the finite experience of the transcendent God communing with us in every moment of life. This is what Jesus meant when he said that when we see and know the Son we come to experience in a finite way (within the immanence) the eternal Father.

Thus the 'line' that exists between the eternal transcendence and the immanence in creation exists only on the side of finite man. It is no barrier to the Father, who comes into our lives in the Son at every point of space, time and experience. This is why Scripture says that ultimately there is 'one God and Father of all who is over all (things) and through all (things) and in all (things)' (Eph. 4: 6). The transcendent Father, one with the Son, comes into every point in space and time in the Son to fill all of creation with his person and presence. 1 Corinthians 8:6 is very helpful in establishing such an understanding. It says that 'there is but one God, the Father, *from* whom are all things, and we exist *for* him; and one Lord, Jesus Christ, *through* whom are all things, and we exist *through* him.'

Transcendence and immanence – one with each other

It is this relationship between Father, Son and creation that brings transcendence into relationship with immanence. They are not categorically distinct, they are not removed in any way from each other – they are eternally one. The transcendent Father comes into the Son and the Son is in, through and over all of the creation – throughout every facet of our lives. From that life in creation in the Son we live, move and reach out into the immanence. In that immanence we are known by the transcendent Father who comes into all of our space, time and experience. The Father sounds into our lives and we cry out into his. The Father moves into our desire and we reach out into his. He speaks of our identity and we speak of our love. He ignites our purpose and we proclaim his glory. And we in the Son reach out into the fullness of that Son, that being the eternal Father. It is in this way that transcendence and immanence are more than reconciled; they are, as they have always been, forever one and manifest in eternal relationship between Father, Son and all of creation in the Son.

At this point I call to the stand the evangelical theologian we heard from (via some editorial leanings) in chapter 4. He disregarded the spatial view of the heavens and the earth because what was up for someone on one side of the world was down for a person on the opposite side. The solution to this (your Honour) is really very simple. The infinite Father God encompasses the Son in eternal relationship within himself. The Son creates and encompasses within himself the creation and all things within it. From this cosmology we can logically conclude that for every person at every place on the globe the third heaven (in the Son) and the transcendent God within and beyond these heavens are always 'up' or 'out' there. Thus the vision of the Hebrew worldview easily holds its own logical space right down to this partially informed time.

There is one more thing to say here to bring a sense of closure to this heavenly vision. It is more accurate to name the line (we finite beings feel) between the transcendence of God and the immanence of God as a horizon. For even though we will never fully know, so as to define or encompass, the transcendence of God, we will ever journey into him. When we arrive in the third heaven we will, in the Son, ever expand the horizon of our experience out and into the eternity and infinity of God. In the ages to come the Son will keep on showing us the surpassing riches of the Father's glory. The vista and depths of the God of forever will continue to unfold before us. Astronomers tell us that the seen universe is expanding into the infinite. In the immanence of the Son we will forever travel into the transcendence of the Father. With such a comfort and assurance, we can confidently turn to the present age to see all that can be seen with God-given 'twenty-twenty' Hebrew vision.

Creation and Revelation

We could turn from here and apply the Hebrew vision to many areas of Christian life and experience in creation. But, as mentioned, it is a change in our understanding of and approach to divine revelation that will be foundational to the paradigm shift the saints need to accomplish at this time. For this reason I will continue to apply the truths of the Hebrew worldview to God's coming to, and being in, the world. I have mentioned the way in which, down through much of church history, general revelation has been played off against special revelation. The fear that keeps this agenda in place is that if we alter this arrangement we might somehow dilute the divine nature by making it appear in any way to be 'natural'. Hence the polarity between sacred and profane, material and spiritual and so on. These divisions have to be removed if we are to see life and encounter God the way he intended. They need to be dismantled carefully so as not to limit God in any way in the creation. However, we must bring them into the relatedness that God intended them to have. We must emerge from the compound made by Plato.

We were made to encounter and worship God in, through and over all of creation. So, if we localise God in rational or removed realms, usually focused on the church event, or when we put heaven in eternity, we effectively create a vacuum in much of life. A space is made that nature abhors and what we find is that the most unusual things rush in to fill it. Saints can so easily become preoccupied in the veneration of leaders and buildings, traditions and creeds. They find themselves clinging to a limited band of religious frequencies and moral activities they associate with God. In many instances God has become localised, like a tribal deity, in sacred plots and special rites. This leaves many believers with a kind of muddled version of idolatry. If we will not see the divine person in and through all things, then idolatry is the only other option. We may believe that there is a separate spiritual realm apart from the present creation, and as a consequence deny, or greatly diminish, the world and its material and relational reality. But the realm we have constructed is as much prone to idolatry as the realm we think we have left behind. We must turn away from such limited vision and decidedly engage the full revelation of God's person and presence in, through and over the all things of creation.

The Son, through and through

As we know, there exists an infinite distinction between natural things and the transcendent God. Once that is established there is no more we can really say or learn about such a statement of fact. By definition, if something is infinitely distinct from something else then there is no comparison, no relationship and hence no finite way of understanding either of them in relation to each other. That is why God made us in the immanence of the Son to know and be known by him. When God describes the relationship between humanity's order of creation and the highest heavens he says that, 'As the heavens are higher than the earth, so are my ways higher than your ways and my thoughts than your thoughts' (Isaiah 55:9). Clearly God does not refer here to any discontinuity between some infinite heaven and a temporal earth; he simply emphasises the immense distance and difference – space, time, knowledge, glory – between them.

Within the immanence of the Son there must be a direct relatedness between all things in creation and the one who both made and fills them. If all things are brought into being by God, are maintained by his hand and are indwelt by his attributes, nature and power, then they cannot be considered categorically distinct in essence to the divine being. The form, the degree of manifest glory and way of revelation will vary greatly, but in all cases God must be the one who is in, through and over every thing. There must exist a

continuity of divine essence right through the created order.
The creation must be filled by the divine; the natural realm
cannot exist in exclusion to it. It simply cannot be categorically distinct. In relation to transcendence the distinction
holds, but never in relation to immanence.

The cold of ice and the green leaf are the cold and green of
God. The divine attributes, nature and power are not some
separate Platonically-defined substance safely and mysti-
cally gliding between and through the platelets of the natural realm. The divine attributes in all things open the way to

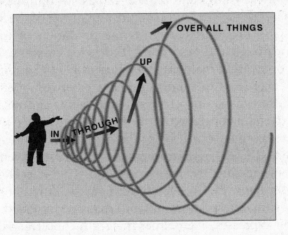

God's nature, and his nature opens the way for his power,
presence and purpose to emerge. Again the divine attributes
are not only in, they are also through and over all things. It
is this relatedness between the in, the through and the over
that makes for the spiritual realm.

This realm is a relational reality to be found, felt and fath-
omed in part right through all things to the very heaven of
heavens. Again I say that the natural realm is not of itself
God. But as is the case with those indwelt by Christ, the
eternal reality in which we live, move and have our being
has at its heart this 'one with but distinct from' way of rela-

tionship. This relational reality arises, of course, from the relationship that exists between the eternal persons of the triune God – Father, Son and Holy Spirit being ever one but three in one.

The Hebrews who wrote the New Testament saw the revelation of the Son of God coming from his life in the eternal Father into the immanence of the third heaven, right down through and into all of creation. Rather than there being any distinction in the heavens and the earth between divine things and natural things, all things express and manifest the attributes, nature and power of the Son of God. God progressively limits the revelation of himself down through the descending orders of creation. Every order of creation manifests the glory of God in a different way. There is no qualitative difference between them; the only difference is one of form (expression) and measure. From the human perspective they proceed from one level of glory to another, one level of the expression of the divine nature to the next, right through to the highest heavens and then beyond into the infinite of God. Paul's teaching in 1 Corinthians 15:40, 41, concerning the different levels of glory (manifest nature of God) that every created thing has and expresses, exemplifies this truth concerning divine revelation.

So it is that the way in which the Son is manifest in the third heaven is different from the way he is manifest in conscience. The way he is manifest in language is different from the way in which he is manifest in nature. The written Word is God-breathed, but it is not totally distinct from all other divine speech emerging from the creation reality. Every day the psalmist heard the heavens speak the glory of God. The way in which God is manifest in Christ, who is the fullness of the deity existing in bodily form, is certainly the highest revelation we have of God. But this way of revelation, rather than being absolutely 'other' to all else, was in fact given to light up the way of God's presence in all things. Every expression of the revelation of God must be understood by its relationship to every other facet of revelation and appraised in line with the level of glory it occupies in the created order.

Rather than this way of divine revelation diluting the divine nature in the natural order, it establishes the place and purpose of that nature in all things. That is, it identifies and distinguishes the attributes, nature and power of God clearly and decidedly in the all things of creation right through to the most glorious manifestation of God in the third heaven. It does not diminish the authority of divine inspiration or the uniqueness of the incarnation; rather it establishes their primary place in relation to all things. This does not mean that we will necessarily compromise with, or accept without question, systems of thought or belief that are in error. Rather it will enable us to see more clearly what is in error through a better discernment of the attributes and nature of God these systems are drawing their power from. That is, we will see light more clearly in all things and thus overcome darkness more effectively.

☞ If we take Hebrew insight we can unify our vision and experience of God and our vision and experience of life all at once. We will see God, as he always intended to be seen, in all things, through all things and over all things. Once this paradigm is established and we no longer have to fight that Enlightenment mind battle, we can begin to look at the powerful and strategic relationships that God intended to exist between all things and different orders of creation. These inter-relationships, as we shall see, are crucial to the divine strategy God has put in place for the new man who forms his body, the church.

A Man and his Car

The Hebrew vision of the universe, and the way of divine revelation it presents, may take a little time to get a handle on. If George gets round to reading these chapters, he might well come away with the impression that the Sunday night sermon he has just heard was a little more accessible than what was written here! And yet, as George ponders the past, present and future, he does so while standing on this created earth. His life resounds right through those heavens above him. He is seated with the Son of God made man at the right hand of the Majesty on high in the heaven of heavens. It matters not that he is in his car heading home to his wife and family. He is existing within this infinite God-given reality. It is on Hebrew foundations that George can begin to really picture just where he is at. He can know and feel that it is in the Son of God he lives, drives and has his being. This vision will enable George to see clearly into the people, the issues and the choices he has to make in the following days. With such a view of reality he can begin to search out the Son of God who is to be found in each of the facets of life he is trying to fathom and needs to engage.

GEORGE THE ELDER (3)
George comes home

The car pulls up at home, George turns off the engine. On its way to sleep the cooling motor ticks like a clock, reminding him to tread carefully. The light is on in the kitchen and it's ten forty-five in the evening. Mercifully he can hear no sound from a crying baby. He turns the key, comes in and there is his waiting Rebecca.

'Hi there,' he says with an up-beat chirp. 'Here's the bread and milk, honey, like I promised.' George chuckles

until he realises that Rebecca doesn't get it. She doesn't mention how long it took to get from the church to the home, but George is more than ready to fudge his way through that one if necessary.

Rebecca, realising it's her call, says, 'How was it?'

'Good,' George replies.

'Many there?'

'Numbers down a little,' he says.

'Good sermon?'

'Funny, very funny,' George discovers himself saying. George looks into his wife's eyes and wonders for the first time in a long time who she is. His convictions immediately tell him she is his wife. But he keeps on looking for a while, trying to see more.

'What are you looking at George? It's late.'

'Oh it's nothing, it's OK, I was just thinking.'

Ten past eleven, five minutes after lights out, Rebecca says, 'George, what were you thinking about?'

'When was that, honey?' George answers, pretending ignorance.

'When you came in, sweethead,' Rebecca shoots back, frustrated in the knowledge that George knows full well what she is talking about.

George doesn't know how to answer so he says 'Adam and Eve,' and chuckles.

'Very funny,' she replies. But before he goes to sleep he makes a decision to seek out the first couple God made and find out some things.

That night, with the permission dreams give one to see, George goes to visit Adam and Eve on a good day.

Chapter 8

The Garden and The Eternal Purpose

Adam has just named the giraffe. It took him days to finally work it out. The last time he tried to name this amazing thing with the long neck he was overcome with the sense of being alone. This unusual feeling had made him feel drowsy, another new sensation for the man. All he could do was curl up under a tree and sleep. Afterwards, when he awoke and saw Eve for the first time, he forgot about the long-necked animal. But now the time had come. Eve suggested 'goraffel' but it didn't seem right. So, while Eve was off looking round the Garden, Adam decided to decide – and giraffe it was. The animal seemed pleased and headed off into the bush. Adam was also pleased he could name and relate more closely to yet another one of the creations of God. Eve was pleased with the name. She said it contained all the best elements of the one she had thought of. Adam didn't disagree.

The late afternoon rolled on and the wind began to blow. In the breeze came that familiar sound, the sound of the Creator coming to commune. They always looked forward to this time, wanting it to be much more than it was. 'Why can't you stay and speak to us all day?' they would often

*ask. 'Why must you leave us alone here?' The sound of God
would say it was for their good. He would ask them about
the names, the decisions and the discoveries of their day. He
would speak to them of heaven above and their life and
work beyond the Garden where the rest of creation awaited
their arrival. Far too soon he would be gone, returning into
the quiet, moving on the winds of heaven. They would
never know quite where he came from or where he was
going. But they always heard the sound.*

In the Beginning

George's dream in the Garden of Eden did not take into
account the record that suggests that Adam gave names to
all the animals before Eve came onto the scene. Dreams are
like that. But that being said, there are many telling facets of
this dream that speak of the creation reality God put in place
in the Garden. This amazing place, planted in Eden, was the
arrival point and focus of all of the creation of God in the
Son. It is essential that we touch base here before we head off
into an application of Hebrew cosmology to the present age
of the church. It is here that we gain the clearest vision of the
strategic relationship God intended to exist between all
things and all orders of creation. It is from the Garden that
we get our bearings. As we do so we will be able to journey
with far greater confidence towards the divine strategy God
has put in place for our lives as his people, the church.

It is a simple setting this Garden. There is play and work,
talk and sleep. But, like a cloud, it holds a thunder of potential, speaking volumes concerning the nature of life in the
creation. So let's look around. The first observation we
make is that the physical and relational facets of the creation were more evident to Adam and Eve than the manifest
presence of God. The creation was open day and night

whereas the Word of God only came in from time to time, generally it seems towards the end of the day. The literal Hebrew informs us that this coming, rather than being a visible person walking, was actually the sound of the Lord coming on the breeze of the day. This description calls to mind Jesus' words to Nicodemus concerning the sound of the Spirit coming on the wind to lead those born of God into the divine purpose.

We learn from the record that Adam was called to enter into the creation and 'subdue the earth' (Gen. 1:28). Through this engagement he would come into maturity and ultimately into his rule over the works of God's hands. Adam and Eve were in effect called to serve an apprenticeship. Like children they were created in innocence and called to grow through life and work to reach their full potential and thus come into their inheritance. It is these simple observations that serve to inform us of the strategic relationship God intended to exist between humankind, the creation and the Word that came on the winds of heaven. Let's look at the set-up and see the plan.

Hide and Seek the Inheritance

God gifted a facet or expression of himself in the creation to humanity, giving us the freedom to choose and act within the boundaries set by moral and physical law. God in effect 'hid' himself within all things with a view to humanity searching him out. This discovery would happen as people named, related to and worked the all things of creation. As they engaged life in this way they would enter into the divine essence (attributes, nature and power) of every created thing. As Scripture says, 'It is the glory of God to conceal a matter. But the glory of kings is to search out a matter' (Proverbs 25:2). You may not identify immediately with being a king. However, if you are to 'reign in life' as a member of the 'royal priesthood' it will be necessary to take hold of the invitation to search out the treasure God has hidden in all things. So it is that God in his glory concealed the 'matter' of creation and we, for our glory, were to search it out. God, I believe, has established 'hide and seek' at the very heart of the creation purpose. Before we look in more detail at the reasons for this strategy of 'hiddenness', we need to turn and listen to the sound of Yahweh coming in on the breeze.

Besides the 'hiddenness inviting discovery' in all things we read of a more direct revelation of God coming to speak with people. Even though God had given himself to humanity in all things, he was definitely not excluded from speaking into and taking initiative on the earth. Yes he had given the earth 'to the sons of man', but the heavens overhead were still very much the 'heavens of the Lord' (Ps. 115:16). From these heavens the eternal Logos (Word) came in finite language to commune with us in relation to our identity and purpose. This Word was also an expression of the immanence of God. The Logos came incarnate and limited, clothed in language and delivered in - immense simplicity. Even in the Garden, the Word speaking would, I believe, have contained many mysteries, narratives, prophecies and dreams alongside clearer statements of divine truth and intent. That is, even in the more direct language spoken by God there existed a good degree of 'hiddenness inviting discovery'. So, why were there two ways of revelation in the creation and what is the relationship between them?

The need for a counterpoint

Firstly, it would have been essential for Adam and Eve to be aware that at the beginning and culmination of all things there existed the person of God. It was not the 'all things' *of themselves* that were God. It was the one who communed with them who was the creator God. He had called them into relationship and he had placed them in the creation with an eternal purpose in mind. Thus the verbal/language encounter on the breeze gave to the image bearer a more direct and personal communion with the divine being of God. This understanding and sense of a personal creator God over all things would give humankind the perspective and understanding needed to discover the attributes, nature and power of God in and through all things. Truth from God is always the starting point. As the Colossians' truth says, it is the 'knowledge of *his* will' that begins the journey into life towards the inheritance. This personal Word spoke of the unseen in the seen, the purpose in the plan: not fully, but enough for Adam to perceive the evidence and get a taste for the substance. It was then up to him to mix it with trust and live by faith to see the desire of the ages come.

Further to this, for the revelation of the Son in and through all things in creation to make sense it had to have another way of revelation to speak it. That is, there was a need for a verbal/personal counterpoint to this 'hiddenness inviting discovery'. It is a part of creation reality that things are defined only by their relationship to other things. Words are defined by other words. An individual cannot know who he or she is apart from another. Male without female has no definition. A number standing alone without any others in existence means nothing. The eternal relationship between the persons of the Triune God speaks to us concerning the foundation of such a way of reality.

In the creation order God's revelation in all things was met with, and related to, his revelation in the language encounter. Apart from the 'speech' of God the creation would not have been definable. This is one of the main reasons why after the Fall creation no longer fully revealed the divine nature. Creation without the divine language has no counterpoint to speak of its nature and purpose. This relationship between Word and creation works both ways in that the verbal encounter by itself would not have meant anything apart from the creation. This is because the words spoken by God would have not referred or related to anything found in human experience.

Questions in the Garden

One dare not presume to know all the reasons why God set it up this way in the beginning. However, I believe we are meant to search out the matter as much as we can. Such an engagement of the Garden reality will deliver many good returns to our present understanding of life, work and the divine strategy. I believe the main dividend will come from the understanding we will unearth concerning why reality is the way it is. Remember the questions I noted that people ask concerning the way of God's coming to and being in the world? How is he present? Why is he so silent? How does he relate to everyday life? Why doesn't he simply walk down the street and say hello, just once? Such telling issues and questions can be addressed in the light of the creation reality established by God in the Garden. So why did God hide himself in a creation that was humanity's major visible reality and then speak more directly in an unseen word that came from time to time on the breeze? I believe several reasons present themselves from the Garden setting.

- Such a creation reality would ensure that humanity's encounter with God would incorporate the entirety of human experience of life in creation. That is, through such a way of life, people would come to understand, see and thus relate to God in all things, through all things and over all things. God did not limit the revelation of himself to communication through concepts conveyed in words. He did not remove himself from the rest of creation and become only a vague reflection in all things. Rather he purposed that all of the creation would hold the vista and breadth of revelation and divine encounter. God concealed himself in every facet of life that humanity dealt with so that from and through all things a relationship with the real God (rather than a postcard from the God of elsewhere) could progressively develop.

- This creation reality meant that when Adam experienced the good in Eve or in relating to and naming the plants and animals he was able to go through that encounter and experience the very goodness of God himself. Adam was able to decide to relate to the person, event or thing or he could relate to the presence of God manifest within, through and over them. It was this choice and this relatedness that enabled Adam to forge the crucial link between his life, work and relationships and the unseen creator God.

- Adam was created to personify and thus relate to the divine nature within all things. That is why idolatry was so prevalent in the human condition following the Fall. It was only when we stopped at the thing itself and no longer went through to encounter God that we hit the wall of idolatry. Because we are persons, we have been designed to go in and through all things to arrive at a personal knowledge of God. There is no other way for people to know and be known by God. This is why the Hebrew psalmist, when it came to ice and snow, had no trouble feeling 'His cold'.

- This way of revelation meant that the depth of our encounter with God would always be commensurate with the level of maturity in life and work we had reached. That is, people would not be able to know more of God than their life could encompass and their maturity could handle. This balance between revelation and reality would ensure that people would progressively move towards their inheritance as their relationship with God deepened. God ensured that no dislocation would arise between our knowledge of God and our standing and progress in life.

- Rather than the earth arriving in humanity's lap already named, subdued and complete, people were called to work the creation to make it their own. If God had delivered it complete and perfect, humanity would no doubt have been impressed, but would have developed no backbone, little wisdom and a stunted character. If God had done it all and filled it all there would have been no room for humanity to grow. And it was that growth towards maturity in the heavens that was the very purpose of God in creating humankind in the first place.

- As men and women, in relationship with each other, discovered, named and related to all things, their sense of ownership and bonding with the entire creation would develop as a strong and lasting reality. Through such a way of life and work humanity would be able to engage the creation God had called them to rule over. As they did this they would be able to carry *all* of creation with them towards its fulfilment and their maturity. It would be incorporated into their reality and encompassed by their character. The divine purpose ensured that, rather than arriving in the heavens having bypassed the creation, humankind would come into their rule as stewards that held the creation firmly in their hands because it had become one with their heart.

A whole lot like life today

Do you see the way in which the Garden reality is a whole
lot like life today? The manifest presence of God is not obvious all day, every day. The Word of God comes to us, but it
does not dominate the foreground of our experience. It is
life, work and relationships that are most evident to us. The
Word written and spoken by the Spirit of God heads us into
life to engage and gather our inheritance and thereby discover the person, nature and purpose of God. Rather than
being the focus or goal of all of life, the Word initiates and
then gives us the ongoing encouragement and wisdom we
need to further experience God in, through and over all
things. The Colossians' truth that we looked at speaks to us
clearly of this process. What we see and understand from
the Garden setting gives us the vision we need to fully
engage all of life and work in this new day.

Bringing Language into Worship

All this experience in creation, with others and with the
Word spoken by God, drew together to bring man into a
fullness of relationship with the Father of that creation. It is
in the Garden that we learn of the powerful relationship
that God intends to exist between his Word, our life in creation and our worship of the Father. Jesus said that his Father desired to be worshipped in spirit and in truth. What is
the relationship between the creation reality and this foremost desire of the eternal Father?

When we sing, 'Father God I trust you, hold me close,
take me home, bring me into the abundance of victory,' the
content of these words is not found in the worship event
itself. Rather it comes from our experience of life in the creation. Certainly our worship songs do indicate what is out

> They shall call peoples to the mountain; there they shall offer righteous sacrifices; for they shall draw out the abundance of the seas, and the hidden treasures of the sand. (Deut. 33:19)

there and up there to be found in creation, speaking as they do of the unseen truth within the seen. These words, however, can only be filled by the substance found in creation. Certainly there is value in crying out to God for what we do not have or have not experienced. And God's answer does often come by way of direct comfort and healing in response to such a cry. However, the strongest renewal comes as we move on from there to fully engage, redeem and restore the 'substance' in creation to our lives.

God has given us the privilege of filling up our words with creation content, gathering our inheritance into the finite Logos we carry and speak into life. We, like the Hebrews of old, are privileged to worship God with the produce of our hands in festivals of harvest and history. Like them we can to this day draw from God's invisible attributes, eternal power and divine nature in all the things he has made, and come to celebrate together the goodness we find. The rational concept or some mystical other has not superseded such creation-filled worship. Our life in the Son in the creation is meant to continually and progressively attain that worship in spirit and in truth which our Father seeks and loves to welcome.

Treasure hunt

The father got up early before the children and wrapped the gifts in paper; he had chosen colours that camouflaged them well. He went out into the garden and looked around, smiling as he thought about the soon commencing game of hide-and-go-seek the treasure. His heart was in those gifts; he had chosen them well and paid for them dearly. And now for the joy of the giving, which he had decided to multiply by the joy of the finding. He placed some on the ground to be picked up at the first rush of little feet. Others he placed high so that only those who looked high would find them. One gift he placed in a special place his youngest daughter knew well and would search out first. All in all he had fun hiding the children's joy.

They emerged into the day and rushed out to get the first and easy rewards. Spurred on they raced around the garden, hardly looking in case they missed something elsewhere. The youngest raced to the fork of her favourite tree and turned with delight to the father's face to welcome and appreciate his heart gift. The middle brother kept looking at his father for clues, asking him if he was warm, cold or hot. He found what he was looking for. The older sister, as the gifts became more difficult to locate, began to follow what she thought would be her father's logic and sense of the ridiculous to search out the remaining treasure. And it worked, for there, running around in an equal frenzy on the collar of the Labrador, was the final prize of the day. No one missed out.

The Eternal Purpose

The question at the end of George's Garden tour 'on a good day' is: what has all this got to do with the present fallen age? Some would say: 'Shouldn't all of this be forgotten now that we have a marred and dark creation ruled over by the prince of the air? Isn't all of this earthly stuff redundant and aren't we now simply waiting for heaven? Shouldn't this "natural" realm now give way to the new realities of the "spiritual"?' My answer, as you may well imagine, is both no and never! God did not reject the creation at this time. Rather he subjected it to futility in hope of what was to come. Creation does not wait for annihilation; it waits for release from its 'bondage to decay'. The truth is that to this day the creation, even though fallen, still exists in the Son of God. When we tune into the New Testament book of Ephesians we hear a message broadcast by the apostle Paul. His calling, he said, was 'to bring to light what is the administration of the mystery which for ages has been hidden in God, who created all things; in order that the manifold wisdom of God might now be made known through the church to the rulers and the authorities in the heavenly places. This was in accordance with the eternal purposes which he carried out in Christ Jesus our Lord' (Eph. 3:9–11).

☞ The God who created all things did not come up with a new plan because of the Fall. No, the plan is the one that he has always had – it's eternal. The divine strategy that he began to unfold in the Garden is the same strategy he has in place for the church today.

There are of course new and tremendous things God has done since the Garden. All that he has done since the Fall, however, is in line with, rather than separate from, the eternal plan he purposed for the image bearer from before all time. As we shall see in the following chapter, the incarnation was never intended to put the eternal creation purpose off line; rather it served to bring all of it back on line. We will come back to this eternal plan and its outworking in this age. For now we need to look into the Garden one more time on what amounts to one very bad day.

On a bad day

Satan had been watching all that God had done in the creation. He no doubt knew a great deal about the eternal plan and definitely knew a lot about the way in which the creation was structured. He had taken the power of choice and the power to do good and turned them both against the divine person and purpose. Satan is nothing if not a strategist. We can learn a great deal about the war by noting the way in which the enemy thinks and manoeuvres. Satan picked his time and moved in. As we shall see, in everything he did there is an indication of what we in Christ must now counter.

Satan came into the Garden, into the innocence, and renamed God's intentions. Adam and Eve fell for the lie and from there they kept on falling. Thus Adam's hope of coming into his stewardship over the created order was destroyed. The descent into sin was swift from that time on. God came in with judgement and creation's full inheritance was submerged behind the thorns and the pain. Creation was designed to mirror and act as a counterpoint to humanity's own identity and purpose. For this reason when humanity fell, it fell too. If creation had remained the same a 'dis-reality' would have been established between it and humanity. Also the evil that fallen humanity could have accomplished in an unfallen world would have been far greater. The judgement of God to confuse the language at Babel (because 'now nothing which they purpose to do will be impossible for them' Gen. 11:6) indicates this principle. We will come back to the strategic judgements God enacted after the Fall in the next chapter.

How could something evil exist in God?

'If the creation exists in God, then does it not follow that now, because of the Fall, evil resides in God? How could that be possible?' The evil found in the cosmos as a result of fallen humanity and angels is not an infinite substance. Rather it is the eternal quality of good going in the wrong direction. Luther called evil a 'metaphysical lack'. The person involved in the unrighteous act is certainly responsible – theirs is certainly an act of evil. That evil is, however, ultimately defined as being, firstly, the lack of good and, secondly, the power inherent in good missing the mark and being turned against its created purpose. Suffering, the consequences of the curse and the effects of sin are in essence the effects of this good as it 'goes wrong'. Also they can be a manifestation of the righteous judgement of God on sin. Such an understanding of evil enables us to see how the fallen creation can still exist in God.

When human choice is wrong or sinful the underlying creation reality and divine presence is not threatened or withdrawn. If this were the case then it would mean that the possibility for such an action would not exist (it would be snuffed out just before or as it happened). When good goes wrong and becomes evil, God does withdraw his manifest fellowship. However, for him to take away the potential realisation of the attributes, nature and power of God (that is, his essential person/presence) in that misused opportunity would be nothing less than the end of finite existence.

Such a view of evil and suffering sheds light on

how God can still be present in all things and events even when they go against their creation purpose. It also helps us understand the capacity God has to directly use human evil (as it is happening) for the good without being compromised within it like people would be if they attempted the same.

From that first bad day Satan moved down throughout history to deceive and place his own inscription on all created things. Over every land came a dark 'principality' and over every sphere of creation came a 'power' stamped with a lie. The heavens above were obscured as the fallen angelic hosts moved in and behind the idolatry that soon followed the Fall. Humankind was brought under the 'weak and elemental things' (Gal. 4:9) through the deception that bound them to serve the creature rather than the creator. They took the things that God had made and named them to make them fit a now fallen image. No longer choosing to see, humanity drew further away from the searching light of God and into its own dim-lit world. Each became 'futile in his speculations and his foolish heart was darkened' (Rom. 1:21).

Twisting things away from the good

Satan moved to compound the growing darkness after the Fall by taking male and female identity, twisting their sexuality and turning it against the creation purposes. He laid siege to marriage and waged war against the family. He took a hold of such things as government and business and, using the power of law and wealth God had placed in them, made them instruments of despair and domination. At first Satan ruled the created realm through idolatry and materialism; then, from the sixth century BC, via Plato and Buddha, he moved to name and further obscure the image of God in all things via a life- and world-denying spirituality. This mixture of idolatry and its Western cousin materialism, married to a split universe, has produced the muddy waters and dark skies of our present day. This is the battlefield on which we stand; this is the earth we contest to win as our inheritance in a new day.

> **GEORGE THE ELDER (5)**
> **Monday morning dawns**

The alarm went off: 6:10 a.m. Four times at four-minute intervals George punished the sleep button. At 6:26, George emerged into the new day. Monday, the day of reckoning. He grabbed a coffee, shunned the morning paper and headed straight for the closet to pray. He was still undecided on his course of action. The Garden dream was good and certainly got him thinking. But he was still waiting on the word that would break open the day. God, as was often his custom during the days between sermons, had been quiet. So George went into the quiet to seek him.

He tried to sing 'This is the day that the Lord has made', but the melody kept on being interrupted by his intense need to yawn. After that, with only eighteen minutes to go, he got straight down to business. His tired brain offered God several options including: performing a miracle (any miracle would do), destroying the building, bomb scare, revival breaking out in the director's meeting, plus a few others that would be difficult to describe. George's eyes were, of course, intensely shut during this process, waiting for an anointing to fall on something. He concentrated hard and then . . .

It was two times four minutes later that George came back from what one conference speaker termed 'spiritual sleep in the presence'. When he focused and tried to remember where he had left off he could not, but pretended he did. 'Ah, yes – the God of the breakthrough,' George said to cap off with conviction what he had plain forgotten. And then something sprang into his mind. It had to be God because he'd stopped thinking. His mind dismissed this assumption with a sentence from a conference speaker from the States he had heard last May speaking against such a practice. But there was the word, clearer than Monday, 'Christ in you, George, the hope of glory, the hope of glory.' George engaged the revelation by asking, 'Is that an answer God or is it simply a truth?' He left it five seconds and God didn't say any more and by then it was time to rise and build; that is, it was time to awaken the car, head off down the freeway and meet Rob at the crossroads.

The Garden was big; the incarnation was bigger! To the coming of the Son of God as man we now turn. It will complete the journey from eternity past to the present age of the church. It will bring us through every barrier and elemental thing that stands in the way of life. And it will enable us to access and enact the eternal purpose that will lead us into our inheritance in, through and ultimately over all of creation. Like George was encouraged to do, let's look into the person of the Son of God coming through the heavens to the earth, to become within each of us Christ, 'the hope of glory'.

Chapter 9

The Son Comes In

There are, of course, many amazing facets of the incarnation that we could look into here. The history of the church is replete with writings that speak of the wonder and the power of God's coming as man. Here we want to look at the incarnation specifically as it relates to the all things of creation given to us by God as our inheritance. In particular the question we want to answer is: in view of the work of Christ, how do we, in a fallen age, enter into the creation to gain our inheritance? The answer to this question incorporates all of the divine strategy God has put in place for the church. In this chapter we will begin to look at that strategy, specifically in the light of the incarnation event that initiated the new era of God's eternal purpose for humanity.

The work of the Son of God as man won back all of the rights and standing humanity lost through the first Adam's disobedience. This 'last Adam' became the head of a new creation made up of believers in Christ. Christ fulfilled all righteousness as man, he ascended through the heavens as man and he entered into his rule over the creation as man. Because of this there is now a man seated at the right hand of the Majesty on high in the third heaven. In one powerful life and act of righteousness he accomplished all that was needed to ensure that the way through the creation and into the heavens was ours again. In the first creation we were called to relate to God in and through our standing in Adam. He was the mediator. Now, in the new creation, we are called to stand in the person and heritage of the Son of God made man. As Paul says, 'There is one God, and one mediator also between God and men, the *man* Christ Jesus' (1 Tim. 2:5). Once we stood in Adam, then we fell in Adam. Now we stand in relationship with God through our life in the Son of God made man.

As God incarnate, Jesus Christ is, of course, far greater than the first Adam. He is the life-giving Spirit, whereas Adam was a living soul. Our destination in the first Adam was to rule over the earth as far as the first atmospheric heavens. Our ultimate destiny in Christ is nothing less than the third heaven. We must still travel through the all things of creation to get there. For, as Paul says in Corinthians, 'We are sown in a natural body and raised in a spiritual body' (1 Cor. 15:44) and 'the spiritual is not first, but the natural; then the spiritual' (15:46). To reach the essence, or spirit, of all things, we must journey into that which contains and expresses that essence, that being the all things of the natural and relational created order. So it is that the rights, the position and the calling we lost in the first Adam have now been restored to us and lifted even higher in the last Adam. The eternal purpose is back on line!

Incarnation and inheritance

From here we turn to look at what the incarnation accomplished in relation to our inheritance. What follows takes us into an understanding of that unusual phrase of Paul's in Romans 8:17. He said there that we are 'heirs of the Father and joint heirs with the Son, if indeed we suffer with him'. Note the positioning of this verse. It comes just after our cry of sonship to Abba, Father and just before the cry of creation calling our name as sons. The reason it is placed here is simply because the creation that cries *is* our inheritance. This is what we are heirs to. The eternal Father gave it to the Son of God made man and all of those who are in him. If we are to welcome that inheritance into our lives we must suffer with him.

Here we come to an amazing dividend of the Hebrew worldview. Here, I believe, we come to the crucial difference between the sons of this age and the sons of light. Fallen humanity can discover many truths, can travel a long way into the creation reality and can even do the good that will, as Jesus said, have its reward. But there is a place it reaches where it can go no further. Humanity may hear a cry from creation, but cannot fully answer the cry placed there by God.

☞ The reason why fallen humanity can go no further and the new creation can press on past that point to gain the inheritance is crucial to the divine strategy. This essential difference has all to do with the way and why of suffering. We need to know why we must suffer with the Son to enter into our inheritance in, through and over all things.

In the last chapter we saw the enemy take the power inherent in the all things and rename them so as to deceive and rule over the systems of humanity. Since the Fall he has been carrying out a very definite strategy. However, I draw your attention to the much larger change in the structure of the creation brought about by God after the Fall. The judgement of God profoundly affected every facet of the created order. The thorns, the birth pains, the dislocation, sweat and death were all brought in by God to bring home to humanity the reality and consequences of the place it now occupied. Satan's activity after the Fall was only possible because of the creation reality God had set up. Satan intensified and multiplied that fallen reality but he was not the creator of it.

All that God did at this time of judgement was strategic and ultimately redemptive. In this regard we read, 'The creation itself was subjected to futility, not of its own will, but because of him who subjected it, in hope.' Paul goes on from here to say, 'in hope that the creation itself will be set free from its slavery to corruption into the freedom of the glory of the children of God' (Rom. 8:20, 21). It is this subjection of the creation to futility 'in hope' that holds the key to the strategy of God for the church. What we learn from this statement is that, rather than completely setting aside the initial creation reality, God only removed the full inheritance within creation out of reach of fallen humanity and wicked angels. He did it through darkness: humanity not able to see or go into the depths of creation. He did it through futility: humanity not permitted to build anything to the heavens. He did it through death: humanity not living to multiply evil over aeons of time. The fullness of the Son in, through and over all things was now disengaged (as it were) from the form of created things. There was no longer a way through them to the fullness. The fallen creation could now only wait 'in hope' for the coming of the Son and the sons to begin the time of liberation. It was only the coming of the Son that could put an end to the dead end God had placed in the creation.

Enter the Son

So how did the Son of God as man relate and respond to the darkness, futility and death in creation? The answer is that he came to encompass, fill and fulfil each of them. The Son came into all of humankind's fallen experience. He suffered his way through every judgement arising from the Fall. He entered into the fullness of sin, which is death. He was engulfed by the divine darkness at the cross. His majestic life was consumed by a futile dead end – thirsting, alone, naked and rejected by the Father. All the darkness, futility and death that were brought in by God after the time of the Fall were taken on by God to begin the time of restoration. And then, after judgement was complete, the Son came out and into resurrection life. He forgave us, breathed his breath of life into us, ascended into the heavens, sent the Spirit in power and commissioned us to live and give his life.

What this means for us is that futility, darkness and death are no longer standing in the way of our inheritance. Because the Son has come into each of them, fulfilled them and now fills them, he has radically renamed them (redefined them). Rather than being a barrier we cannot overcome, they are now the very means of entering into the inheritance.

☞ The Son of God made man went through the pain barrier set up by God after the Fall. He came in the power of righteousness and entered into all of human travail, thereby forging a strategic relationship between himself and every facet of fallen humanity's experience. He went into futility, darkness and death as a man; he went through to the essence of all things to secure the inheritance in, through and over all things.

And as he entered in and through these things he suffered. That is why we read that, 'it was fitting for him, for whom are all things, and through whom are all things, in bringing many sons to glory to perfect the author of their salvation *through* sufferings' (Heb. 2:10). 'And having been made perfect, he became to all those who obey him the source of eternal salvation' (Heb. 5:9). The wall that faces fallen humanity is now the gate for the redeemed. How do we get through that gate to gain the inheritance? To zero in on the answer, we turn to consider one of the most intriguing judgements delivered at the time of the Fall.

The telling sign of birth

God said to Eve, 'I will greatly multiply your pain in childbirth' (Gen. 3:16). Countless women have wondered at this (some men have as well!). I believe that God established this powerful and painful sign as a testimony that the inheritance (the child, the promise, the fruit) would now only come via the way of suffering. The inheritance still existed, but the sign showed that it was now concealed behind darkness, futility and death and would only emerge through the pain of travail.

Pain existed before the Fall. Without the ability to feel pain (physical, moral, psychological) humanity's ability to relate to the outside world would be impaired. Pain was not created after the Fall: rather it was 'multiplied'. Pain is given as a reality sign. The work of Dr Paul Brand in the area of leprosy has brought out into the light the nature and blessing of the gift of pain. Leprosy is a condition that causes a person to lose the ability to feel pain. Their limbs don't simply fall off: rather they are damaged and lost because these people cannot relate properly to the physical world. Pain is the signal that something is wrong, it directs us to the wound wanting and needing to be healed. Pain arises from our experiences of life and is multiplied by the futility, darkness and death we encounter. Pain is the gift that, try as we might to run from it, draws us to address the wound that is bleeding our life and inheritance away. Where are we situated in the feeling of this pain?

Suffering Through to Your Inheritance

When things and events become evidently futile and seem to work against you, where are you at that moment? Right

then you are touching the very inheritance that God himself
has rendered fallen and wounded.

☞ The things you call futile, decaying and even dark hold
within them your inheritance. They are the gift of the
Father wrapped in thorns and covered in sweat.

You can walk away down easy street but it is only a dead
end. What, in essence, is this futility? Is it not simply a
reflection of your own wound, given to you by God? Is this
not the very sign to you of what was lost in the Fall, both
individually and universally? We read in Scripture that creation itself 'suffers the pains of childbirth until now' (Rom.
8:22). The way in which creation now (dys)functions is not
a basis for our abandonment of it as saints. The opposite is
in fact the case. In the dysfunction is an opportunity for
change in us and change to the thing, person and event we
engage. Pain connects us with all fallen things as 'we also
groan' (8:23). The place where we meet is the very place
where the 'dis-reality' started – that place where sin and its
strongholds enter into creation and into our life.

The creation reality is in fact a reflection of your fallen image, both individually and corporately. Its cry in pain for restoration, heard through the futility, darkness and death all
around you, is an invitation you must accept. Can you walk
away from a birth that is coming? Many women would like
to, but they cannot. You must go through. Behind that
wound is a life waiting for restoration. In that complex and
fallen relationship is a person who is your eternal inheritance. Only by restoring and joining your diverse and complementary lives will your own heart grow. And only as that
relational reality grows will the body, the church you are one
with, come to fill the heavens. It is only by pressing into the
suffering that the thorns can be bypassed, the fruit seen, the
sweat spent and the bread of life tasted.

No fallen person can get past the futility, journey through the darkness and transcend the death that so vexes human existence. It is only the sons and daughters who have the ability to enter into the travail these experiences bring and go through to discover the land promised as their inheritance. I hasten to add that I am not referring to suffering as a virtue in itself. Nor am I in any way proposing we should be passive in the face of injustice or oppression. If you get a toothache, take an aspirin and make an appointment with a dentist! In life we should not search out suffering for its own sake. It will, however, find us. The way in which it finds us and the way in which we respond to it are the key to God's strategy in suffering. How then might this divine plan work for people like George on Monday morning as he drives into town to face his own particular brand of fallen reality?

Meet me at the altar

A friend once said, in relation to her struggle for a meaningful marriage, 'I wouldn't have changed but pain drove me to do so. It was not a noble idea that moved me; it was a wanting to stop the hurting. And to stop the hurting through my marriage being healed. Pain became my ally. It showed me, through the process of my change, that I was really doing something. I set up an altar in my marriage, a place of sacrifice and worship, and I met Jesus there and we built together. I thought it was my husband that was going to change, but over the years it was me who changed the most. My marriage is not perfect, but it's restored. My husband is free from so many of the expectations I used to place on him. He's not perfect, but he's changing to be the man God has made him to be.'

Here we see a person faced with the reality of relating to one of the major spheres of her life – marriage. Her marriage, family, home and all that these contain and express make for her inheritance. In a fallen world the pain and struggle found in this sphere of life is more than evident. When we go into any creation sphere it is not long before we come up against challenges. In every facet of life the reality of a fallen world has to be reckoned with. Whether or not God planned the challenge or trauma is not so much the central issue here. The matter has all to do with the way in which we will respond to the suffering we are now beginning to engage. The issue, in terms of the divine strategy, is how we are going to relate to the Son of God who indwells this life struggle.

As we know, it is strongholds in our minds that structure our perceptions and our language. These determine the way we relate to people and ultimately build our reality. It is our strongholds, raised up against the knowledge of God, which keep us from our inheritance. Our problem is not so much with fallen angels. These do not create our reality, they only back up and intensify the 'dis-reality' we establish. This is why God made creation as our counterpoint. It is a mirror that reflects back and portrays who we are in our strengths and weaknesses. Our strongholds trigger reactions in the relational reality around us. They evoke a response from creation that sends back a confirmation of where we really are in life.

When fallen humanity is faced with trauma, challenge and opposition it generally reverts to fallen responses. As it does this, the immediate problem may well be overcome, but the God-given essence of the created thing is not encountered. Even though the individual may succeed in the world's terms, the creation treasure remains beyond their reach. When the saints enter into the creation reality they also hit up against the same obstacles, travail and limitations. In these they also come face to face with their own strongholds and those of others. Things don't work out, people let you down, you fail and disappoint others, the job doesn't come through, the house didn't sell, the husband leaves, the church splits – on it goes! Paul speaks of perplexity and confusion, of being afflicted, struck down and persecuted and he names these things with a marvellous new name. He calls them the 'dying of Jesus' (2 Cor. 4:10). Futility for the fallen becomes the dying of Jesus for the sons and daughters. Darkness becomes light. Death (to self or life) is now named as 'his death' (Phil. 3:10).

Pain that teaches

When we encounter what we will inevitably encounter, when the reality time is reached and the suffering begins, there is a choice to make. They can either keep going into the particular thing or relationship or back off by choosing any number of the world's options. These options are also on offer in many religious environments established to safeguard the saints from the cost and reality of entering into a complex and fallen world.

If, however, there is an understanding of the creation reality and the nature of the incarnation, the saints are in a position to press through the pain barrier to gain a lasting inheritance in Christ in the creation. How? Firstly they need to understand the place of pain: what it is signalling in terms of the situation or relationship in which they are engaged. Rather than running for painkillers they need to use that pain to prayerfully locate the wound that is being exposed. This pain will move them towards a place of 'sensitivity' where someone very special is waiting. As they enter into the suffering they are surprised to find much more than pain. They discover the person of the Son of God existing *in* the place of trial. They also find that they are able to 'fellowship with him in (what the Son now names as) his sufferings' (Phil. 3:10). The person of God is actually present in the disappointment, the setback, the obstacle and even the injustice. He is actually present in your suffering as God made man.

When we first locate Christ in our sufferings, our conversation with him tends to consist of such pressing pleas as – get me out of here quick, validate me, make the money appear, show everyone how wrong she is and other such notable supplications. These may be options that the Son of God will consider. However, his overriding passion is more for our life and inheritance than for our immediate comfort and vindication. So he is often quiet for a time until we turn to really 'fellowship' with him in our sufferings. When we respond to him the pain does not disappear. Rather it takes on a divine dimension that transforms it into a travail that begins the work that can deliver the child of promise.

From temporary shelter to eternal home

When we fellowship with him in the furnace of affliction, the temperature is raised as divine reality comes to bear on fallen thinking. This heat works to expose our strongholds in the light of the eternal day. Here joint starts to divide from marrow and truth is discerned from error. Sometimes we are aware of the thinking that needs to be changed. Often the process runs far deeper than our capacity to understand. We find ourselves giving up on a position or stronghold, not because we want to, but because it has become useless and unworkable in the present environment. It has become too painful to sustain that unforgiveness or that attitude any longer. Often we have to let go of positions that are right in themselves. It is only later that we discover that it was our need to be right at all times, fuelled by an underlying fear of failure, that was making us cling to validation. There are many examples that could be covered here. His death works to take it all – the seemingly good, the bad and the ugly – along with us, into death. The resurrection will tell us what can and will live before him.

So it is that, rather than taking us out of our suffering as we demand, the Son of God takes us into the very death relating to the strongholds that surround the particular sphere of life being dealt with. We become 'conformed to his death' (Phil. 3:10). This divine dying is final for the stronghold but for us it is a gateway into life itself. The dark and futile thinking that kept us from our inheritance in life is overthrown in that death. This abiding with him in death may last a month, sometimes it lasts a year, sometimes, in particular areas of our life, we can remain in the dust of death for a decade. There we abide alone; yet we are not alone, we are with him. In that place we hear things and come to know things that we could never hear or understand elsewhere.

Then, in the fullness of time, we hear the trumpet sound. We see the banner unfurled as we journey 'cross the borderline. It declares our emergence from death into the new creation waiting. We will feel the moment when freedom comes. We will see providence arriving from several directions at once. And we will know that the mind that controlled certain responses and structured that part of our reality is no longer thinking for us. We will reach for it but it will not be there. Its counsels will still be resident in our sin nature and we can still tune in to their frequencies. But 'his death' has separated us from their constant and insidious domination. We have emerged into what Scripture names the 'out-resurrection from among the dead'. Such a life will, of course, culminate in the final resurrection, but this phrase from Philippians refers to our immediate entry into newness of life in Christ in this age. It is in this way that our 'outer man' (fashioned after the world system) decays and our 'inner man' is 'renewed (restored to its true nature) day by day' (2 Cor. 4:16).

Change

As one might well imagine, in this amazing process we are changed! That change happens in our own character and in relation to the person, thing or work we have been dealing with. It is not to say that all of a sudden the world dances to our tune and does our bidding. Rather it means that our relationship to that facet (or facets) of the creation is forever changed. Fear, insecurity, rejection and the lust, pride and greed that they fed on and existed through no longer have the power to keep us from the relationships that are our inheritance. We can begin to take hold of the attributes, nature and power of God found in the relationships and works that that particular sphere of creation holds and accesses. That part of our life has been redeemed by the Son. And that facet of the creation is now accessible, ready to be progressively restored to us – brought on line to find its own fullness in relation to the image bearer. We have seen through the darkness, reached through the futility and journeyed through the pain to arrive at the beginning of our inheritance in the all things of creation. This is why Jesus came, suffered, died and rose again. This is why Jesus said that, if we are to enter into the kingdom of heaven, we must do so through much tribulation. This is why we *must* suffer with him to enter into our inheritance.

> And I will give you the treasures of darkness and the hidden wealth of secret places. In order that you may know that it is I, The LORD, the God of Israel, who calls you by your name. (Isaiah 45:3)

Who would have structured such a way of reality except God? Fallen humanity could never even imagine such a process. They are not looking in the direction of suffering, let alone death, for an answer. Only God could make such a way through. Only God could arrive in fallen reality through a doorway like this. So it is that, through this incredible way, sons and daughters can go through suffering into the fallen creation and emerge into the eternal purpose. This purpose of God moves on from the initial phase described here, but apart from an understanding of the role of suffering we cannot reach the first base of the divine process of restoration.

Light in the Darkness

This incredible journey into the Son of God profoundly influences another facet of our inheritance in the Son. It has to do with fallen men and women who struggle under futility, crying out, along with the rest of fallen creation, for release. The new man's journey through suffering, death and into life is also for them. How so?

The people of this creation, crying out under the burden of sin and decay, are searching for an answer to their travail. How are we as sons and daughters of God to connect with them? God has called the body of Christ to join with the created order by sharing in its experience of suffering ('we also groan'). It is in this relationship of mutual travail that God is able to do a profound work. The outcomes of suffering for saint and sinner are radically different. It is in that difference we come to touch God's way of reaching into a lost world.

The travail of fallen humanity can only end in futility and decay. They search, but cannot find a way out of their situation. If the saints are removed and distant from such travail then people will never come to know God's way out. So the saints enter into their fair, and at times seemingly unfair, share of trials and suffering. The 'new creation' in Christ is able to emerge from the afflictions common to every person into life. Observing such a process, fallen people begin to see in us the resolution to the aching problem of their futility and travail. They may not want to see, but God is at work to draw their attention to the saints working and relating alongside them. They come to hear the heart's cry of the Father sounding through our suffering to them. They begin to see the fruit and the life such struggle generates and they are drawn to the quality and strength of character it produces within us.

☞ Fallen people see mercy and joy at work in the midst of our struggles, not as a denial of reality but rather as the heartbeat of divine reality. They see the very presence and power of God in our life circumstances, not so much always getting us out of difficulty, but rather taking us through and into life.

So, it is in this resonating together with the fallen that God comes to sound the sound of his love and power to save. It is in that union that the redeeming light reaches out to dispel the darkness. They now see that their suffering and futility need not end in death: rather it can embrace the Cross of Christ, move into the dying of Jesus and from there come out into his resurrection and life. In this way the gospel becomes more than a message preached, it travels into the heart of fallen humanity as a reality demonstrated before their eyes. It is understood not just as religious history, but also as a whole way of living and being.

This is why God works through suffering to bring us close to those outside of Christ. For they are a part of the Son's inheritance in the Father and as such they are a part of our fullness in the Son. We must allow God to bring us alongside them. For that to happen we must allow the Spirit of God to take us into the suffering of creation to bring in the restoration. God has concealed the produce of the earth behind the thorns, he has placed the child behind the birth pangs and he has hidden the bread behind the sweat. When the Son of God came he took the thorns on his head, he bore the suffering on his back, he travailed in naked shame on the tree and then he declared 'It is finished'. He took them all into death to complete the incarnation and emerged, beckoning us to follow and share now in the inheritance reclaimed for the sons and daughters.

The new man emerges to answer the cry

It is this way of suffering that prepares the saints, like nothing else, to be those who can answer the cry. The doctrine can inform them, the fellowship can encourage them, the vision can inspire them, but the suffering will enable them to resonate in such a way as to attract the inheritance into their hearts and lives. It is this new man or woman for whom creation waits. It is these men and women who are the church, the body that Christ came to create and release into the earth.

What kind of man is the new man? What kind of woman does this way of travail and divine death create? What does a person who can embrace 'his suffering' and no longer fear 'his death' look like? How do they function, relate and respond to life? Who is this Spirit-filled Hebrew creation emerging from the furnace of affliction to answer the cry? Paul, the foremost sufferer, gives us a masterly portrayal of them in 2 Corinthians 6. There we read of the many and varied places they can live and serve; we see the tensions that keep them moving and reaching out. This new man can survive and thrive in the emotional states of affliction and confusion, can go through the physical stress, can take the knowledge, the love, the power and the weapons and really live and war with them. These saints can live between the glory and the dishonour, the evil report and the good report. It matters not if they are regarded as deceivers when they are in fact true, if they are well known or unknown. They can be dying daily but ever living, sorrowful yet always rejoicing, poor yet making many rich. They know that it is relationship that is the heart and essence of life – not the concept, the set position, the title or the law.

These ones are able to engage the created order relationally without being subject to any elemental thing or definition of fallen humanity. These are able to impact the earth without having to own it so as to control anything within it. They are able to sound the sound of the Father in love, in empathy, in power and in truth out and into creation. Ultimately they can live as 'having nothing yet possessing all things' (2 Cor. 6:10). The 'all things' these people can possess refers to all the created order. For the suffering of the heirs of God works to bring forth saints who are able to resonate with and lay hold of their inheritance in and over the creation.

This reality, with its cry of travail, is happening in and around us at this moment. Will we name it in accordance with the divine strategy? Will we see and respond to it in line with the eternal purpose? Will we take it up and suffer it through to the inheritance, our inheritance? The challenge of going into creation to gain our inheritance may well be greater than that faced by Adam. But the one who leads us and the rewards that await us are also far greater than at the first. Because we have a high priest who has passed through the heavens we can hold fast and journey through. The incarnation brought us out from condemnation and into life. Now redeemed and restored through his suffering and death, that life is ever before us. Christ's body, the church, has all of this and all of him resounding and coursing through its blood.

With this in heart and mind we now turn to look with Hebrew vision at the church, the creation and the plan. Before doing that let us, by way of summary, refocus on that God-given vision.

Chapter 10

Brief Snapshot of The Hebrew Worldview

God taught the Hebrews that creation was made up of three heavens (orders of creation) existing from the earth right through to the highest heaven. People lived on the earth and inhabited the first heaven. The second heaven was the dwelling of angels who visited the earth and interacted with humanity. The third or highest of these heavens was the place where the throne of God was established. The place of the dead was called Sheol. It was under the earth. Through this vision of creation the Hebrews came to understand that heaven (the heavens) and earth existed in space/time relationship with each other.

Further to this we read in verse 20 of Romans 1 that in the beginning God made us and intended that we come into relationship with our creator through 'that which is made'. It was through every facet of our life in the creation that we finite beings were meant to encounter the infinite God. This verse from Romans reveals the amazing extent of God's revelation of himself in and through the created order. Paul says that God's 'invisible attributes, his eternal power and divine nature' were to be 'clearly seen' through all the things he had made. As Paul said in Ephesians, God is not only over all things and through all things, his attributes, nature and power are in reality also in all things. Scripture plainly teaches that God's unseen nature exists in, and is expressed from, every created thing.

Bringing these two foundational Hebrew truths together we can conclude that God's revelation of himself is manifest from every created thing, from the earth through to the highest heavens above. For the Hebrew the spiritual or unseen realm was one with the created realm. It did not exist in a separate or removed dimension; it was in union with all of life in creation.

The Son and the Creation

The next foundation stone of the Hebrew worldview has to do with the place the Son of God occupies in relation to the Father and the creation. We know from Scripture that before the creation was brought forth the Son of God existed eternally with and in the Father. The Son of God brought all things into being and is the ultimate purpose of all things. He is the pre-eminent one *over* all of the created order. Paul also says of the Son of God that 'in him all things hold together' (Col. 1:17). What he is saying is that all of the creation exists in the Son of God. Paul told the Athenians the same thing when he said that it is 'in him we live and move and exist' (Acts 17:28).

The Son of God exists in and through the entire created order – incorporating time, space, atmosphere, matter, events, person: everything in which we live and work. The attributes, nature and power of the Son of God reside within every created thing; he is the essence and substance (as in 'the substance belongs to Christ', Col. 2:17) of all things in finite creation. The Son of God, ever radiating from the Father, brought the creation into being within his eternal person. He is before that creation, he is the purpose of that creation and he is in, through and over all of that creation.

The Hebrews who wrote the New Testament saw the revelation of the Son of God coming from his life in the eternal Father into the immanence of the third heaven, right down through and into the all things of creation. Rather than there being any distinction in the heavens and the earth between divine things and natural things, all things express and manifest the attributes, nature and power of the Son of God. God progressively limits the revelation of himself down through the descending orders of creation. Every order of creation manifests the glory of God in a different way. There is no qualitative difference between them; the only difference is one of form (expression) and measure. From a human perspective they proceed from one level of glory to another, one level of the expression of the divine nature to the next, right through to the highest heavens and then beyond into the infinite of God.

Creation and the Fall

In the beginning God gifted a facet or expression of himself in the creation to humanity. He gave to the image bearer free will to live and act within certain limits. God in effect 'hid' himself within all things with a view to people searching him out. This discovery would happen as they named, related to and worked all things in creation. As people engaged life in this way, they would progressively enter into the revelation of the divine essence (attributes, nature and power) in and through every created thing. In this way they would come to maturity (and thus enter into their rule over all creation) and progressively enter into deeper relationship with their creator God.

Besides the 'hiddenness inviting discovery' in all created things, we see a more direct revelation of God coming to speak with humanity. From the heavens the eternal Logos

(Word) came in finite language to commune with humanity in relation to his identity and purpose in creation. This way of revelation ensured that Adam and Eve understood that it was not the 'all things' *of themselves* that were God: rather, before all things came into being there existed the person of God. This verbal/language encounter gave to humankind a more direct and personal communion with their creator God. It enabled them to make sense of life and work, and correspondingly the creation reality enabled them to make sense of the word spoken.

When humankind fell into sin the creation reality was not destroyed: rather the fullness of it was placed behind thorns, sweat and travail. Futility and death came in to stand in the way of humanity's journey into the attributes, nature and power of God in and through all things. Satan acted within this fallen reality, but he was not the creator of futility and death. These divine judgements came in so that fallen humanity could no longer access the full resources of the creation and thus maximise the evil they might accomplish. Also they were a sign to us of our fallenness and separation from the creator. All that God did at this time of judgement was strategic and ultimately redemptive. In this regard we read, 'The creation itself was subjected to futility, not of its own will, but because of Him who subjected it, in hope that the creation itself will be set free from its slavery to corruption into the freedom of the glory of the children of God' (Rom. 8:21).

Incarnation and Restoration

The Son of God came and became a man to re-establish the eternal purpose. He suffered his way through every judgement arising from the Fall and opened up the way through to the inheritance again. He came in the power of righteousness and entered into all of human travail, thereby forging a strategic relationship between himself and every facet of fallen humanity's experience. He went into futility, darkness and death as a man; he went through to the essence of all things to secure the inheritance in, through and over all things. The outcome is that the wall of futility that faces fallen humanity is now the gate for the redeemed.

This is the reason why the Bible says in Romans 8:17 that the way through to our inheritance is through suffering. Pain is a reality sign given to us by God. It is a gift of God that connects us with physical and moral reality. When we engage fallen life we are sure to encounter pain in one form or another. It speaks to us of the reality of the universal fall and of our own and others' fallenness. Because the Son of God made man now indwells our pain we can now come up against the thorns of life's experiences and go through into the attributes, nature and power of God. We can come up against situations of travail and challenge and, rather than running away by following the world's options, we have the ability in Christ to 'suffer' our way through.

In the place of the 'fellowship of his sufferings' (Phil. 3:10) God works to overcome the strongholds in our thinking and ways of relating that have held us back from entering into our inheritance in creation. The Spirit of God takes us into the place of 'his death'. Here the old things and old thinking are 'done away with' (Rom. 6:6). In God's time we emerge out of this place into the 'out-resurrection from the dead' (Phil. 3:10). In this renewed life we find that the way we relate to the people and situations that once stood in our way is changed. We have been transformed and equipped to live a life that is now able to deeply engage the attributes, nature and power of God in, through and over all things, events and people. The futility is overcome and the creation is again opened up before us.

It is in this way that our 'outer man' [fashioned after the world system] decays and our 'inner man' comes to be 'renewed [restored to its true nature] day by day' (2 Cor. 4:16). Through this way of suffering and change we come to resonate with the struggle and futility of fallen humanity. We are able to demonstrate, in a tangible way, the reality and relevance of the suffering, death and resurrection of Christ. Through this way of the Cross we are able to enter into life, gather our inheritance, answer creation's cry and ultimately enter into our rule over all things as God intended from the beginning. There is more that flows on from this process, but suffering our way through the judgements that God brought in after the Fall is the definite starting point for the divine strategy of redemption and restoration.

THE STRATEGY

Chapter 11

Jesus Christ – The Church – The Plan

Did Jesus have a particular strategy in mind when he said 'Go into all the world'? If this is war, then are we presently fighting according to the master plan? Following Paul we have preached the gospel, gathered disciples, appointed elders, taught sound doctrine and established congregations. However, under the influence of the Greek grid we appear, for the most part, to have halted at that point. That is, we have stopped at the gathering, stayed in the building and focused on the activities therein and not moved ahead to engage the creation. Against this backdrop, in this postmodern time and in the light of the Hebrew worldview, we ask: is there a divine strategy that arises from this God-given creation reality? I believe there is.

To understand this divine strategy we need to begin with Jesus Christ. We have looked at the coming of the Son of God as man, entering in to fill all the dimensions of fallen human experience. After he had entered into the final fallen outpost, that being death, he began an amazing journey through the heavens. Why did the Son of God choose that particular route through to the right hand of the Majesty on high?

Paul tells us the reason in Ephesians chapter 4 verses 9 and 10. He says, 'Now this expression, "He ascended", what does it mean except that he also had descended into the lower parts of the earth? He who descended is himself also he who ascended far above all the heavens, that he might fill all things.' This work of Christ to 'fill all things' refers to the created order that the Hebrew people saw and experienced around and above them.

Jesus came from heaven, to the earth, to the regions of death. From there he rose to the earth and then kept on rising until he reached the third heaven and sat down at the right hand of the Majesty on high. His purpose was to fill every thing, every order of creation and every facet of fallen human experience. Hence the strategic relationship that must exist between the work of Christ and the all things of creation. So, what is the creation that the Son of God came to fill made of?

Understanding the Make-up of the Unseen Created Order

Because general revelation has either been ignored or pushed into the background, our insight into the testimony of God in and through the creation has stopped far too short. Our preoccupation with the rational or removed realm has meant that we have not pressed in to discover the way in which God reveals his attributes, nature and power in all things. We know from Genesis about the creation of the heavens and the earth, the fish and the birds, the plants and the seeds and humankind. These are the 'seen' things of creation. To look more closely at the 'unseen' things of creation we turn to Genesis chapter 1 verses 27 and 28. There we read: 'And God created man in his own image, in the image of God he created him; male and female he created them. And God blessed them. And God said to them, "Be fruitful and multiply, and fill the earth and subdue it; and rule over the fish of the sea and the birds of the air [first heaven] and over every living thing which moves on the earth." '

Looking at this foundational verse in Genesis, we can see three unseen and created spheres that God has made for humanity. The first is *marriage*, the second is *family* and the third is *work*. These three spheres are the primary building blocks of humankind's created reality. They set the context and agenda for all created things. That is, the character of all creation – work, relationships, the heavens, earth and the angelic realm – is predominantly determined by and oriented around these three spheres.

The first ceremony God conducted, after Adam had named the animals and Eve was created, was to join male to female in marriage. The blessing of God was on them to multiply and create the family. Humanity's purpose unfolded from this place of identity and nurture. God placed them in the Garden and called them to cultivate it. As we saw in the Garden setting, the divine call to rule over the works of God's hands was to be accomplished through work. The systems of created reality, through which our work engages the world of humanity and nature, are government, health, education, business and recreation. We could place recreation in a distinct category, for as God said, he established six days for work and one day for rest. However, as so many people work in leisure, arts, sport and other fields of recreation and creativity, I place it here under the sphere of work.

Because every man, woman and child's reality is wrapped up in and one with the creation spheres of marriage, family and work, we definitely need to take account of their place in the divine strategy. It follows that if Christ is to 'fill all things' then he must fill these unseen spheres of the created order. So how does Christ do this? To answer this we need to consider the purpose and strategy of God for the church.

There is no better place in Scripture to gain insight into the nature and purpose of the church than the book of Ephesians. In this God-breathed Word we discover the primary definition of the church. In chapter one we read that God, after raising his Son Jesus Christ from the dead and seating him at his own right hand in heavenly places, 'put all things in subjection under his feet and gave him as head over all things to the church, which is his body, the fullness of him who fills all in all' (Eph. 1:22, 23).

There is perhaps no more crucial place to apply the Hebrew vision of the creation than right here. It is only with our spatial creation-oriented Hebrew insight into the spiritual realm that we can ask certain questions of this key verse and receive surprisingly clear answers!

Firstly: Where are the feet of Christ? Because of the incarnation they are now established on the earth. Hell and death and the lower regions of the earth are now in subjection under his feet. Secondly: Where is the head of Christ? Right now, God-made-man is in the third heaven, seated at the right hand of God. He is the 'head over all things', over and above all the systems of humankind, the sky, the stars, the angelic realm, nature, every creation sphere and unseen authority, every name and every thing! And finally: Where is his body? Well, it can only be between his feet and his head. And so it is! Scripture reveals that Christ's body, the church, exists right through the created order. And what is the purpose of this church? The body of Christ can have no other purpose than that of Jesus Christ, and his purpose is to 'fill all things'. This is confirmed by the

> Thus says the Lord, 'Heaven is my Throne, and the earth is my footstool. Where then is the house you could build for me? And where is a place that I may rest? For my hand made all these things. Thus all these things came into being,' declares the Lord. (Isaiah 66:1, 2)

phrase – 'his body . . . (is) the fullness of him who fills all in all'. Hence we conclude that the purpose of Christ for his body the church is that it be the fullness of all things seen and unseen of the created order.

The Church – the Fullness of the Created Order

☞ It follows from this revelation from Scripture that the church can only come to fill the creation through the spheres of marriage, family and work. These are the means by which we access and relate to the all things of creation. Only through these spheres of creation can our identity and purpose be expressed and realised. It is through these, and only through these, that we can grow, mature and reach the 'stature that belongs to the fullness of Christ' (Eph. 4:13) in the heavens. There is no other way for his body the church to become the fullness of him who fills all in all. In this unambiguous way the Word of God, via the Hebrew vision of all things, speaks to us of a divine strategy for the church that encompasses all of our life in creation.

What does it mean to 'fill' a sphere of the created order? I will go into more detail further on, but briefly, the best way to explain this concept is to look at the word 'fulfil' that takes up the sense of the word 'fill'. To fulfil something is to realise or draw out its full potential or maximum benefit. For us this will be the discovery and enjoyment of the nature, attributes and power of God within the creation spheres. Everything in creation contains the glory of God in different measures. We are called to search out that glory and thus inherit the measure! We can see immediately how this relates to our experiences in marriage, family and work. To draw out and realise the full meaning and divine intention of these creation realities is the fullness and privilege of the saints. To do this we will have to journey through the suffering and the dying of Jesus. But our resurrection into our inheritance is assured because of the finished work of Christ. This inheritance is ever waiting for us in and through life in the three unseen spheres of human existence.

Thus says the Lord, 'Heaven is my Throne, and the earth is my footstool. Where then is the house you could build for me? And where is a place that I may rest? For my hand made all these things. Thus all these things came into being,' declares the Lord. (Isaiah 66:1, 2)

The vision splendid

If such a vision of creation and perspective on the nature and purpose of the body of Christ is accepted, the way in which we see and do things will change. So much of what the saints (and the church they embody) need at this time can, I believe, arise from the Hebrew vision of the divine strategy. Before we look at its outworking in the life of the New Testament saints, let's bring together some of the elements we have examined thus far.

Third Heaven

Second Heaven

Work

Family

Marriage

First Heaven

Sheol

> And he put all things in subjection under his feet and gave him as head over all things to the church, which is his body, the fullness of him who fills all in all. (Ephesians 1:22, 23)

We conclude from the above-stated truths concerning the body of Christ that the church is not something separate from marriage, family and work. Rather, the church is the people of God living and impacting in and through these key creation spheres. God did not create a special, separate thing and call it 'the church'. He created a body, the head of which is Christ, which would encompass and become the completion of the created order.

Once we grasp this vision of the church, many truths presently stuck under the grid of the Greeks can emerge into the light of the new-creation day. We will be able to establish a vital link between the church gathered (at various places and times) and the church as 'fullness' (existing in marriage, family and work). Scriptures, such as are to be found in Ephesians 4:15, will come on line. There we hear Paul's clarion call to 'grow up in all things unto him, who is the head, even Christ'. Often we have taken this phrase 'all things' and applied it, for the most part, to Christian character development and ministry involvement in the local church. However, what is referred to here is the all things of creation. It is the entire created order, made up of things seen and unseen, that we are called to grow through in order to reach the full stature of Christ. Rather than travelling to a conceptual or spiritual 'other' realm, the saints are called to journey into the fullness and revelation of God in marriage, family and work.

It is in the light of the above that we understand the great commission relates to more than simply establishing physical church gatherings in premises throughout the world. When Jesus said, 'Go into all the world and preach the gospel to all creation' (Mark 16:15), he was telling us we had to engage all of the seen and unseen systems of humankind.

☞ Church is not only an activity that happens in certain
   buildings overseen by pastors. It is in 'all the world'

and 'all creation' that we are all called to be the body of Christ – to see his church built in our marriages, our businesses, our homes, our work, our gathering together, our entire lives. We must release the powerful name 'church' to define all of life, work and relationships.

This will not take away the authority of the elders over particular localities and/or different gatherings of the church; in fact it will enlarge the scope of their God-given authority. It is with such a vision of church and of life that we, as saints who are that church, will be able to see, sound and work right through the created order.

An immediate reaction to all this might be 'Too far! Too fast!' But just such a change in the status quo is what is being called forth by our present situation. Mike Regele says we are heading into death as the church, a death coincident with the death of modernism. It is time to envision the form and the paradigm that might best serve the church resurrected in a postmodern era. The Hebrew worldview opens up a vision of the church and a strategy for the saints that can, I believe, bring us across the border to that new place for this time.

The Battle Plan of Jesus

In the remaining chapters of this section of the book we will look at how the divine strategy was accomplished in the New Testament. We will see how the saints, by following the battle plan outlined by Jesus, became the fullness for their time. Jesus said, 'The kingdom of heaven is like a mustard seed, which a man took and sowed in his field; and this is smaller than all other seeds; but when it is full grown, it is larger than the garden plants, and becomes a tree, so that [recalling the creation mandate from Genesis] the birds of the air come and nest in its branches' (Matt. 13:31, 32). We will follow the course of this seed through the lives of John the Baptist, Jesus the Christ and Paul the Apostle. Through them we will see how the divine strategy emerged from the prophetic voice in the desert, through the words and the blood of the saviour, into the passion and zeal of the apostle to touch the cities and transform the world. The ancient city of Ephesus will be the showcase for our survey of the battle plan.

We will look at the divine strategy unfolding in Ephesus through three distinct phases. The first phase sees the gospel breaking into the city, placing the seed of the kingdom into the lives of the people who respond (and hence into the ground of the city). The second phase sees this 'little flock' (the body) begin its growth through the unseen spheres of the created order towards the heavens. The third and final stage sees the little flock come through to the place of standing in Christ in the creation, so that the body now determines the very make-up of the heavens. This standing effects a change in the counsels of the heavens over the earth and thus brings change to the whole culture of the city. This transformation ushers in the restoration harvest – a time of reaping that brings substantial restoration and lasting salvation to a nation of many peoples, tribes and tongues.

So, with map in hand, let's travel first to Jerusalem and then on to Ephesus.

Chapter 12

The Restoration of All Things

The last and greatest prophet of the old covenant burst out of the wilderness and ushered in the age of the gospel. Jesus said of John the Baptist that 'Elijah does first come and restore all things' (Mark 9:12). Here we encounter the term 'all things' mentioned alongside a process called 'restoration'. The word occurs again in Acts 3:21 where Peter said of Jesus, 'whom heaven must receive *until* the period of restoration of all things'. We are used to hearing about the need for the gospel to be preached to every nation as a witness, but here is another criterion to be fulfilled before the end comes. John the Baptist ushers in the period of the restoration of all things and Jesus awaits the culmination of such an event before he comes again. This restoration must be a crucial part of the purposes of God for it to feature so prominently in this way in Scripture.

☞ What is this 'restoration of all things'? I believe it refers to the process whereby the body of Christ comes to occupy the unseen spheres of creation – marriage, family and work. As the saints live in accordance with the purposes of God in these spheres, restoration comes to them.

Through restoration the darkness and futility that came into the systems of humanity at the time of the Fall are reversed. Once again light is able to shine through the all things of creation and mankind is able to experience God's invisible attributes, eternal power and divine nature in a tangible way. Restoration enables the attributes, nature and power God has placed in all created things to be released to work towards his eternal purposes. Through this process of restoration the believers in Christ take up the mandate given to the first Adam. They enter into their stewardship of the earth, they come to maturity and ultimately they enter into their rule over the works of God's hands.

This perspective on the restoration of all things flows on logically from the Hebrew worldview, the purpose of Christ to fill all things and the call of the church to be the fullness of him who fills all in all. This leads us to an obvious question: how does God work through the saints to accomplish the restoration of all things? In answer let's take up this powerful truth about the restoration of all things and, with our Hebrew vision and understanding of the divine strategy, journey with it through the New Testament record.

The Prophet, the Father and the Family

Where else does Scripture speak about this restoration of the spheres of the created order? In the Old Testament book of Malachi we read, 'Behold I am going to send you Elijah the prophet before the coming of the great and terrible day of the Lord. And he will restore the hearts of the fathers to their children and the hearts of the children to their fathers, lest I come and smite the land with a curse' (Malachi 4:5, 6). God left these words ringing in the ears of his people until four hundred years of silence were broken by John's proclamation in the desert. It appears that John's ministry was primarily directed towards restoring the relationship between fathers and their children (Luke 1:17). Why was this so important? We learn from Scripture that the unseen sphere of creation called family was made by God to reveal the person of the Father to humanity. It is from the Father that 'every family in heaven and on earth derives its name' (Eph. 3:15). The identity and name of the family is that of the Father, its meaning and its power takes us into his life, his nature and his eternal Father's heart – hence the central place of the family in revealing the reality of the Father God to all creation.

We don't have an extensive record of John's preaching, but we know he moved with passion straight to the heart of every issue he tackled. Why was it important for John to restore the relationship between father and child? As we know, Jesus expressed and held within himself the Father's heart and purpose. It was John's ministry that prepared the way for Israel to behold the Son of the Father God. As Jesus said, no one knows the Father except the Son and no one knows the Son except the Father. It was John the restorer who readied the creation path of family for the Son to walk upon.

Following on from John's work, the Son of God was able to come and speak to Israel about his Father and theirs. John's ministry pushed back the darkness that had invaded the creation sphere of family, alleviating the curse that had come on the land because father and child were divided. With these mountains brought low and these valleys lifted up the Son of glory could come and journey through the land into the very heart of Israel. This is the power and the place restoration has in the purposes of God. It appears from Scripture that when we restore a sphere of the created order we prepare the way for its fulfilment by Christ. We make it useful, cleansed and clear so that people can see the attributes, nature and power of God through it and, in its light, understand and encounter the reality of the gospel and the kingdom.

The Bridegroom Speaks of Marriage

John thought that it would all happen right then and there. However, the prophetic immediacy in which he declared was intended by God only to initiate a process that would extend far beyond his short life. At the height of John's ministry Jesus came to be baptised. After some questions of doctrine were settled, the clouds burst open and the Father shone through, declaring to the heavens and the earth, 'This is my beloved Son, in whom I am well pleased' (Matt. 3:17).

The eternal Son was ready to reveal the Father and that he did in a most powerful and complete way. Jesus then prepared the ground to reveal another amazing mystery that for ages past had been hidden in God. During his short earthly sojourn he made the way clear for us to behold the reality and importance of a unique relationship that believers would come to have with God the Son. The Spirit of God would soon join those who responded to his call in union with the Son. They would become the bride,

> So that what was spoken through the prophet might be fulfilled, saying, "I will open my mouth in parables (the story); I will utter things *hidden since the foundation* of the world." (Matt. 13:35)

the very body of Christ. To enable people to see the reality of such an astounding promise, Jesus, like John before him, had to work to restore another of the powerful spheres of the created order. To see this process in action we turn to the key manifesto of the kingdom given by Jesus in the sermon on the mount.

Jesus begins by speaking about the heart of the new man and the attitudes and actions that flow from him. It is from the redeemed and purified heart that the restoration of all things must begin. It cannot arise from an external Law manipulated by Scribes and Pharisees. The holiness that comes from the Father of lights is not a burden to be carried: rather it is a gift enabling us to see, enjoy and keep on going into all of life in the created order. It enables us to search out and engage the attributes, nature and power of God in every relationship and work. The call of Jesus for our lives to be perfect does not speak of exacting conformity to a code of conduct: rather it proclaims that it is time for the sons and daughters to reach for and arrive at their created purpose. This call to 'go for it' combines that well-known human curiosity to uncover and discover with the strong desire to create eternal marks in time.

Jesus moves on to speak against anger and lust. Anger works to undermine relationships by destroying love, and lust takes away one's ability to really belong by polluting the streams of identity that are at the heart of relationship. If these works of the flesh choke the rivers within, then blood will not flow and light will never shine from the body into the world. Sin is a pleasured pain that cuts against good tissue until, drained of blood, it becomes a dull thud demanding more, forcing man to evil's dead end unless held back by common grace and common sense. So the redemption that pays the price paves the way for those who are in Christ to emerge into a more radical righteousness than the Law could ever imagine.

So that what was spoken through the prophet might be fulfilled, saying, "I will open my mouth in parables [the story]; I will utter things *hidden since the foundation* of the world." (Matt. 13:35 *italics mine*.)

After applying this 'fullers soap' to the Law, Jesus moved to bring restoration to one of the most significant spheres of creation. He was ready to breathe life into something that he himself had created, something he held a strong and eternally decided passion for – the creation sphere of marriage.

The Son of God did not care for Moses' easy divorce bill: rather Jesus declared that 'from the beginning of creation

God made them male and female'. He went on to say 'for this cause a man shall leave his father and mother, and the two shall become one flesh; consequently they are no longer two, but one flesh. What therefore God has joined together, let no man separate' (Mark 10:6–9). Jesus' forceful message on adultery, divorce and remarriage, as hard as it was to hear, was intended to cleanse and thus bring restoration to this foundation sphere of the created order. Later on the 'Pauline privilege' (1 Cor. 7:15) would come in, but here Jesus was not addressing the complexities of individual situations. He was dealing with the very nature of the created order.

His listeners would not have known the full meaning of what he was saying. The many more things that Jesus wanted to teach had to wait until he was glorified. Even the twelve would not see the entry of the bride, the body of Christ, into this restored sphere of creation until after the Spirit had joined them to Christ on the day of Pentecost. After this came ministry gifts whose purpose was to reveal the fullness of what the Son had prepared for those who believe.

It is from Ephesians in particular that we learn about the nature and purpose of marriage and its relationship to the second person of the Trinity. It is amazing the extent to which this sphere of creation unlocks and reveals the person of Christ and the relationship he desires to have with his called-out people. 'The mystery (of marriage) is great,' says Paul, 'but I am speaking with reference to Christ and the church' (Eph. 5:32). In marriage we are able to experience what it is to respond and be in submission to the lordship of Christ, our husband. We come to know the work of the bridegroom to wash, keep, value and thus unveil the glory of the bride. We gain clarity and insight into the relationship between the Father from whom we originate and the Son to whom we are joined. Paul shows how we who are betrothed to Christ in marriage come into the fullness and consummation of that bond as the very body of Christ himself. We read that, 'Husbands ought also to love their own wives as their own bodies' (Eph. 5:28). Our love for Christ and his love for us as his body is a reality because we have become one through the marriage union. In marriage, faithful to one, we prepare for, and are carried into, the ages to come: towards that time when our ultimate intimacy arrives in one Son – one with the eternal Father. Solomon's Song of Songs takes this truth concerning the betrothed deep, and then deeper, into the beloved.

Thinking about all this for a moment can take your breath away. We are called to take hold of, to comprehend and to feel the reality of Christ as the bridegroom and head of the body in and through the creation sphere of marriage. From this place of encounter with the divine attributes, nature and power we discover no less than the person of God the Son. The concept from the Word of God might inform us, and the worship of God in song may inspire us; however, it is the experience Scripture speaks of and the relationship the songs illuminate that outline the possibility of, and invitation to, our greatest encounter with God the Son this side of eternity.

☞ Marriage is not simply an analogy or example to help us understand a complex truth about God, with the ultimate experience being found in some abstract conceptual or removed spiritual realm. Rather we are called to move *into* and *through* marriage to discover and embrace the Son who is the heartbeat and ultimate goal of this creation sphere.

Marriage and singles, divorced and widowed

How is God able to do this work in something so frail and personal as marriage? The Word says simply that God is able to *make* light to shine through this sphere into the darkness. This was why he created marriage in the first place. This creation sphere was made to reveal the divine nature, attributes and power of the Son of God. 'What if my marriage is struggling or broken, does that exclude me from this revelation of Christ?' The answer is a definite no. Those who stand in the truth in Christ through a marriage breakdown, even if the partner leaves permanently, go on in life with that sphere of creation strong and intact for themselves in relationship with Christ. Many saints who face disappointment and betrayal in their marriages are able to powerfully sound and demonstrate the truth, the love and the power of the kingdom through such times of difficulty. God is able, Scripture says, to perfect divine power even in the weakest part of our lives. Our suffering and the attitude and heart we have through that time of the 'dying of Jesus' enables life to come to us and light and resurrection power to resonate out to those whose struggle is similar.

'What if I am not married, am I out of the picture?' Again the answer is no. You came from a marriage union and are headed for a union either in this life or with Christ in the one to come. This is the reality that sets the context for this life. Your husband is your maker and he is able to come close to you in many ways of revelation available in this fallen and fractured world. The love and friendship of brothers and sisters in Christ, God's beauty in creation, the fruit of your good work, as well as the marriage bond, all minister in different ways the life of Christ into your life.

Of course, much more could be drawn from the wells of these creation spheres. However, space does not permit us to go into greater depth here. In the final part of the book I will be concentrating on the creation sphere of work, knowing that the truths we draw out in relation to work apply equally to our experience of life in marriage and family. In summary at this point: the divine life and reality experienced when two become one, the invitation to encounter the bridegroom in each other and the sound and light from Christ that marriage is, make it one of the most powerful and strategically placed spheres in all of creation.

John and Jesus and the Spheres of Life

While we are studying the ministries of John the Baptist and Jesus we will look briefly at the way in which they dealt with the many issues of everyday life. John would speak to tax gatherers about their work, to soldiers about justice, to people about poverty and equity. Jesus spent a great deal of time speaking about money, its use, its power and its potential danger. He touched on practically every sphere of life – family, marriage, business, government, agriculture, law and so on, stamping them with kingdom life and divine purpose.

One of the major spheres he worked to restore was that of government. He directed much of his teaching against the controlling alliance that existed between the religious and political overlords. He established an understanding of how one should relate to them as individuals with wrong motives and behaviour and how to respond to them within the divine office they occupied. He was outspoken against the former but redefined, restored and thereby filled the latter. Jesus cleansed the temple, restored the Sabbath and fulfilled the Law. His life, his work and his example opened again the spheres and administrations used to engage the earth, clearing the way, readying them for the body of Christ that would soon emerge to fulfil them.

The seed that became a mighty tree

Many of the disciples expected Jesus to usher in an earthly kingdom. Even John the Baptist was confused. Throughout his ministry Jesus would declare and demonstrate the kingdom and then, when the crowds got excited about the new political power-broker in town, Jesus would draw back into the wilderness. When they came to make him king by force, he passed through the crowd to go have lunch with Zaccheus. The disciples had their swords at the ready but Jesus just kept on talking about little seeds and bits of leaven and, near the end, the subject that particularly occupied his thinking – dying. The confused disciples followed him right to the garden of Gethsemane but finally fled at the sound of soldiers' footsteps. They left this unique person to be lifted up in crucifixion, fall to the ground in death and be buried alone.

The twelve could not grasp how the divine seed of the kingdom could rise from death and become a tree that would come to fill the heavens. Jesus knew full well the divine strategy of redemption and restoration. That is why he gave his life and that is why he rose again and ascended to fill all things. Once seated at the right hand of God he moved to fill the church at Pentecost. On that great day his body, the church, rose in Spirit and life to begin its calling to be the fullness of the created order. It was from this time that the Holy Spirit, the third person of the Trinity, began to equip and release the saints of Christ to do the 'works' of ministry. As we shall see further down the track, this third sphere of the created order came into prominence at that time as an integral part of the divine strategy to bring restoration to the heavens and the earth.

The church that was birthed on the day of Pentecost shook the city with resurrection life and it looked like nothing would stop the occupation. The saints tried to stem the tide by staying and building a 'granary' at Jerusalem. However, Paul, who was used by God even before he was saved, scattered the seed of the kingdom right through to Antioch. Then, after he was saved, he kept on scattering it to Syria, to

Asia Minor, to Europe, until finally he landed at the centre of the arc of light God had established through him. Paul came to Ephesus. At that focal point between Europe and the Middle East we see three phases of this divine strategy of restoration unfurled. This war plan is so complete, so strong, so life integrated and all-encompassing it could only have been designed by God. So let's make the move to Ephesus.

Chapter 13

The Divine Strategy – Phases I & II

In the city of Ephesus the kingdom of God exploded in the most powerful way seen in the New Testament era. The initial impact on the city was so forceful that the commercial dimension of the chief deity Diana came close to collapse. We see the outworking of three phases of the divine strategy at Ephesus in three different books of the New Testament – the first in Acts, the second in Ephesians and the third in Paul's first letter to Timothy at Ephesus.

This city and its region call for some comment before we proceed. The fertility cult of Diana in Ephesus was a major focus of activity for the whole area. To give you an idea of its importance, the temple of Diana was four times the size of the Parthenon in Athens. E. M. Blaiklock said of Ephesus and its strategic place in the purposes of God:

> Paul was, in fact, assaulting a stronghold of pagan religion together with the active life and commerce associated with a vast heathen cult, in a key city of the central Mediterranean and a focal point of communication. Ephesus was also a seat of proconsular power from which the whole province of Asia could be influenced (*Pictorial Encyclopedia*, vol. 3, p. 328).

The temple of Diana was the centre of worship and ritual prostitution as well as the city bank. It's no wonder Paul had to fight some 'wild beasts' in the place!

We need to look briefly at the preparation by God leading up to the initial invasion that heralded the beginning of the occupation. Firstly, we note the divine work carried out in the history of the territory and the culture, readying the region for the coming of the kingdom. We see this process plainly in Israel, God making the way through word, sacrifice and feasts for the time when the Son would come. We see it in the altar to the 'unknown god' (Acts 17:23) in Athens, the one who was thought to have stopped the plague in the city, thus becoming established in the thinking and expectation of the people. There is the 'man of Macedonia' (Acts 16:9) who called for the apostle to come over and begin the liberation of Europe. Throughout the Roman Empire we find synagogues and God-fearing proselytes prepared by Moses for the good news. God, who has his witness in every generation, is not far from any of us. Paul sought out these divine preparations at the beginning of the gospel push into each city or region.

We then see a reviving of this 'redemptive purpose' that serves to water and soften the ground, readying it to receive the seed of the gospel. We see this in John the Baptist's work as the forerunner of Christ in Jerusalem: the Baptist, in the spirit of Elijah, preparing the way for the one who came in power after him. I have always thought it interesting that when Paul finally arrived in Ephesus he found twelve disciples of John the Baptist (Acts 19:1–7). God had set them in the city to prepare the way – to make ready the ground and supply the necessary seedbed into which Paul could plant the gospel of the kingdom.

The First Phase of the Offensive

The Ephesian revival must rate as one of the most dramatic and exciting events in Acts. Paul comes into town, baptises some Baptists, makes his way to the synagogue and launches his campaign. The 'extraordinary miracles', the book burnings and confessions, the 'word of the Lord growing mightily and prevailing' (Acts 19:20) all inform us of the impact the kingdom of God made when it first burst into town. Paul was based there for three years, a long time compared to the apostle's usual timetable. Finally a riot by an irate crowd, instigated by businessmen, gave him the signal that it was time to leave. It appears from Acts that Paul would often go to a place, preach the gospel, make converts, stir up the city and then move on. It was as if a city in uproar was an indication that a particular phase of the divine strategy had been completed. Why else would Paul see a riot as a reason to move on? He had no fear of death. In Ephesus he was actually pushing to be allowed on stage to address the fuming multitude. It would appear that riots and disturbances were a signal to Paul that the ground of the city was now sufficiently 'turned upside down'.

☞ I believe, from the record in Acts and from the history of revivals, that the initial gospel push in a city or region is designed by God to plant the 'seed of the kingdom'. It comes with miraculous signs and strong moral conviction to break hearts and the power of principalities. It works to establish the 'little flock' within the territory. This first phase then gives way to a period when the seed takes root in the city and begins its journey up through the heavens.

Continued ploughing of the same ground over a prolonged period of time would be counterproductive. To keep on stirring up a city, to keep on militantly proclaiming and pushing against the powers, could well harden people against the church and possibly extinguish the flickering light now burning in a dark place. As we shall see, God has a much more pervasive and overwhelming strategy to win the cities.

The Second Phase

We turn again to the letter written by Paul to the Ephesians a year or so after he had left the city in an uproar. This 'book of the church' unlocks so much for us concerning the nature, identity and purpose of the body of Christ, the church. I remember leaving a conference given by Ed Silvoso, a prominent church strategist from Argentina, thinking, 'I have a new book of Ephesians!' Silvoso said that the body 'fitted and held together by that which every joint supplies', spoken of in Ephesians 4:16, is the same body standing against the rulers and powers in the heavenly places referred to in 6:11f. Once this is seen, the overall strategy of God revealed in Ephesians comes into view in a most profound way. This perspective enables us to see Paul's teaching between chapters 4 and 6 as the key to our overcoming on the earth and thereby our coming to stand in the heavenly realm. It informs us of how we can 'grow up in all things into him, who is the head, even Christ' (Eph. 4:15).

I draw attention here to the way in which the teaching of Jesus in the sermon on the mount (starting in Matthew 5) parallels the teaching of Paul in Ephesians (commencing with 4:17). The similarities between them are striking and strategic and demonstrate the importance of Paul's teaching in the last three chapters of Ephesians. A brief comparison will suffice here. Paul says, 'Be angry, and yet do not sin' (Eph. 4:26). Jesus said, 'Everyone who is angry with his brother shall be guilty' (Matt. 5:22). Jesus then speaks against looking 'on a woman to lust for her' (Matt. 5:28) while Paul goes on to talk about not letting 'immorality or

any impurity' be found among you (Eph. 5:3). Paul then
applies these principles of the kingdom to the three major
spheres of the created order. Jesus applies them to marriage
and from there to other key spheres of life and work. Both
Paul and Jesus finish with an emphasis on 'standing', Paul in
the heavens and Jesus on the rock. The same strategy for
standing in life from the earth and through the heavens
resonates in both Christ's and Paul's teaching. The longest
recorded teaching of Jesus concerning the kingdom of God
corresponds directly to the key teaching of Paul the apostle
concerning the way in which the church is to stand and
overcome in the created order. For these truths concerning
the spheres of creation to feature in this way, both in the
teaching of Jesus and Paul, indicates the critical importance
of what is being taught here. Something is definitely happening at this point in the epistle; something to which we do
well to pay attention!

Between Ephesians 4 and 6 a lot happens!

It is essential that we bring to our survey of Ephesians
the Hebrew vision of creation, the revelation concerning
the call to the body of Christ to become the fullness of the
created order and, finally, the divine strategy that speaks of
the restoration of all things. These truths must set the context for our consideration of the strategic teaching found in
this epistle.

Before I made the connection between chapters 4 and 6
I used to question Paul's ability to keep to the point and
maintain a sense of drama in his writing. Christ ascends on
high, gives the five-fold ministry gifts, equips the saints for
ministry, moves them to maturity, weaves them together as
one body in truth and love and then, all of a sudden, instead
of taking off into the heavens, we drop back to earth! Paul
breaks the momentum by talking about everyday subjects

like our thought life, relationships, anger, immorality and singing songs to one another! I confess to often moving hurriedly through this section, nodding my approval, but impatient to engage in mortal combat the principalities and powers in high and wicked places spoken of in 6:10. However, from the vantage point the Hebrew worldview has given us concerning Christ, the church and the plan, we are ready to enjoy every moment of the ride from 4 to 6! Our take-off point is located at verse 17 of chapter 4.

The new self – freed from the Gentile mind

It should be no surprise that the first obstacle to our journey to maturity in Christ is the mind we inherit from the world system. I have spoken of the pagan and Platonic make-up of the Gentile mind at this time and the worldview that arose from it. Paul deals strongly, even savagely, with this mind, endeavouring to draw the Ephesian saints away from its lure and power. He spares no facet of this 'ignorant', 'hard', 'callous', 'impure' and 'greedy' way of life. Then he sends out a further challenge to the saints at Ephesus: 'You did not learn Christ in this way, if indeed you have heard him and have been taught in him, just as truth is in Jesus.' If indeed! You can hear the response of the readers: 'Well certainly we have nothing to do with that old, useless, futile, stupid way of thinking. Now, tell us again Paul, what is the new way of thinking you have in mind? Once more for those who may not have been here long.' In answer Paul speaks of the emergence of the 'new man', coming forth through the 'renewal of the mind'. A way of life and thinking once dark, futile and deceived is to be overthrown so that the 'new man, which in the likeness of God has been created in righteousness and holiness of the truth', can come forth to answer the cry of creation.

From here Paul speaks of the works of the flesh that

churn at the heart of Satan's strategy to destroy the image of God in humanity and thus render the eternal purpose ineffective. He places them under three categories – relational dysfunction, sexual impurity and chemical intoxication. The alternative to anger is love, the alternative to immorality is purity and the alternative to intoxication is 'Spirit-filled' fellowship. These works of the flesh take God-given life and power for good and spend them in wasteful 'dissipation'. Rather than fuelling our journey to the heavens with the power inherent in relationships, sexuality and joy, the treasure is spent and the life spirals down, ending up trapped under the elemental things of earth.

Sexual purity and evangelism!

Paul, in chapter 5, speaks about an evangelistic strategy based, amazingly, on sexual purity. I had always thought it strange that we could expose the deeds of darkness, the disgraceful things done in secret, by not talking about them! The only way to resolve the apparent dilemma here is to understand God's strategy of using every aspect of our lives as saints to illuminate and thus expose the darkness. God makes his light shine through the purity that exists in the marriages and relationships of the saints into the darkness and futility of fallen humanity's confused and destructive sexual pursuits. From our lives the sound of the Father is heard in resonance with that light: 'Awake sleeper, rise from the dead, and Christ will shine on you.' Many commentators think that this phrase from Ephesians 5 is drawn from Isaiah 60:1–3. There we read, 'Arise, shine; for your light has come, and the glory of the Lord has risen upon you. For behold, darkness will cover the earth, and deep darkness the peoples; but the Lord will rise upon you and his glory will appear upon you. And nations will come to your light, and kings to the brightness of your rising.' It stands to reason that God should cause light to shine first from this sphere of human life. In the beginning he made them male and female. It was from there that the journey began. Restoration light begins to shine from male and female, the image of God. To think – if this is the impact of something as hidden and personal as sexual purity in relationships, imagine the impact God intends to make through other more overt facets of the life of the saints!

Divine life and divine government

Now the unseen spheres of creation that enable the image bearer to encompass all things come into view. These unseen spheres, for so long defined and kept down in dark names by the enemy, are ready to receive the light that will restore them. Relational love, sexual purity and Spirit-filled joy are now breathed into the three major spheres of the created order. Paul establishes the divine order in the unseen spheres of marriage (Eph. 5:22ff), family (Eph. 6:1ff) and work (Eph. 6:5ff). He reveals the way in which these spheres are meant to function so that the divine nature, attributes, power and creation purpose might be drawn from them.

The person and presence of Christ is seen as the heart of the marriage sphere of creation. The purpose and meaning of the family is unlocked as children honour their father and mother. As they do this children are drawn into the divine image of God resident within their parents. The promise is that it will be well with them throughout life. The father is called to give the children room to grow, not exasperating them lest they lose heart: rather bringing them up in the way and the word of Christ. The father stands within the eternal Father to bring his purposes, his image and his growth into the young lives he stewards. Workers are called to unlock the divine image in work by responding to and obeying their masters 'as to Christ'. Their service is to God and every good thing they do will have its response from the Lord. Masters are called to 'do the same', to give up threatening, for ultimately there is only one Lord and master over both slave and free, worker and boss. It is his image they represent and express and it is to his impartial nature and character they must be true. As it was in the beginning, the unseen creation spheres of marriage, family and work are brought into focus as the key to our inheritance on earth and occupation of the heavens.

Into the heavens to occupy

What Paul has been saying leads naturally to the consideration of the field of battle inhabited by principalities and powers. The body of Christ, by growing through the spheres of creation, now begins to reach and fill the heavens occupied by fallen and holy angels. Hence the positioning of the teaching concerning 'spiritual wickedness in high places' at this point in the epistle. It is important to see that our arrival in this arena was not accomplished through a concerted binding of the enemy or fervent loosing of angelic allies. The disarming of these principalities was already completed and assured because of Jesus' ascension through them. The triumph is in the Cross. This impact by the saints in the second heaven is happening because of the life they are now living in and through the spheres of creation. Intercession and prophetic declaration over a region are certainly an important part of this process. But in the final analysis all things are on the move here because the saints are coming to fill the unseen things God made for just such a purpose as this.

Too often we have dislocated this section dealing with the heavenlies from what precedes it. It is crucial to understand that the phrase, 'having done everything, to stand firm. Stand firm therefore' (Eph. 6:13f), refers to an action in the past tense. The illustration of the armour of God is not the key to effective spiritual warfare, offering new concepts about the helmet, the shield and the belt. Rather it is simply a summary, clarifying what Paul has been speaking about in the preceding sections of the letter. We do not occupy the heavens with words alone; we occupy them through life and work in the spheres of creation. It is the relational atmosphere in creation we must fill, not some conceptual or Platonic removed realm.

It is this second phase of the divine strategy, where the body grows strong through the spheres of creation, which is the most overlooked in our present patterns of church life and evangelism. Look around you on any Sunday, do a brief read-out on your friends and family, look at your own life: Where are the real struggles? Where is the most hurt, pain and desperation? In what areas of life are the big decisions made? What matters most to people in life?

☞ There is little point in having strong congregations if marriages are falling apart all around us. It doesn't matter if our song service is contemporary if people have no strength or time to nurture their own families. It is of no consequence if the preaching is good, funny or brief if the day-by-day work of the saints is ineffectual. The real battle and place of standing in life and in the heavenly realm is in marriage, family and work.

Only when the saints stand in power in these spheres of creation will the church stand in power on the earth and through the heavens. With this in mind let's look at the last unusual directive given by the apostle to the Ephesian saints.

Final orders for phase two

Again I admit to having wondered why the saints, locked in dire conflict with the principalities and powers, armed to the teeth with spiritual weapons and brandishing the mighty sword of the Spirit, received that rather limp command to pray for each other. One would think that at such a crucial time and place in this heavenly battle we would be encouraged by Paul to bind the devil, maybe declare against a fallen angelic majesty or at least let go a volley or two at a stray demon! We think we are about to deliver a final death-blow to the enemy, but instead Paul tells us to get on our knees and pray for one another. He then adds a PS about praying for him as well, tells the Ephesians that Tychicus is coming, declares a final blessing and signs off. Is that it Paul? Are you going to leave us there for several years? What's the story?

The only resolution to this seemingly anticlimactic ending is to understand the truth about God's way for his body, the church, to stand and overcome in the heavens. In Ephesus, as in much of the church today, some saints were standing strong in marriage, family and work, but many were not. We can leave many of these behind in the rush to the next crusade or we can sit down, determine our troop strength, and work out whether the body is ready to face the armies of darkness in the next level of engagement. A good general first prepares the troops and then places them in strategic positions to engage the enemy's territory. Hence this final strategy given by Paul calls for the saints to put their energy where it is most needed. That is, to ensure that a substantial number in the body of Christ are standing in the creation spheres of marriage, family and work. Those with standing in the heavens have the ability and the authority to intercede for those still struggling. They have the God-given responsibility to effect a change in the heavens over the entire body of Christ. They have the ability to change the relational atmosphere over those they are one with. Such prayer, wisdom and encouragement enables those who choose to respond to rise up and take their own place in the body of Christ in the heavens.

The kingdom's coming, just you wait!

This is a difficult time for trigger-happy leaders who live for the sound of guns and war. The saints and other people of the city are not feeling the radical push of the gospel campaigns and book burnings as in the early days. This is because something more powerful than a crusade is growing in their midst. Something is happening in, through and over the earth more far-reaching than we could imagine or that could be expressed in a public event. As Jesus said, 'First the blade, then the head' (Mark 4:28) – these are the beginnings of the process. In the third phase of the divine strategy we will see this tree of life and righteousness filling the canopy of the heavens over the city. One can see the birds of the heavens making ready to come and settle on the branches.

The principalities and powers know something is stirring. They are beginning to feel the pressure of the body of Christ as it takes its stance in the created order, rising in stature in what was until that time a relatively uncontested heavenly place. They are starting to tremble at the sound of prayer declaring the eternal creation purpose of God. The strategy for life and intercession given here has to work first in the context of the body, for in time it will be used to impact an entire city. Already the powers are losing their hold over the mind of the redeemed. Soon their grip as principalities over the city will be contested. The church, as Jesus commanded, is beginning the occupation. In a little while the final orders will be given.

Chapter 14

The Divine Strategy – Phase III

Three to five years after the epistle to the Ephesians was sent, Paul wrote to his son in the faith, Timothy, who was ministering in Ephesus at the time. Timothy was experiencing his share of confusion, opposition and affliction; daily dying so that life might come to others. Paul encouraged him to keep standing and be strong 'in accordance with the prophecies previously made concerning you, that by them you may fight the good fight' (1 Tim. 1:18). He needed to be encouraged to rally, because a new offensive of the kingdom was about to be launched in the city.

It appears that those prayers for all the saints Paul had encouraged in his prior epistle had been effective in drawing a substantial number of the church in Ephesus to stand on the earth and through the heavens. By this time the seed planted by Paul in that first revival had grown to become quite a tree. It was reaching out into the heavens, even in the midst of the struggle against the currents and culture of the city. Timothy, wrestling with the day-to-day challenges, perhaps could not see the strength of the church across the city. He appeared to be more focused on the ongoing opposition and challenges to his ministry. It often takes someone from outside to give what is necessary for God's new season. Here Paul is given the privilege. By the Spirit he saw that the church at Ephesus was ready for the third and most

expansive phase of the divine strategy. He knew that it had
the standing necessary and the troop strength available to
occupy and restore the very atmosphere of the city and
region. The troops are ready; no terms of peace will be
sought. What are the orders now?

The Orders Are Given

What we are about to look into must be the most amazing
passage of scripture concerning the divine strategy found in
the New Testament. It is from 1 Timothy 2:1–4. Had not
the history of the Ephesian church and city borne out its
contents, it would be hard to believe that such things were
possible. Let us look closely at the remarkable orders given
there and the impact God intended for them. Paul says,
'First of all, then, I urge that entreaties and prayers, peti-
tions and thanksgivings, be made on behalf of all men, for
kings and all who are in authority.'

At the end of the book of Ephesians the prayers were
made on behalf of all the saints. Now Paul directs the
prayers of the saints towards the people of the city, specifically towards those who occupy the places of authority.
These strategic prayers are not aimed at angelic majesties;
they are directed towards leaders in line with the creation
spheres they represent. These leaders occupy their particular administration only by God's permission. God had
called them to be instruments for good in those places of
authority. They stood for God to serve those who were
daily influenced by the attributes, nature and power inherent in, and expressed through, these administrations. In a
fallen world their ability to accomplish this had immense
limits set by futility and darkness. They carried the burden
of this fallen reality every day and as such came to personify
the travail of creation in their city. It was these people, given

the right relational atmosphere in the heavens, who had the potential and authority to call forth the sons and daughters in answer to the cry.

We note here the inclusion of thanksgiving in the prayers of the saints for those in authority. What is the relationship between giving thanks and answering the cry of the city? Remember that the fall of humankind into darkness and futility occurred because they did not 'honour . . . God or give thanks' (Rom. 1:21). When you give thanks you necessarily focus in on the qualities that make for good. The giving of thanks for those in authority enables you to call forth the creation purpose and establish the counsels of God over a person, place or authority.

Apart from thanksgiving you cannot know the goodness and hence the divine nature God has placed within all created things. Giving honour enables you to behold the divine image and presence in a created thing, and thanksgiving is God's ordained way of drawing out the goodness of God within it. This great truth gives us the key to drawing out the creation purpose of those in the place of authority.

Moving into the spheres of creation over the city

From time immemorial these authorities of government, education, health, recreation and business in this city had been ruled over and predominantly defined by the counsels of spiritual wickedness in high places. Because of this the people who expressed that rule had – some to a greater extent, some to a lesser – come under the influence of these dark forces. Now there had been a change in the make-up of the heavens over the city. The body of Christ had come to stand through the creation spheres to occupy and fill these heavens once ruled by Satan. Once they were only a 'little flock', a small seed planted in hostile ground. But they had grown and travailed through suffering and death to emerge into resurrection life. This life was now breathing restoration into the spheres of marriage, family and work. This had happened to such an extent that now the city itself was calling them forth. It was inviting them to come and heal its very heart. Holy angels, ministers to these heirs of salvation, had been moving into place in response to the life and prayer of the saints. Now they were established and strong in sustaining the creation reality the saints had restored to the city. These angels had been waiting for this day – no doubt wondering about the delay!

The second phrase of this passage speaks about the intended outcome of such a living, powerful and occupying intercession. This strong sounding into creation is done 'in order that we may lead a tranquil and quiet life in all godliness and dignity. This is good and acceptable in the sight of God our Saviour'. It is easy to read past this sentence without catching what is really being said. The reality is that this prayer, at this time, actually brings about a transformation in the very atmosphere and culture of the city! What is being said here in the Word of God is astounding. When the saints attain standing in the heavenly realm through the spheres of the created order then, in answer to their prayers, the relational atmosphere or culture of the city will change! How?

☞ The saints, through kingdom life in marriage and family and through the administrations engaged by work, had seen substantial restoration come to these spheres of life. Because of this the attributes, nature and power of God were now becoming visible and known to the people of the city. The body of Christ had lived and worked in such a way that the goodness of God was now established in the land of the living.

This manifest goodness of God, like leaven working its way through the lump, was now working to conquer from within. From their standing in the heavenly place the saints, with words filled with the substance that belongs to Christ, began to prophesy and declare into and over the unseen spheres of creation in the city. The body of Christ, standing through the heavens, was now determining the counsels in the relational atmosphere over the earth. Is it any wonder that the words God spoke when he had finished creating the heavens and the earth make another appearance here? Paul says, simply but profoundly, 'This is good' (1 Tim. 2:3). The reason for this declaration becomes clear in the following and final part of the passage from 1 Timothy.

The Restoration Harvest

God had worked through this incredible strategy in Ephesus because he 'desires all men to be saved and to come to the knowledge of the truth'. This is the outcome, this is the fruit, this is the finale of the divine strategy! It is nothing less than salvation to all, nothing less than the city coming to know and experience the grace and truth of God. Way back in the beginning God wanted humanity to know him through the things that were made. Satan had blinded the minds of the unbelieving and futility and darkness had entered in. Now the Christ had come, now the price was paid, now the saints were living in the creation spheres, now these were cleansed and substantially restored, now the heavens were changing, now the prince of the air was falling like lightning. Now the silent God sounds his answer to the cry – breathed from every breath of atmosphere, radiating from every moment of time, emerging from earth beneath to heaven's sky. The idols are exiled and the life of the Son, the fullness, the radiance, rushes out from all things, comes down over all things, travels in relationship through all things and fulfils the life of the city. The rivers, whose streams make glad the heart of God, wash over the land, renewing the all things of God's creation.

Jesus, lifted up through the heavens in the lives of the saints, now draws all unto himself. The heavens now tell the glory of God. Day to day they pour forth speech and night to night they reveal knowledge. The creation spheres are fragrant with the unity, humility and love of the saints. People now know that Jesus, from whose face the light of the knowledge of the glory of God shines, is alive. To their surprise they see this Christ in these seemingly ordinary saints. It compels them to ask after and call forth the hope that God has placed within them. The fallen can now see something they want, and it is God! The season of reaping begins, the earth opens wide and salvation springs up. People begin pressing into the kingdom, some even taking it by force.

How different it is from that time when the gospel first 'broke into' the city. This time is the time of the 'restoration harvest'. This is because the third phase of the divine strategy speaks of a victory that arises from *within* the city. As Jesus says, in conclusion to his teaching about the seed, the plant and the harvest, 'When the crop permits, he immediately puts in the sickle because the harvest has come' (Mark 4:29). The crop itself is calling out to be harvested at this time, it is permitting us, it is calling for us, it falls into our lap!

☞ The city is taken without a vote being cast or a weapon being used. The saints have lived as having nothing and now possess the all things in a relational matrix that no one person, movement or ideology can rule or fathom.

It is for this reason that the impact of the divine strategy on the city is so far-reaching. This harvest becomes anchored and fixed in the very creation spheres; it is established in every authority of the city. It is not contained in a series of crusade meetings or inside a church building or programme; it is expressed in and over and through all things in the city. Because of this its impact goes deep, its staying power is strong and sure. It will not be blown away by some new fad or phenomenon. It has become intrinsic to the life of the city. The gospel has ushered in the kingdom and the kingdom's rule is here. The new creation seed planted has now become a tree of life – matured and trained, a tree of righteousness, able to discern both good and evil, having grown up through all things into the heavens – its scent attracting the birds of the heavens, its branches offering a place to nest, its fruit feeding the young born safe for heaven's sky.

Epilogue on Ephesus

The above account may sound too idealistic and appear to tilt at Christian triumphalism this side of the age to come. I could have tempered it with references to ongoing struggles experienced by saints in their everyday life. I could have mentioned that many in the city would have still remained outside the kingdom. Pockets of darkness would no doubt have still been in operation after the restoration harvest had come. I mention these fallen realities here to balance the account and to allay concerns that I have crossed the border into paradise with language alone and left reality behind in the rush! I am not advocating a perfect triumph at Ephesus. I am, however, trumpeting the victory of good over evil in this city at that time.

History does tell us that this divine strategy impacted the city of Ephesus to such an extent that the church grew in a short time to become the dominant force in the city. Around the year AD 110 Christianity had so changed the region of Bythynia directly to the north that the temples were mostly deserted, the ceremonies to the gods neglected and it was difficult to sell fodder for sacrificial animals.

The coming of the Catholic and Orthodox systems to Asia Minor in subsequent centuries would have strongly influenced this state of affairs. It follows that the same principles that win the victory for the body of Christ, if neglected or rejected, will become the means of its demise and regional defeat. Also, each subsequent generation must rise in maturity to answer the cry for its time – the prior generation can bequeath a heritage, but it cannot guarantee the following generation's God-given inheritance.

To give an indication of the staying power of this restoration harvest I cite F.F. Bruce, who says of Ephesus and the region that, 'The christianisation of the province of Asia was carried out during those years by Paul and his colleagues so thoroughly that for centuries the churches of Asia were among the most influential in the world; they survived the Turkish conquest and did not come to an end until the exchange of populations which followed the Graeco-Turkish war in 1923' (*New Testament History*, p. 309). That is what you call a long and distinguished career!

What great pleasure God must have had in seeing this outcome of the divine strategy commenced in John, carried by Jesus, ignited by Paul and fanned into flame by Timothy. It was in this way that the sons and daughters of God, called forth by this great city of Ephesus, fulfilled the age-old prophecy: 'Those from among you will rebuild the ancient ruins; you will raise up the age-old foundations; and you will be called the repairer of the breach, the restorer of the streets in which to dwell' (Isaiah 58:12). Should the body of Christ, brought into being through the sacrifice of Calvary, be called to do anything less? What a strategy! How connected it is to life. How in line with the nature of the created order. How rich is God's answer to the cry of his creation. John the aged apostle decided to retire in Ephesus – in fulfilment, I believe, of Jesus' prophecy that 'there are some of those who are standing here who will not taste death until they see the kingdom of God *after* it has come *with power*' (Mark 9:1).

Again the question is asked, if this is war, are we presently fighting according to the master's plan? It behoves us to set the largest of contexts when looking at the field and scope for our ministry and life as saints. After all, we *are* dealing with the infinite and eternal God! I believe God has given this strategy to his body the church, the fullness of him who fills all in all: a divine plan and eternal purpose that encompasses all of our life and all the creation he has made for us. Should we expect anything less from our eternal Father? Our world is moving rapidly towards a fragmenting future and leaving the church behind in its wake; surely the time has come to look again at our paradigm and look again at our plan.

Chapter 15

The Church as Pillar Meets The Church as Fullness

Increasingly the call is going out for a more radical and far-reaching approach to being the church. As popular as the megachurch has become in certain countries and as relational as the house church movement might be, I believe their scope and strategy needs to move far beyond their present focus on the campus or the house cell. Our challenge is to take hold of a paradigm and a strategy that will enable the saints to move beyond the multiplication of meetings and on into their life and work in the entirety of the created order. I believe that the divine plan from the ancient city of Ephesus can deliver what we need at this time. With the creation as our context and with this divine strategy in focus we are in a far better place to fathom the nature and purpose of the gatherings, the mission and the ministry gifts of the 'local' church.

Paul, in his first letter to Timothy in Ephesus, said this of the gathering of the saints: 'I write so that you may know how one ought to conduct himself in the household of God, which is the church of the living God, the pillar and support of the truth' (1 Tim. 3:15). In this phrase we find a second definition of the church. The first, from Ephesians, speaks of the church as Christ's body being the fullness of him who fills all in all. These two definitions, combined with Jesus' words concerning the church being built upon the rock of confession of Christ as the Son of God, complete the list of more direct descriptions we are given of the church.

Paul calls the church gathered 'the pillar and support of the truth'. This phrase indicates that this expression of the church is intended to be a *support* to a larger reality or truth. It appears that, of itself, it was not intended to be the central or complete thing. I believe we can conclude from this verse that the church gathered must be called to be the pillar and support of the church as the fullness of the created order. This interpretation arises from the text itself and it follows on logically from what we have seen of the description of the church in Ephesians. What other reality in the created order would the church as pillar be called to support except that which is the fullness of the created order?

Some might say to this: 'Is it not the church's faithful preaching of the word of truth that is in view here?' Yes, the preaching event at church does proclaim the truth from the pulpit. However, God's eternal purpose is ultimately to proclaim his wisdom 'through the church to the rulers and the authorities in the heavenly places' (Eph. 3:10). This kind of proclamation can only be accomplished in the life and work of the saints who occupy the spheres of creation.

☞ The 'local' church cannot reach the heavens via its words, programmes and meetings. The Son of God stands not so much in the truth concepts spoken on Sunday: rather he stands right through the created order in the body of Christ. This is the all-encompassing truth that the gathering is called to be the pillar and support of. Once this relationship is established in our thinking we can begin to consider the strategic relationship God intends there to exist between the church gathered and the church as fullness.

The Pattern for Life and Living

Again I draw attention to the way in which the early church was defined as the saints living, working and worshipping in the context of a whole city or region. The containment of the church in denominations and buildings was not a part of early Christian experience. Paul calls the church gathered 'the household'. The gatherings, like the kitchen or dining room of the family home, were places where the extended family, made up of brothers and sisters of the one Father, could get together. There they would catch up, encourage each other, eat and be nourished, plan and dream, have some fun and then, when the day was over, each head back into their broader lives and work. The love feast, the spiritual gifts for the common good, the teaching of the Word, the worship of almighty God, the reading of Scripture and the settling of family disputes were among the many good and essential things on offer at the gathering of the household.

As in any good household, one of the most powerful elements of the church gathered is its ability to establish the pattern for Christian living. Paul wanted elders to be the husband of one wife and to be good fathers of their families. Why? Because there is a need for church leadership to be a pattern for the way marriage and family are meant to be. The best place for new converts from a pagan world to start learning how their own marriages and families are meant to function is in relationship with leaders and in fellowship with other mature saints. The church gathered is the place where we learn to name life again, where we learn to relate to each other and to God in a whole and healing way. It is the place where our gifts and identity are drawn out. What is agreed upon, what is bound (not permitted) and what is loosed (permitted) when two or three are gathered establishes the kingdom culture and sets in place a relational matrix that serves to impact the life of the body, right through to the heavens (Matt. 18:18–20). The gatherings of the people of God certainly have an important function. Scripture, however, places them in a servant rather than a central role.

The Epistles, because they deal mostly with the time after the initial planting of the gospel in the city do place stronger emphasis on the gathering and the nurturing phase. This emphasis, combined with the dramatic evangelistic activity in Acts, has tended to set the agenda for both the evangelist and the pastor. This of itself is not the problem. Our problem is with the leaven of the Greek mindset working its way through the record of these events. One of the many consequences of this influence is that we have come to believe that the church gathered is the major vehicle for evangelism and the saints' work of ministry. Yes, individual ministry is encouraged, but the powerful name 'church' is reserved only for those activities directly sponsored by pastors and elders of local congregations. Leaders will at times preach the importance of the saints' work. But most of what is said and done in preaching, planning and resource allocation by leaders indicates to all and sundry where the action really is and where the future really lies. This arrangement ensures that most of the momentum for ministry (and thus Christian maturity) ends up travelling towards the buildings, the meetings and the programmes of the local church. The end result of the Greek infiltration is that we are kept in the crusade, tied to the nest and are unable to fly very far into the creation before we are drawn back to support the pillar.

Health and church life

I did a weekend conference for health workers during
which I had various discussions with the people in
attendance. Many told of the years that they had spent
working in very difficult areas, often under great stress.
Every so often their pastors would ask them how they
were going, but they never engaged and sought to
empower them directly in relation to the work they did.
They all knew that the pastor's major concern was
how the church was going. His relationship with them
was on the basis of the work of the church he
pastored. If they had a problem and needed
counselling he would of course be available. However,
apart from that he kept to his speciality, which was the
church work, and they were meant to keep to theirs.
They would overlap on Sunday in relation to spiritual
and moral matters. But the pastor's main interest and
passion had to do with the next sermon he would give
and who would be there to hear it.

Looking at the Church Containment Policy

It is the concentration of the activities and passion of 98 per
cent of the ministry gifts of Christ in and around congregational settings that sets the agenda for what does (and does
not) happen with 98 per cent of the body of Christ. We
need, I believe, to take Hebrew sight and begin to look beyond the crusades, the appointment of elders in every city,
the preaching event, the directions for the proper use of
spiritual gifts, the protocols for church discipline and other
important elements of a strong local church community to
see the eternal purpose towards which they are all meant
to be working. These things are not given just to build the
church localised and organised: they are given to build

the church as the fullness of him who fills all in all. That church exists in marriage, family and work. It cannot live and bear the fruit that God intends within programmes, buildings and meetings. The church gathered must ultimately exist to equip and resource the body of Christ with a view to the saints coming into their fullness in, through and over all things in creation. It simply cannot be the other way around. A pillar is made to support.

The church as pillar and support must be the servant of the church as fullness of the created order. We were made, as Paul says, to grow up in and through all things in creation. The entire creation is the setting for the body of Christ, not the congregation. So many things in life and in revelation cry out this logic: the Garden given to prepare Adam and Eve for the creation outside the gate which waits to be subdued; the child that learns on its mother's knee in readiness for the day he takes his place in the world as an adult; the mare that kicks her growing foal at the right time to establish its independence; the eaglet pushed from the nest by a mother demanding that it learn to fly. The Garden is not the creation, the nest is not the sky, the nursery is not the city, the mother's milk is not the only thing on the menu of life. Everywhere we look we see the progression from initial safety and simple definition into a more complex and far-reaching world where maturity waits for us alongside our inheritance. We know the principle from nature and life well. Our challenge is to set a paradigm in place that can discern the difference between these phases and facets of life in the church. In the past three decades our ability to make such a distinction has become more and more difficult. The reason for this relates to what might be termed the corporate take-over.

The corporate church

The Church Growth Movement began in earnest in the '70s to position the church to compete in the modern market-oriented world. It was from this time that the church took on the identity of the corporate model of business. Throughout most of its history the church had been something separate from the saints, oriented towards the 'truth' or 'spirit' realm. However, from the early '70s another dimension of this congregation-focused paradigm came in. Many churches began to operate as business organisations overseen by either an owner/operator or, if the church was large enough, a Chief Executive Officer. With this corporate reality came things like vision or mission statements, pitching meetings to the market, intensification of competition between fellowships, departmental structuring of local church life and many other attachments that served to further distance the household of God from the everyday life of the family members.

The third force

A Christian friend who works as a lawyer for a transnational corporation was entering into a partnership with another Christian. In this venture he did not want to establish a company structure to express the business relationship. He said the reason for this was that a company takes on a life of its own. It has a certain culture, regulations and practices that eventually become a kind of third entity in the relationship. This third player imposes its own definition of the way the relationship will work, what can happen and what cannot. He said that every time he, as an individual, wanted to do business he would have to take into account the company. He was not opposed to companies existing for other reasons, but he did not feel it would enhance his partnership with another brother.

The present containment of the church in corporate structures is perhaps one of the least questioned but most
important concerns we will face when it comes to releasing
the saints to engage the created order. I am not saying that a
fellowship (of 10 or 10,000) shouldn't have an organisational dimension that assists its activities. The challenge is
that we have taken the organisational dimension of life and
placed it over us. We named it an organisation and we
brought it to life. We stamped a vision statement on it,
placed it in a legal construct, gave it a brochure and a building and sent a cash flow through it. The outcome is that
most leaders and saints now live to serve it. It is beyond the
scope of this book to go into detail concerning many of the
psychological and strategic implications of the church func-
tioning as a corporate structure. Here we briefly consider
some of these implications in the light of the creation reality
we have looked at.

The church trying to sell a product

A company operating in one of the spheres of the created
order, such as business or health, can achieve a tremendous
amount by having a singular focus and an organisational
structure that serves that focus. The problem the church
faces when it functions in this way is that God did not intend the church to occupy a distinct sphere of creation. It
was not given its own product to make and market. In contrast to a business producing services and commodities, the
church has no unique sphere of creation to inhabit. These
spheres produce their results because they exist in reality.
The church's reality can only arise from being the fullness of
them all.

☞ In very practical and obvious terms the local church
    operating as an organisation simply cannot occupy or

fulfil the created order. Marriage, family and work fill the creation; meetings, programmes and buildings cannot. When the local gathering attempts to encompass the impossible it cannot help but falter. It is only the saints, individually and in relationship, who can (and already do) work, live and relate in all of creation. They are already there but the church gathering is not. They will always live there whereas the gathering will never be able to occupy that place of the fullness, no matter how many departments and programmes spring from any one church.

That is not to say that individuals cannot undertake organised initiatives as an expression of the church gathered. The distribution of food to the widows 'on the list' in the time of the early church is an example of such a practice. There is certainly much we can do together. However, when such is deemed to be the primary work of the church we in effect relegate the major work of the saints to the background. The outcome is that the church's ability to engage the created order is drastically reduced.

I believe many of the strategies the church continues to adopt in its attempt to discover and define its identity and purpose in a postmodern world are self-defeating. Rather than being the fullness of creation and mobilising the gathering to resource the saints in their life and work, we have chosen instead to identify our local congregations with one or the other of the spheres of the created order engaged by work. We noted in chapter 11 that these administrations are named – government, health, education, business and recreation. Of course every gathering of the saints should use a good sprinkling of these elements of creation. However, the church 'localised', allied to the corporate structure, has mixed these elements to form some rather unlikely compounds! The Church Growth Movement taught leaders to find their niche by specialising in one or the other of the above. How else, it said, would people be able to make their decision to purchase the particular brand of church they were shopping for?

The outcome of this trend is that we now find ourselves with some churches that are predominantly entertainment centres. Others exist to produce life-enhancing merchandise. Many churches operate as perpetual educational and personal development institutions. Others go for the governmental or hierarchical approach, taking charge of people's lives and superintending their decisions, always doing what is best for the citizens of their congregation. The final sphere is that of health. Here people are nurtured, healed, revived, taken care of and carried within the church subculture from the cradle to the grave. The outcome of all of this is lots of activity and advertising. However, the results are, to say the least, problematic! The church was never designed to be a marketable item or to market items. It was designed to be a body of people, the very body of Christ – the fullness of him who fills all in all.

What are the problems that arise from this niche-marketing enterprise? Each of the spheres of creation the church is endeavouring to specialise in are defined, for the most part, by the world system. The reason we use them to promote 'our' church is because people readily identify with them from their own life experience. Does it not stand to reason that by employing such a strategy we in fact ensure that people will increasingly relate to our church in accordance with the world's definition of these spheres? Such things as entertainment and 'infotainment' derive their substance and meaning from the media culture. Their definition does not originate in the church. As much as we try, the church in the first and second phases of the divine strategy cannot fundamentally redefine these things. As the saying goes, 'If you live by something you may well have to die by it'.

If the saints begin to treat the church like another entertainment event, if they get bored and want to switch channels, can we blame them? If they no longer have the time or the ability to put the last ten sermons and five conferences into practice because the next ten and five have arrived demanding their attention, can we charge them with the crime of sermon tasting? If they are not healed and still remain emotionally challenged should it surprise us when they head off to the next ministry promising deliverance? If they become wary of expectations promised but not delivered and begin to modify the degree to which they respond to the next build-up, can we charge them with a lack of commitment? This is how things like entertainment events, health facilities and other institutions are treated in the world; this is in time how they will be treated in the church. It is we who are leaders that have set up the parameters and organised the agenda that determines the saints' response. It was not their worldliness, it was our paradigm. I am not saying that such an outcome is a given in every circumstance. I am, however, drawing attention to a trend that sees a growing army of uncommitted saints migrating from one local church to the next, on the look-out for that well-advertised, but elusive, 'right product'.

I am not advocating we be insensitive to our present culture. In fact it is more discernment about the way in which our society has been programmed by the market place that is needed, not less. I believe this will help us understand why the move by the church to set up shop in one of the creation spheres not only increases the divide between church and life, but also further diminishes the identity and strength of what we are trying to build. There is a purpose for the creation spheres that has to do with the church as fullness. There is a purpose for the church as pillar and support and that is to *be* a pillar and a support. It should be noted that the world has a bigger budget and a far less morally challenging product. Not only are we mostly competing for a market of the already saved, but we are also setting up against business operators for whom the creation supplies an overwhelming competitive advantage.

The church operating in a non-sphere of creation

I believe that the church has established itself in a sphere of creation uncreated by God. The consequence is that we are left without the resources and the definition we need to impact the creation. We have moved away from the diversity and richness of God-ordained unity and substituted it with a self-limiting and narrow uniformity tied to one organisation and often one individual.

☞ We have failed to make the connection between the congregation context and the spheres of the created order around us. Because of this we have had to make the congregation a whole world in and of itself. The outcome is that the church has become something that is disconnected from the world and dislocated from the very life and work of the saints themselves. The consequences are taking their toll on leaders and laity. The leaders are losing their hold on the people of God and the people of God are being deprived of the necessary resources and affirmation they need to make it through their daily struggle in life and work. The sad irony is that each holds the key to the other's life and calling.

The societal trend to amass more and more information, the push to place your church's ministry out where people are buying, and the incredible pressure from within to fill the building have brought many to a place where they believe their own advertising. Through it all we are laying heavier and heavier burdens on our gatherings and our pastors than our forefathers ever had to bear. The larger and more extravagant our events, the more diminished the saints who attend and admire them become. Certainly encouragement and solidarity can come from these large events. However, on their own they only offer pseudo-strength simulated by association. Some churches have the ability to put these mega-events on, but the market in any one area can only handle so many. Also most pastors are simply not trained in their colleges for market warfare with glamour weapons. In all, like a beast of burden trying to make it up the hill with too much baggage, our meetings and our pastors are increasingly not making it to their projected sales summit. The church bell is beginning to toll and starting to tell in the lives of an increasing number of pastors buckling under the demand to do or die. Many do not choose the latter option; it is picking at them. Almost all the surveys bring out the difficulties inherent in the present church paradigm. They are obvious to anyone who has been around long enough to survey the landscape. These may not appear in the church brochure but the writing is everywhere else. What we have promised the people of God we have not really been able to deliver, and it has not been for want of trying.

Our present struggle for identity will not be resolved by the education-oriented churches telling the entertainment churches to come back to the Reformation or by the entertainment churches telling the education churches to come 'back to the future'. The issues run deeper than which sphere or which era of history we should specialise in.

The Greek mindset now married to the consumer age is working against the very things we are trying so hard to accomplish. We are not getting out of our buildings; we are staying in them. They are to this day our 'Christian Centre'. Yes, there is much good being achieved in the localised expression of the church. However, this good is not only not travelling the distance, but in far too many instances it ends up actually working against itself. The social and ministry context the local church offers, even if large, soon becomes too small to match and resource the growth in individual lives. The result is that most of the saints' life happens beyond church, which creates the well-known sense of divide and tension between church life and the rest of life. Another outcome is that many people's Christian life becomes dependent on and narrowed down to the limited programme on offer at their church. Many of course do manage to build a workable bridge between life and church, but this begs the question: if the saints are the church, then why do they have to work so hard to build that bridge in the first place?

The Work of the Ministry Gift

No matter how many ecclesiastical or market expectations pastors are presently dancing to, there is the beat of another drum they are called to minister in time with. In Ephesians, the book of the church, Paul gave the ministry gifts the job description put in place by their ultimate employer. He said that the ministry gifts of Christ are called to accomplish 'the equipping of the saints for the work of service, to the building up of the body of Christ'. Their work goes on and through 'until we all attain to the unity of the faith and of the knowledge of the Son of God, to a mature man, to the measure of the stature which belongs to the fullness of Christ'. The outcome or result of their ministry, Paul says, will be that, 'we are no longer . . . children, tossed here and there by waves and carried about by every wind of doctrine, by the trickery of men, by craftiness in deceitful scheming' (Eph. 4:14). And here comes the crux of the matter – 'Speaking the truth in love, we are to grow up in all aspects [things] into him, who is the head, even Christ' (Eph. 4:15).

If this key passage is to come on line for this time, we must set its truths in a creation context rather than a congregational one. If the Son of God stands in, through and over the all things of creation, if he is head over his body, the church – a body called to be and become the fullness of him who fills all in all – then it follows that the ministry gifts must give saints a knowledge of that Son and live to build that body. The job description from Ephesians, unlocked via Hebrew cosmology, must set the overriding agenda for both the preaching and practice of the ministry gifts.

☞ Ministers must equip the saints for every level of their engagement with the creation. From the moment of salvation, through the nurture stage, into the time of maturation, restoration and occupation of all created things, the ministry gifts must stand with the saints.

The ministry gifts can only gain their inheritance when they equip the saints to be apostolic – breaking ground in their own life and work; prophetic – speaking words full of creation content into their God-given land to see the bones live and the plants thrive; good-news tellers – reaching those who come within the borders of their land with the message of salvation; pastors – caring for those who are won within that matrix of relationship and work; and teachers – ready and able to speak the truth in love and build those who come into the body. If the apostles are first in the church and they are exhibited last of all, what then must be the place of the other gifts derived from the apostolic? The first and foremost exhibit is not the pastor or the teacher or the prophet. The hope of all glory and the fear of every fallen principality and power is an apostolic, prophetic, evangelistic, pastoring and teaching church standing up in the stature that belongs to the fullness of Christ. It is such a body of people, served by the ministry gifts of the risen Lord, which will progressively occupy right through to the heavens.

Where to now?

A solicitor, married with two children, working in his own community-based business, came one day to an unexpected decision. He realised that he couldn't run a business, put time into his marriage and be with his children as well as run a house church that reached out to the lost and attended to the spiritual and social needs of ten or so Christians. He said to me, 'All of my church life had prepared me to take up leadership of such a group. That role was held out as being the pinnacle of lay leadership and I couldn't do it and do all of those other things as well. So I stepped down and gave the group to another person. I hadn't counted on the guilt I would feel arising from such a decision. It took me the best part of a year to get over it and rest in the truth that I was not being selfish. My family and my job were my ministry.'

The next unexpected surprise arrived for this solicitor soon after the guilt had subsided. He went on to say, 'There I was with my work my focus. Soon I began to realise that all of my Christian/church life to date had only really prepared me to work ethically and witness opportunistically. Apart from that it had given me no tangible ability to really "go into" my work as a Christian. So here I am, yes, still in fellowship, but not quite with the church programme. I have a staff of five, a building and resources worth lots of money and I'm open five days a week. I'm ready. Will the church please send somebody to help *me do what surely must come next. I know there must be more to do in this place than ethics and witnessing, as important as those things are. But will somebody please tell me what it is?'*

The gathering fills up

Right now there are incredible resources, strong passions and an immense momentum moving with the life of every saint who attends on a given Sunday. Why try to establish a separate momentum going in the other direction? If we want to see the impact made, why not move the works of the kingdom in line with the saints' life and work in every sphere of the creation? It is only when a continuous highway is established between the 'household' and the 'fullness' that we will be able to mobilise the incredible resources of the church gathered.

Such a way of 'doing church' will initially appear to diminish the clarity and centrality of the Sunday meeting. However, as the saints discover the attributes, nature and power of God in the 'all things' of their own life and work, they will increasingly carry the meaning and treasure they have found into the church celebration. Those leaders who release such momentum will find a greatly enlarged and diversified ministry role as they stand with and serve the saints in all their life and work.

The words of our worship songs will increasingly fill with the content and substance the saints have found and restored to themselves in the created order. The strain of marketing our meetings and selling our products will be gone because the saints themselves will become the main light and best attraction to a world in darkness. We will no longer have to keep them at the boiling point of expectation. Instead they will gather momentum in life, work and witness into their own reality and thereby taste the fruit of their inheritance. Rather than such a focus on life and work in creation diminishing our Sunday morning service or Wednesday cell night, I believe we will see vitality and validation return to the gatherings we are presently trying so hard to fill with purpose and with people.

The Spirit-filled new creation was never intended to be limited to the congregational setting. The call to release it is strong and growing stronger. In it we can hear the hope of glory and the cry of so many saints trying to survive in and reach out to their world. The call is to make the creation context *the* context for the works of ministry of the saints and the life and identity of the church. Before we look into the nature of these powerful works and the relationship of the ministry gifts to them, we need to travel into and through that precious and long-awaited time of revival.

GEORGE THE ELDER (6)
Journey through the lines

It was Monday and George was heading down the freeway, weaving his way across to the fast lane, heading towards his self-made front line. No clear answer from God had come. He was still surrounded by 'should do's' and didn't know what to do. From his morning quiet time he had been reminded that Christ was in him and that was reassuring, but he was having difficulty taking that truth further at this stage. As he moved towards the speed limit, the struggle inside started to manifest in a battle between his accelerator pedal and his feeling of helplessness. When he pushed down he felt powerful but whenever he let up the dread of what was coming closed in. Trouble was that if he kept pushing he would soon be up over a hundred, he would get booked and lose any anointing he might have had stored up. 'Snap out of it George,' he said, 'the pedal's not your problem!'

Things settled down in the fast lane. George was most comfortable praying in the car; he sometimes called it his prayer chariot. He began the proceedings by saying, 'All I need is a revelation God. I'm sorry for asking for more than "Christ-in-you" but in twenty-five minutes I'll be there, they'll be there, and we'll all be standing toe to toe on that line. You remember Elijah and Mount Carmel.' George remembered that God never forgot, except, of course, in relation to our sins when we repented. For a moment he dipped into the matter of the sea of forgetfulness and hoped he wasn't a part of the eternal not knowing. Things were getting a bit deep so he waded back to life on Monday.

In an unconscious act to clear his thoughts, George pushed the button that activated the water spray and turned on the windscreen wipers. As they swished to and fro across his field of vision, their rhythm reminded him of a song, which in turn brought to mind a sermon he had mostly forgotten. All George could remember was pastor Steve leaning over the pulpit one Sunday night, smiling and pleading at the same time, saying, 'When it's all over, come on home.'

George started to interrogate the statement. On the night it had made perfect sense, said, as it was, with great conviction. But now George wondered, 'When what's all over, and which home – heaven or the church? Christ in you the hope of glory, and when it's all over come on home.' He browsed through this small collection of words for a while. 'It's no good, I don't know how to use them,' George said, helplessly. 'Maybe I'm just not getting it.' He shook his head to refocus his thoughts. Then he saw it up ahead.

It was a slow car in the fast lane. George knew the Ten Commandments and wondered why this obvious crime wasn't listed as one of them, or at least an addendum to the donkey-coveting one. This was an area that George had always struggled with. Paul the apostle had problems with coveting. For George the elder it was slow cars in the fast lane. *Paul's struggle was evident; he named it sin. For George the issue was hidden deep below his ability to justify the contempt he held for anyone guilty of this modern transgression. To add fuel to this righteous fire, George was in the mood to put his frustration to work. His anger had been building over the past few days, and here was a chance to vent it with the help of some moral outrage.*

He hummed up behind the offender and wound his window down (just a little in case the guy was a criminal), waiting for the moment he could cut inside, pass him, look righteous and discharge justice. George had learned the art of swearing without using 'bad' words. All you had to do was take the swearing emotions and house them in innocuous words like 'what, how dare, listen you' etc, with 'jolly well' reserved for when things got really hot.

'Sickly green. Needs a wash. Earlier model than mine.' George was building up the case for his planned offensive. It was up to him to make the world a fairer and better place. The moment came and he took it. He planted his foot on the pedal, hit the wheel, jumped the lane and tore up beside the offending car, ready to make a citizen's arrest with his face. He jerked his head sideways, and called out some 'sanitised' swear words.

To his chagrin, instead of taking offence, exhibiting shame or simply ignoring him, the man in the car smiled and waved at him. Before George knew, the moment was over. He was back in the fast lane and the bad green car was behind him. Instead of the anticipated satisfaction, George was left with a slightly uneasy feeling and an impression in his mind of a waving hand and a round, grinning face. 'Idiot!' George muttered at the memory of the grinning face.

His attention turned sharply to a sign telling him that the end of the freeway was at hand. Soon he would have to leave the security zone and engage the enemy. Terror struck. The more helpless he felt the more he tried to bolster up some, any, kind of righteous anger against Rob. But by now it was too much effort. He looked around, up and sideways – nothing.

To add insult to George's growing list of injuries, the green car had moved up on the inside lane to overtake him. Again he was confronted with the face of the offender with the stupid grin and the slow-waving hand.

'What are you looking at moon-face,' George yelled out, but the green car just sped off in front of him. As soon as the words 'moon-face' passed George's lips the stern countenance of Churchill made an appearance in his mind's eye. It was the same face he had seen last night at the lookout.

Winston stared impassively at George and then asked, as if he already knew the answer, 'How is it going?'

'Badly thank you. This could be my last day and you . . .' he hesitated, unsure of the connection between the man in the green car and the image of Winston Churchill. He went on '. . . and he's made me late.'

'You'll get there on time,' the calm, gruff voice expressed in disregard of George's concerns.

The next question came out of the blue. 'What do you see George?'

'I see nothing, nothing,' George said.

'Look!' said Winston.

George hesitated. 'Look? Look at what?'

But even as he formed the question he knew what it was. For the first time since the crisis began, he looked at what it was he might lose that day – at what it would be like not to leave home each weekday morning and travel on this highway into the city. He saw the guys in the Friday meeting. He felt their desire for things to work out for the company. He read the fear in their eyes, the fear of anything that threatened their world and undermined their security. He understood why these men had no alternatives.

George had become so accustomed to wading through the mud in his mind that he was taken aback by such a sudden rush of clear thought. Quickly, before it faded, he looked again into the best vision he had had for days. He saw the company like a giant tree falling in the forest, and he felt his colleagues' terror as it took them all silently screaming down with it. No one else would hear and the city wouldn't care. But he would care, because he was a whole lot like them.

Winston broke in again. 'So what do you want?'

Alone, in the sanctity of his car, as the city traffic furled around him, George knew what he wanted, and he said it out loud.

'I want to work with the guys. I want to work it through.'

Winston smiled and looked anointed. George didn't try to work that one out because he was busy with some unfamiliar but welcome emotions. He felt strong and new at the same time. It was like getting something you really wanted, something you'd been searching for for a long time, and it felt good. During the remaining minutes it took him to reach the building he breathed in the new sensations and breathed out the clarity they gave him. These emotions surged as he pulled in to his car space. He looked at his watch and declared, 'OK George, it's time.'

Chapter 16

When Revival Comes

How great it is when revival thunders into town and lays claim to many a hard heart, breaking them open and winning them with the gospel. When we read of such times in history, or even experience such seasons of visitation, we are drawn out and changed by this intense touch of eternity. But when reading the accounts of great revivals we are often left wondering why they don't stay around for very long. In Finney's time they moved into town, churned up the place like a tornado and then headed off down the road to the next county. We read of the Great Awakenings under Whitefield and Wesley and witness the fire of God descend and then move on, leaving the life of the city to find its own level in the post-revival period. We wonder why God doesn't just keep the revival fires going until the job is done. Then the country would be won, the kingdom would come and all would be well. What on earth is the problem here?

We may wonder if it is sin, disunity or misguided zeal that turns off the torrent of revival. But how could the sovereign purposes of God in times of revival be thwarted again and again simply by human failings? Certainly, these will influence the course of events, but the truth is human sin was taken into account by God long ago when he paid the price and declared it was finished. If God draws back from revival because of certain people's misconduct, then the creation will wait forever for the fullness to come. There must be more happening here than simply sin. Why does God not pursue a scorched earth policy with the infinite revival fire he has on call?

Our journey to Ephesus revealed that times of intense revival cannot, of themselves, produce the maturity God desires in the saints. Revivals carry people along in their fervour like a mighty wave, with a power hard to resist. It is after the revival moves on that the time comes for the saints to build a life with the truth given to them. The difference between the intensity and activity of Acts and the straightforward and practical teaching of many of the Epistles about everyday life and relationships is evidence of the difference between these two seasons. God, in his wisdom, calls us to 'grow up in all things' into the fullness of the stature of the man Christ Jesus. This maturity and standing in the heavens over creation thus becomes ours for both time and eternity. Seasons of revival break open hearts filled with years of futility and pain. This is why the apostolic, expressing the Father's heart, turns from the crusade and even the miracles to begin the work of restoration of hearts.

It is interesting to note here that Jonathan Edwards, the church leader and theologian involved in the American revivals of the early eighteenth century, speaks of an emotional backlash that occurred after seasons of revival. At such times depression swept over the region and many saints had quite a struggle making their way back to everyday life. We have been accustomed to ascribing such influences to the devil alone. No doubt he was in there intensifying the struggles of people. However, we need to consider the possibility that such unusual phenomena following times of revival may have a whole lot to do with the way God has ordained things to be. People were not made to live for extended periods in such an intense emotional climate. Elation gives way to fatigue that calls the people to rest and then emerge into the struggle and blessedness of everyday life. It appears that revivals are gloriously unusual times, rather than being the usual times God ordains.

What Revival Does Not Do

Most of our society will not really be able to see God in crusades, overwhelming emotional experiences, moral conviction or even in miracles. These are not the primary means that God uses to reveal himself to people. They are, without doubt, a very important part of God's purpose; however, they alone will not bridge the tremendous gulf that exists between congregation and society. This is particularly true nowadays when so many gurus, spiritualists and false prophets are performing signs and gathering eager crowds after them. Divine light does not shine so much from the sign itself. The signs are given by God to demonstrate the power of the kingdom breaking in. The signs do not establish divine reality: rather they serve to highlight that reality. We see this brought out in the teaching of Jesus when he stressed the limited value of signs to reach an unbelieving and perverted generation. In a life replete with miracles he stated plainly that 'the kingdom of God is not coming with signs to be observed . . . the kingdom of God is in your midst' (Luke 17:20, 21).

Jesus said we would only ever win from within, influencing, leavening, growing and overcoming through our lives and our works. These would shine the light to the world and salt the entire earth with divine savour. Without the life and the work that goes with the supernatural events there is nothing to distinguish them from the great signs we read about in the book of Revelation, signs that deceive through their brazen display of power.

Revival and reaction

Revival, as we have noted, does not of itself usher in the long-term restoration of the city or region. Many times we read of revivals that came and went in a year or two with powerful immediate results but little lasting effect. The Welsh revival at the turn of the 20th century comes to mind here. It is said that a little over two years after the revival fires died down, in many places in Wales there was no lasting evidence of it ever having been. In these regions the remnants remain only in songs sung in stadiums where sport is king. What a tragic waste of the divine outpouring.

Human nature, being what it is, can often react against a time of intense revival. It can become hardened against something that outlasts its welcome and seems so unlike the normal life or aspirations of the city. Witness the process of revival in many cities impacted by the apostle Paul's visitation programme. First there was revival and then there was reaction. The power of God healed the lame man at Lystra in full view of the city. At first they applauded the divine manifestation, until they realised that it had naught to do with their own familiar spirits. The result was the stoning of Paul by the angry mob, with a quick visit to the third heaven thrown in for no extra cost! As we have noted, Paul marked such times of backlash as the signal of the end of the first phase. He knew that it would be in the third and final phase that the church would win from within, securing a lasting result in the city by standing mature and strong in Christ.

☞ Many are looking to the next revival, believing that it will be the last and the greatest, completing the purposes of God for the ages. In nations like America, with its history of popular revivalism, such thinking runs deep and moves many. In the light of the Hebrew worldview and the divine plan displayed in the city of Ephesus, the pressing question is: Will the next revival move out and into the lives of the saints and penetrate the city, the nation and the nations, or will we leave it boiling in the church or the crusade until the river runs dry and the cloud vapourises into space?

The evangelist and revival

It is telling to look at the relationship between revival and the kind of church life that follows it. Revival seasons are characterised by many meetings in set locations, usually strongly focused on one particular called and gifted individual. Evangelists, as we know, love the meeting, have a passion for the crowd and live for the altar call. They move on after a time and the fierce awakening fires mellow back into the Sunday regime. The revival has, however, left its indelible mark on the patterns of church life from that time on. In effect, what we see in most instances following revival is the great commission fulfilled through the preaching event, mostly on Sunday evening or at special crusade times planned throughout the year. In effect the church does evangelism just like it did in the revival but now in miniature. The result is that the evangelist has profoundly influenced church structure and strategy. Many of the megachurches are started by leaders with a strong evangelistic calling. The way they run their churches has much to do with their gifting, calling and passions. Such expressions of church life, through the conferences and books they produce, have now become the measure of things for other congregations in the cities and across the nations. The evangelist's influence in the current climate is far-reaching indeed.

Apostolic Revivals

In contrast we look at revivals overseen and structured by the apostle. This is clearly seen in the life and ministry of Paul. We find that the apostle follows a very different building strategy from that of the evangelist. That is why Paul's epistles are so different in character from his activities when first arriving in the city. In his writings to post-revival situations there is little or no mention of crusades, open airs, book burnings and other tactics we would expect from this aggressive and fearless apostle. Paul's reminder to Timothy to do the work of an evangelist seems to indicate that gospel meetings were not necessarily a regular part of the church programme. All the verses that relate to evangelism in the Epistles refer to personal evangelism done in the context of everyday life and work. In particular we note 1 Peter 3:15 and Colossians 4:5. Paul knew the difference between the seasons of God. He did not focus on building evangelistic centres: rather he built the people of God and made them intrinsic to the life and destiny of the city.

When we look at Jesus' life we find it was spent at dinners, on the road talking to individuals, engaging people in the market place, in villages and in the cities. Jesus encourages us to make friends in our workplaces and in the context of our financial dealings so that eternal life might be made available to them. In any and every way we are called to go into all that is our world and proclaim the gospel in life, in deed and in word. This does not exclude times of gospel proclamation in large and small settings: rather it sets the larger and overriding context for such strategically timed events.

How not to stop a revival

We see from the record that the most far-reaching revivals in history are those that either develop into missionary endeavour or those that create a movement into the broader streams or spheres of society. An example of the first is seen in the student movement that followed the revivals under Moody and in the Pentecostal revivals flowing from the Asuza Street outpouring. The best of the Welsh revival journeyed beyond its own borders. In these instances the wave of revival was ridden out across the nations and came to break over many lands.

An example of the second is evident in the period following the Methodist revivals in England. Here the saints impacted spheres such as education and health, and men like William Wilberforce worked in government against the injustices of slavery. These revivals carried over into the life systems of society, bringing lasting change and restoration. Wesley's apostolic abilities ensured that Methodism became more than a revival. He structured what was to be for many years a powerful force for good in many nations.

During seasons when the manifest presence of God arrives to overcome us, the challenge to leaders is great. The feeling is that no one should ever touch revival because it is something God is doing. But what separates it from what God does in every season he is sovereign over? I believe that to do nothing but allow the events to take their course is to ensure that in time the revival will default to the preconceptions and patterns of old. The deluge comes and pours across the ground only to disappear like run-off out of the city. It has happened far too many times for this waste to be repeated again.

☞ It must be part of our preparation for revival to be ready, like Paul, to take hold of apostolic wisdom and build according to the master plan. If the church stops at revival, thinking it to be the arrival point of the divine strategy, then the momentum will falter there. However, if we go through revival into the all things of creation, we will see the body of Christ journey through the intensity of that time into the fullness.

I believe that in times of revival leaders need to prayerfully decide how and when to diversify the focus of the saints, directing the course of the river out into their daily life and work. The harvest that awaits us in creation is immense. The great deluge has to saturate as much of the earth as is possible, watering the seed of the kingdom that has been planted, thus ensuring its future growth into the heavens. This is a hard call for the minister and saints who have been experiencing packed meetings and heaven on earth just by coming and sitting in church. However, as the record shows, if we hold on to the patterns established in the heat of revival we will again become preoccupied with the form and gradually lose the content. The next generation arises and reacts against their parents' religion and nostalgia and drifts away into what they call the 'real world'. Many of them think they have rejected God when in fact they have only left a structure which could no longer express and empower their desire for life, identity and meaning.

Revivals need not end up in the settling ponds and holding patterns the church has historically made for them. The church that Jesus came to build is built upon an apostolic foundation that calls for much more than such a limited outcome. The Word of God speaks of the early rains and the latter rains. The first are given for the time of planting and the latter come in the time of harvest. What happens in between these times is growth – growth of the planting of the Lord to become a tree that fills the sky, attracting the birds of the heavens to come and settle in its branches. What takes place is the ripening of the city through to the final stage where the crop permits the full harvest to come. If we have rain, rain and more rain, it will only flood our building and ruin the carpet. We need the soil of the earth, the seed of the Word, and life in the spheres of marriage, family and work to ensure the water produces life eternal on the earth, through the heavens and into the ages to come. Ezekiel, I believe, prophesied the same:

> I shall also take a sprig from the lofty top of the cedar and set it out; I shall pluck from the topmost of its young twigs a tender one and I shall plant it on a high and lofty mountain. On the high mountain of Israel I shall plant it, that it may bring forth boughs and bear fruit and become a stately cedar. And birds of every kind will nest under it; they will nest in the shade of its branches. And all the trees of the field will know that I am the LORD; I bring down the high tree, exalt the low tree, dry up the green tree and make the dry tree flourish. I am the LORD; I have spoken and I will perform it. (Ezekiel 17:22–24)

Growing up in all things

There are three phases of the divine strategy in the apostle's master plan. The first is revival, the second is the saints' maturity (arising from their substantial restoration and occupation of all things) and the third is the time of restoration harvest in the city or region. The gospel proclamation is found in each one and the kingdom of God comes in an ever deepening way as one phase gives way to the next, reaching towards the final move. When seasons of refreshing or revival come, we need to know why they come and we need to be ready to oversee these times as good stewards of the household and the vineyard. It stands to reason that God might well visit us with many more seasons of revival and refreshing if we are prepared to faithfully release the blessing of them into our life in the creation. He is ever looking, as a good investor, for those to whom he can entrust true riches.

Speaking of investments, let's now look at the way in which all the works of the saints are able to impact the creation and produce the returns desired by God.

THE WORK

Chapter 17

All Things Work Together For Good

Dorothy Sayers, a colleague of C.S. Lewis, writing many years ago, had this to say concerning the church and everyday working life:

> In nothing has the church so lost her hold on reality as in her failure to understand and respect the secular vocation. She has allowed work and religion to become separate departments and is astonished to find that, as a result, the secular work of the world is turned to purely selfish and destructive ends and that the greater part of the world's intelligent workers have become irreligious, or at least, uninterested in religion. But is it so astonishing? How can anyone remain interested in a religion which seems to have no concern with nine-tenths of his life? (*Creed or Chaos?*, p. 56)

If this was the case almost five decades ago, then the reality she speaks of is ever more pressing (and depressing!) today. The sad fact is that Satan has worked overtime to separate the body of Christ from the redemptive impact our work is meant to have on creation. Satan always divides to conquer and his strategy is clearly evident in relation to the saints and their working life.

God, however, always unites that he might rule. Such being the case, what are we to make of the third unseen sphere of the created order called work? In this time of great challenge and many changes the answer, I believe, is a resounding – much!

The Everest of Romans

The book of Romans stands as a magnificent mountain of divine revelation in Scripture. We have looked at the summit in chapter 8 and found great insight into the nature of the new man, the all things of creation and the Father who is sounding into and over all. At that place there is a most vital truth to be found. It is, I believe, crucial revelation given to us from the heights of this grand book. To establish its strategic place and to set the context for it let's ascend, starting from base camp in Romans chapter 1.

Romans 1–4

We begin with the gospel, declared to be 'the very power of God unto salvation for all that believe'. From here the creation purpose of God to reveal himself through all created things is spoken of. We see the drastic consequences of the fall of humanity into sin, with idolatry compounding the darkness and futility that had entered into every sphere of the created order. The Gentiles, still having the Law in their hearts, are found to be transgressors of that law. The Jews, having the Law on tablets of stone, are also transgressors. Every mouth is stopped and the entire world is declared guilty before God. There is, however, a way of escape. There is a God-given way of salvation and it comes through the Cross of Jesus Christ. In the Cross is found the gift of God's righteousness. It comes not by any works we do: rather it enters in and embraces us by grace through faith.

David spoke of it, Abraham lived by it and the Law came in to inform us of our need for it.

Romans 5

In chapter 5 the peace with God that comes to us through this faith is heralded. The first discovery we make here is that in Christ our sufferings no longer stand in the way of life. Rather his grace now abounds in our struggles and travail, producing the proven character and strength of hope that enables us to stand in the midst of all that life might send our way. As we have seen, this suffering is the very means of our moving through the futility that besets all of creation into our inheritance.

From here Paul moves again to the creation context to consider the effects of Adam's sin. The first man's transgression brought condemnation and death into the world. Christ's righteousness on the other hand brings justification and life to all. Here we discover the extent to which this righteousness impacts our lives and the creation that calls our name. Through the Cross we receive 'the abundance of grace and the gift of righteousness' to 'reign in life through the One, Jesus Christ'. Here, for the first time in Romans, in line with God's purposes for the creation, we hear a call to the new creation in Christ to come into its rule in and through life. It is important that we see the turning point here in Paul's consideration of the work of God in Christ. The saints are saved from sin for a purpose. It is here in this creation context that this purpose comes into view. In the conclusion to this section Paul states this truth a second time to ensure its impact on the reader: God has purposed that just 'as sin reigned in death, even so grace might reign through righteousness to eternal life through Jesus Christ our Lord'. How this sovereign purpose of God for our lives will come to pass is the question Paul now takes up in chapters 6, 7 and 8.

Romans 6:1–8:13

When we entered into Christ we in fact entered into his death. In that place God broke the chains that bound us to Adam, separating us forever from the old life ruled by sin. In that death we were also separated from the dictates and curse of the Law that reigned where sin had been. We came through that death into the resurrection life of Christ and as a result we are now forever joined to him. Sin may still dwell within our bodies derived from Adam; however, because of the Cross there exists no condemnation for those who are in Christ Jesus. God himself has made a radical separation between who we are in Christ and the law of sin still operating within the flesh. In chapter 8 we discover that works still have a place in the new life. The saints have not been liberated to engage in sin: rather they are set free to pursue the deeds of the Spirit, deeds born of God's own righteousness. It is these very deeds that work to continually mortify the deeds of the flesh and, as we shall see, it is these precious deeds or works that are destined to powerfully impact the entire created order.

I have taken a little time here in our journey towards the summit so that we can clearly see the contexts in which Paul is considering the work of Christ. The first is the judicial setting of the courts, dealing with our need of justification. The second is the historical setting, commencing in Adam and travelling through the chosen line into Israel, towards the fullness of time when Christ, the son of David, came. This account of God's dealings with humanity continues when Paul looks at the place and purpose of the nation of Israel in chapters 9,10 and 11. This treatment of the chosen people takes us through to the very climax of human history. The third context set by Paul is that of the created order. We need to see Romans primarily from this creation perspective, incorporating the judicial and historical work of God in Christ into that overarching context. This is particularly necessary as we approach the summit.

Many commentators look at Romans 8 from a judicial, moral and personal perspective only, seeing the sons' engagement with, and answer to, the creation as something that awaits the distant future when Christ comes again. By reason of their theological heritage they arrive at Romans 8:15 and suddenly fast track their way to the return of Christ. I am not saying the end of the age is not in view here: rather I am advocating that we apply the brakes to our theological wagon and strategically pace the journey God wants us to take to the last day. As we have seen from Acts, Christ awaits the restoration *before* he comes. Although such a restoration will be far from complete when he comes, we are called to work the works that begin that process in the here and now. Yes, our inheritance is kept undefiled for us in heaven, but these heavens are over this earth, an earth that forms a major part of that very inheritance.

☞ It is when we connect Christ's final restoration with our present work of restoration that the future will draw us onward. Such relatedness between now and then will see Christ's coming as a fulfilment, rather than as some disconnected eschatological interruption. Such a perspective enables us to see Paul's teaching here in Romans more as strategy for warfare than doctrine that tells us to patiently wait in our suffering until the end comes.

Romans 8:14–30

Paul moves again from verse 14 of chapter 8 to the creation setting. Here he speaks of the three cries that make for the relationship between the sons in Christ, the all things of creation and the Father who is over all. As he did in chapter 5,

218 *The Church Beyond The Congregation*

Paul speaks in verse 17 of the relationship between our suffering and our inheritance in Christ. We read in Romans 5 of the hope that suffering produces within us. Also we know that God subjected the creation to futility in hope. It is at this stage of the book of Romans that Paul joins God's hope and our hope as one. It is this hope that will answer the suffering creation in a way that will not disappoint the saints, the creation or the Father! We are now ready to fully engage the creation through the righteousness that reigns in life through Christ. Welcome to the high point of the summit of Romans 8.

On another mountain of revelation the person of Christ was transfigured before Peter, James and John. While busy trying to decide where to build booths for the visiting prophets, they heard God's voice from the cloud of glory, calling them in no uncertain terms to 'listen'. Here, too, we need to pay careful attention, for right now, with the sons crying and the creation calling, this same Father sounds through the sons into this creation. His sound through them is deeper than words, moving here from the deep through the Logos to become much more than words. Travelling with the momentum of all that went before, the sound that first touched the creation in suffering moves towards its fullest expression in the proclamation, 'We know that God causes *all things* to *work* together for *good*, to those who love God and are called according to his purpose' (8:28, *italics mine*).

Our first response to encountering a well-known verse, particularly this one, is to recall the times it has challenged or encouraged us. Now I certainly don't want to take away from the comfort this truth has brought and still brings to us in times when life is difficult and we wonder how it's all going to work out. However, there must be more here; the lead-up we have seen, the positioning and the nature of the verse itself all clearly point in that direction. So, with intensity born of Hebrew sight and an understanding of the divine strategy, let's look at this magnificent revelation into God's purposes for the sons and daughters and all of creation.

I begin by drawing your attention to three very significant concepts found in this verse. Firstly there is the use of our well-known phrase 'all things'. Secondly, we see a reference to the third sphere of creation, 'work', and finally we note the tell-tale declaration used by God after he created the heavens and the earth, that being the word 'good'. So there exists, in line with the 'purpose' of God, a powerful and strategic relationship between work, the all things of creation and the 'good'.

Before we proceed I need first to establish the simple but essential link between this work of God towards the good and our own work as saints in Christ. Here I note two statements by Christ: 'We must work the works of him who sent me' (John 9:4) and 'My Father is working until now and I myself am working' (John 5:17); and also Paul's words: 'For we are his workmanship, created in Christ Jesus for good works, which God prepared beforehand, that we should walk in them' (Eph. 2:10).

After God had finished creating the heavens and the earth, he rested from his work. He then called humanity to begin its own work to subdue the creation. So it was that the Father established the pattern, the opportunity and the purpose of all work in the beginning. The Fall came in to thwart this purpose. But now, through the work of Christ, this eternal purpose for humanity's work has again come into view. The new beginning arrived with the incarnation and subsequent work of the Son of God (the last Adam). From here the work was given to his body, the church. The focus of all the works of God is humankind. Hence God's purpose to work 'all things together for good' must refer to our work in him, rather than some separate work of God apart from Christ or the new creation in him. Paul brings this relationship into focus when he states that 'it is God who is at work in you, both to will and to work for his good pleasure' (Phil. 2:13). Let's look at the nature of this work.

The good working verse

The statement 'God works all things together for good' is, I believe, the single most strategic declaration found in Scripture. It brings together all the key elements of the creation reality we have looked at. The creation, as we know, cries out for the sons to come. How can we answer such an immense cry? Romans 8:26, 27 tells us that the Holy Spirit responds to our weakness by searching out this answer from the depths of God. The answer comes as a sound, a groaning 'too deep for words'. This answer from the Father arrives in our lives as intercession. It is a deep sound and travail coming into and through our lives, resonating in us 'according to the will of God'. It is verse 28 that follows which speaks to us of the nature and purpose of this amazing sound.

The verb 'we know' found in verse 28 is in the perfect tense. This tense speaks of a present state arriving as a result of past actions. Hence we could render the first part of verse 28 in this way: 'As a result (of the Spirit's searching out the will of God) we come to know that God continually goes on working all things into [or unto – *eis*] the good.' Here we discover two key things about the sound of the Father coming through the Spirit to the sons. Firstly, as a result of the Spirit's search, we now know that the eternal purpose for the saints is that they work all things in creation together in such a way as to bring about ultimate good. Secondly, we learn that the heart-beat and impetus for this work keeps on arriving in the sons through the sound that comes from the Father.

This teaching from Romans 8 lines up directly with the Genesis account. It informs us that to this day the creation cries out for its completion. We learn also that the sons of God are still waiting to come into their inheritance in and over that creation. The relationship between the creation and the sons is, as mentioned, first established through mutual travail and suffering. From there, as verse 28 informs us, it is the good works of the sons that bring fulfilment to the creation.

This placement of the saints' good works at the heart of the divine strategy arises naturally from the creation reality God established in the beginning. Humanity and creation are mutually dependent, unable to come into their created purpose apart from each other. Creation needs human work to come into its fulfilment and humanity needs to steward the creation through its work to come into its inheritance.

It follows from this that, if God declared the creation to be 'good' and if humanity is called to work the creation, then by this work it must be able to bring forth, or realise, that 'good'. The goodness of creation is another way of expressing its 'fullness'. This is evident in the well-known verse, 'The earth is the Lord's and the fullness thereof' (Psalm 24:1). The goodness of the earth is to be brought forth, made manifest and enjoyed through all of the saints' works in the creation. This amazing verse, found at the very peak of Romans, serves as the most succinct summary of the divine strategy we see unfolded in the city of Ephesus.

Releasing the good

What then is the creation crying out for? It must be crying out for its goodness to be fully realised and fully released. The creation cannot be good apart from the sons and daughters because we alone were given the right to name it;

we are the image bearers who were made to speak moral value and divine intent into it. We were created to draw forth the attributes, nature and power of God in all things.

☞ Our calling to 'good work' the earth is in fact God's way of uniting us to all of creation. It is the God-given means through which we can fully answer creation's cry and thereby come into our inheritance in and over all things in Christ. This is why the creation to this day looks forward, waiting in eager anticipation for the time when it will enjoy the fullest measure of the 'freedom of the glory of the children of God' (Rom. 8:21).

A life lived 'good working' all things in creation towards the good is a life most definitely lived 'according to his purpose'. This is what the sound from the Father comes to accomplish. It is this sound, Jesus said, which we can hear and must follow. Is it any wonder this answer from the depths of God is too deep for words to encompass!

John the Baptist restored the sphere of family to make way for Christ the Son. Jesus cleansed and restored the sphere of marriage to make way for his bride the church to come. From there the new creation, with the power of identity drawn from marriage and family, enters into its purpose. Now the Holy Spirit comes to fill and empower the saints to declare into and engage the creation through the good works prepared for them from eternity. The Fall, as devastating and far-reaching as its consequences were, was only an interruption to the eternal purposes of God to create a people who would reign through love and righteousness and relate to his attributes, nature and power throughout all of life. This sovereign purpose is now amplified and lifted higher by the Last Adam, the life-giving Spirit. Now sin is nullified, death is abolished and the Law fulfilled; now it is the new creation in Christ that has become, as

Galatians 6:16 says, *'the rule'*. The truth seen here at the summit of Romans is a revelation of divine strategy given to us to profoundly influence the whole way we relate to life and be the church.

Good works are everywhere

From here let us turn to look at the numerous places 'good works' are referred to in Scripture. We do this to demonstrate the extent to which our works feature in God's plan for our lives. What we find is that the major focus of Scripture, when speaking of our purpose as saints on the earth, centres on our good works. From the very foundations of the earth these works were prepared for us by our Father, readied by him for us to walk in. As we saw in the verse from Ephesians, we were created in Christ Jesus for the specific purpose of engaging in good works prepared beforehand by God. Again the Colossians' truth comes into view, telling us how the knowledge of God's will journeys through wisdom into a life lived in 'every good work' to produce the fruit that leads to the knowledge of God himself. Here again good works are heralded as the mechanism by which our inheritance in creation and our relationship with God arrive. The Word of God is inspired and profitable for all things, yes, but it has as its stated purpose the equipping of the saint 'for every good work' (2 Tim. 3:17). Also the ministry gifts, those first expressions of the risen Christ, have at the very head of their job description the 'equipping of the saints for the work of service' (Eph. 4:12).

Finally we come to that well-known statement by Jesus: 'Let your light shine before men in such a way that they may see your good works and glorify your Father who is in heaven' (Matt. 5:16). Remember the divine strategy of the restoration of all things? We saw in that teaching of Scripture the way in which the spheres of creation came into darkness and futility after the Fall: how the light of God that was meant to shine through them shone no longer. Here, plainly stated by the Lord of creation, is this same divine strategy. It is our good works that bring in the restoration of the spheres of creation engaged by that work.

☞ Good works, done in God and for God, will unlock the divine intent of the creation itself. They will reveal the attributes, nature and power and, ultimately, the goodness of God in this land of the living. Our 'good work' dispels the gloom, ends the futility and banishes the lies that came into the creation because of the evil works of darkness.

The restoration, accomplished through work, is that which enables divine light and life to shine through the all things of creation. This is why Jesus said that when they '*see* your good works' they will be able to encounter and glorify your Father in the heavens above.

Only via this God-given way can those who are in Christ emerge to become the light of the world. This new creation, coming through suffering to 'good work' the creation, is the one God foreknew, predestined, called, justified and glorified to bring in the fullness. From eternity and into time the purpose of God has never changed. The image bearers were always called to release and realise the image from every facet of creation. They were forever destined to come to maturity through this way of life and work, thereby entering into their rule in the Son over all of creation. That is why God to this day still works all things together for good to those who love him and are called according to his purpose. Yes, Jesus will come again and he will complete the restoration. But in the meantime, while it is still today, we *must* work the works of him who sent us.

Romans 8:31–39

Before we press on into the way of these good works in the creation, let's look around the summit of Romans one more time. Here the great apostle takes the opportunity afforded by the vantage point of chapter 8 to gather all the instruments – the mercies, the grace, the power, the plan, the works, the goodness – and move them in symphony to sound the sound of the eternal. Paul calls us to attention by saying, 'What shall we say to these things?' Look now as he lifts the baton, fixes his gaze on the orchestra and begins the apostolic symphony. This God, 'who did not spare his own Son', is it not his purpose to 'freely give us' all things in creation? Yes, respond the drums of conviction. Will anything get in the way of our journey? Will our sin emerge to accuse us? No, the cymbals crash, never! For it is Christ himself who has justified us. Who then could possibly condemn us? Christ is the one who died for us, who was raised for us. It is he who sits at the right hand of the Father God in the third of the heavens. He is calling us up, declaring over our lives, he is anticipating our arrival into the fullness of the stature he is for us.

Strange and wonderful journey

Paul now establishes the strongest connection between our suffering and our inheritance as heirs of God and joint heirs with his Son. What is the nature and extent of this suffering; where does it start and where does it take us? Here, in the second movement, Paul takes us through the score.

We begin with that which Jesus promised us – 'tribulation', apart from which we cannot enter into the third heaven. This gives way to 'distress', the perplexity and turmoil of heart and mind Paul knew and spoke of as his daily experience. Will this suffice? Can we stop now? For Paul it moves on into 'persecution' – overt harm that comes against us as a result of the evil actions of others. This brings us into the desperation of 'famine' and with it even the shame of 'nakedness'. Surely God must arrive here, surely if he is good and really loves us he will rescue us now – right now! Alas, our journey into his suffering is not over. To the contrary, we find that our lives are now in 'peril'. Will we be overcome? Is there no way of escape? Where is this power that delivers? Here enters the very 'sword' of those who hate us, coming to take life from us. Paul, where is this victory you so confidently proclaim in Christ? His answer at first seems so strange; he says with a careless abandon, 'we are considered as sheep all day long to be slaughtered'. Paul, you seem to be singing this last line with such decided detachment, there's a kind of wry smile on your face. It's as if you don't really care if you die.

Our suspicions prove correct. It appears Paul is aware of something we are not. His preoccupation is not, it seems, with the silence and defeat of death. He is looking further on and higher up than others would ever dare. This Spirit-filled Hebrew man had seen the purposes of God through this suffering and death all along; that is why he did not shrink back. He knew that Christ had encompassed all of our suffering and death into himself. He had become convinced that God had breathed the divine presence into them and declared them to be the very gateway into resurrection life itself: hence Paul's triumphant declaration that it is in fact in all these things that we overwhelmingly conquer through him who loved us. *In them* is found the very victory itself. How could this be true? The reason is that only those who are in Christ can suffer their way through these things and rise through their sufferings into life. No one else can; no devil can arrange such an outcome. He can set up a sign. He can manifest the power. He can turn on the charisma. But when it comes to life out of death, he has no hope and no idea!

We may never be called to embrace a premature physical death; each of us, however, will be called to surrender, to one degree or another, to that dying of Jesus. Those who are decided in this journey into Christ will alone feel the freedom that comes from no longer fearing death. No bondage to and obsession with self-preservation and control will hold them back from entering into his death and emerging to reign with him in life. Who would have thought to encompass the whole of redemption, suffering, life and relationship within one great work of the Christ through the Cross? God would! No one else could deliver such a reality. No one is even looking in that direction for life to come.

Where and how is this resurrection life to be lived? God intended all along to take us through this dimension of the Cross into our inheritance in Christ over all of creation. From the dying of Jesus God quickens the sons to emerge and, through good work, begin to reign in life as servants of righteousness. So it is that suffering identifies us with fallen humanity and our good works reveal to them the attributes, nature and power of the eternal and invisible God. In the resurrection life all the saints' work explodes the divine light and life into the darkness, calling the dead to rise and follow, even to the heavens. This purpose was foreknown, this suffering was ordained and these works prepared from eternity to enable Christ's body the church to become the fullness of him who fills all in all. The earth is open, the heavens await, the destination is assured, the inheritance is ours.

This immense triumph is clearly seen in the third and final movement that begins now, bringing to a climax the apostolic symphony. Here we see the ultimate goal of the divine strategy revealed through the apostle in Romans. The sound begins low and rises in crescendo to touch the heaven of heavens. Trace the resurrection journey of the Spirit-filled Hebrew man one more time. It is your journey, from innocence to maturity, from death to life, from earth through the heavens. This new creation in Christ will not be overcome by the lower regions of 'death'. Nothing in this 'life' will stop them. The realm of 'angels' will give way. Even the 'principalities' and over-reaching 'powers' of the second heaven will bow the knee as they journey through them into the fullness. From space to time Paul moves to declare that 'things present' and 'things to come' will never stand in the way of our own standing through the created order. Indeed, from the 'height' of the third heaven to the 'depth' of Sheol, nothing will ever separate us from the head who is Christ. Every 'created thing' will make way for the emergence of the sons of God: sons who will answer the cry, take the inheritance and live forever to express and enjoy the 'love of God, which is in Christ Jesus our Lord'. Our work, all of our work, matters to God. It matters to the creation and, because of that, it *must* matter to us!

Chapter 18

All The Saints' Work is Good Work

Our heritage has worked overtime to ensure that most of what the Scripture calls 'good works' is considered to be that done in, or from, the congregation context. A businessman I spoke with worked as a consultant to both smaller businesses and larger corporations. He specialised in bringing in ome of the new management philosophies that became popular during the '90s. He had quite a passion for his work and was able to regularly include both his Christian beliefs and testimony in his presentations. I listened with excitement, blessing God that such people were being used to influence hundreds of lives in the business sphere. Then the shock came. He had been made a very good offer by a large company (not Christian-based) for his company and its resources. He told me that he wanted out because it would give him the opportunity to 'go around churches and tell my testimony'. As much as the ministry gifts of this man's congregation had encouraged him to get out there in the harvest, their own actions were all the time drawing the meaning and value of the kingdom in this man's thinking and planning back towards the building, the programmes and the meetings.

The Reformation started well, with Luther and Calvin naming work as a vocation from God, a direct service to him. It is said that over time, as uncertainty grew over the matter of who had and who had not been predestined, one of the sure signs of God's favour became material success. This meant that many Puritans made it their business to work extra hard, making a veritable virtue of being industrious. This cultural leaven made its way through to become the well-known Protestant work ethic. Reformation theology concerning work was a great leap forward from the medieval period. However, it still emphasised work primarily in terms of one's temporal responsibility, as a moral testing ground where one could build virtue and as a test case for the sovereign choice.

Protestantism helped create capitalism but over time was, for the greater part, consumed by it. In this day, even though pastors will speak of the value of work, it still occupies a place in the shadow of the larger building and higher calling we have named church. There is, I believe, a definite challenge before us here. We are losing most of the saints' work in the cracks between their church and their life. Our consultant friend had the luxury, if bought out, to live off the proceeds derived from the sale of the business. Most saints are not in such a position. They feel trapped inside their working life, without the resources they need to work with satisfaction and impact. Hence the importance of determining the place of all the saints' work, in particular their paid work, in the divine strategy.

Paid Work is 'Good Work'

The apostle Paul, in his letter to the saints at Colossae, tells us about the crucial connection God has made between working life and good work. He says, 'Whatever you do, do your work heartily, as for the Lord rather than for men; knowing that from the Lord you will receive the reward of the inheritance. It is the Lord Christ whom you serve' (Col.

3:23, 24). The logic is simple: whenever we work, we work ultimately for Christ. It is him we serve and it is from him that we receive our reward. So it follows that our everyday work should not be named anything else except 'good work'. The setting in which the work is done does not make that work sacred or secular. Evil works can be done in any context, church based or otherwise. The setting is not the thing that makes them either good or bad: rather it is the nature and intent of them that determines their eternal worth.

The difficulty many people have in believing the work they do to make a living is 'good work' arises mostly from the fact that they get paid for it. 'Surely only volunteer or charitable work or one's work for the church can truly be good?' The creation reality clearly informs us that we were made to work the earth in order to bring forth its goodness and its fullness. That eternal purpose has never been revoked. It certainly has never been divided into sacred and secular. So it is that whenever we work we must work for the good rather than for the money. At its heart our work is a giving and a sowing into the earth to release the 'goods' in the creation. When this is done we receive the response of the earth and of others into our life. 'Give and it shall be given unto you' is not just a novel idea, it is a creation secret for all of our work in life. You were created to give to others, so when you serve others and do the good, the return, pressed down and shaken together, will come to you. This creation truth thus unites all of our work under the powerful banner of good.

To add more colour to the canvas outlined above – in Ephesians 6:7, 8 we read, 'With good will render service, as to the Lord and not to men, knowing that whatever good thing each one does, this he will receive back from the Lord, whether slave or free.' Work is clearly listed here under the heading of the good things we are called to accomplish.

From this work we receive back from the Lord the blessing of the return. Paul, in Colossians, calls this return 'the reward of our inheritance', thus pointing us in the direction that our work will take in the plan of God. I also draw attention to Ephesians 4:28 that refers to the place of work in the sanctification and maturation of the saint. Finally, in 1 Thessalonians 4:11 we see that our working life is one of the important things that leads to our living of a 'quiet life'. This phrase makes an appearance in the strategic passage we considered from Timothy where a 'quiet life in all godliness and dignity' is an important part of the divine plan in bringing in the restoration.

There is no dearth of direct teaching in Scripture in relation to the power of our working life. Even here, however, we need to be careful not to limit ourselves to these verses. One of our main difficulties in seeing the place of paid work in the plan of God arises from the way we have been conditioned to view the Scriptures. We look into the Word and see numerous references to good works and on the surface they do not appear to be related to our working life. By comparison we find only a few references to actual paid or slave work. Hence we conclude that this work, though important, must not be central to the divine plan. However, our challenge here does not arise from a scarcity of references regarding working life. Rather it arises from a heritage that has constructed Greek divisions within our thinking. The Hebrew vision, on the other hand, enables us to bring all of the verses and all of the works together for good.

☞ Our paid and personal work is essential to the divine plan. It is direct work for Christ. It releases our inheritance in Christ and over the creation. It unlocks the good things that God has placed in the creation so that our needs might be supplied. It shines light into the

darkness and opens up the reality of the throne of God
above us. It is used by the Spirit to sanctify and mature
us. And it is strategically placed to impact a city by
ushering in and demonstrating the peace and dignity
of God to those outside the faith.

This work can certainly be done in the setting of the church
as pillar and support. However, again I emphasise that it is
only the works done by the saints in the spheres of creation
that have the ability to fulfil the eternal purpose. The church
as an organisation cannot of itself fill marriage, family,
business, health, education, government and recreation.
The saints can and the saints must. The division is over. All
the works of the saints are called to be good works.

A lawyer's testimony – over lunch

'God created me to be a lawyer you know – I may
not be the best and smartest – but that's who he
made me to be. In our corporation people are trying
hard to hold on to and legitimise their positions. They
used to treat me as a lawyer and just want the work
done. I've been there a while and now more people
are dropping in just for a chat. It's like I've grown
larger than a lawyer; they now see me as a person,
someone they can trust. They come and want to
hear what I say. They gain strength. I haven't seen
dramatic conversions but my contacts are growing
throughout the city. Two people I have worked with
are now attending church. I'm planted there and I'm
made to be there for all these people.'

'But I don't like my job!'

Certain qualifiers could be given here, but because of our
old friends space and time, I'll mention only one. A person's

major field of work does not necessarily need to be their paid employment. It is obvious that many kinds of employment do not exactly ignite the saints' passion. In fact they do the very opposite. Saints can have a far greater heart concentration on work (volunteer, local church initiative, hobby, part-time business) that happens outside of their paid employment. If they can best serve and create in and through these good works then their growth and maturity will certainly come through them. However, that being said, the paid work they do does occupy a sphere of the created order. In that work environment there exists a creation purpose. In that place there are many fellow workers struggling in futility and darkness, needing Christ's light to shine. Thus, rather than deciding that you will specialise elsewhere, you need to search out the redemptive potential inherent in the place and time you spend with people. It is only as you move to fulfil that opportunity and substantially restore it that you will know what it contains for yourself and others. Also, if you concentrate on only one area to the exclusion of most other works, be it your local church or your sport, you will miss out on the composite of life and relationships that God intends for you.

The grass is often greener on the other side because we refuse to water our own patch of lawn. We need to dwell in the land and cultivate faithfulness, no matter how mundane and ordinary it looks in comparison with the affirmation and clarity we feel on Sunday or the dreams and visions we feel the future holds. In regards to our dreams – it is only as we discover and fulfil our humble level of glory by being faithful in the little that we have that we are likely to come on line for more glory and opportunity. Finally, if you are certain there is no good at all to be done in your place of work, then I would suggest you consider looking for another job ASAP!

Strategic desires of the heart

So, what motivates the good works of the saints? Who is in charge of them? What safeguards are in place for them? Who and what determines where they start, where they stop and where the benefits that come from them will accumulate? These are leading questions; they draw out the difficulty many leaders have in deeming the main works of ministry to be those done by the saints in their everyday life. However, in the light of the creation call on the body to work all things towards the good, where does God place his emphasis?

In the divine purpose the Spirit does his work, the Word does its work and the ministry gifts do their work as well. However, as important as these are, they are not the finale of the plan. Rather they are all given by God to ensure that his sons and daughters emerge to fulfil the creation and accomplish the eternal purpose. How do the resources of Spirit, Word and ministry gift work to release them into this destiny? Is it through the written command of Scripture? Through the direct promptings of the Spirit to do this or say that? Is it through the vision of the leaders or the programme of their particular local church? Yes, partially, is the answer to all these questions. Ultimately though, in line with the journey to maturity that God intends for our lives, the initiative for our good work comes from a place far deeper, a place far more at one with and intrinsic to our heart.

In 2 Thessalonians 1:11, 12 we read, 'To this end we also pray for you always that our God may count you worthy of your calling and fulfil every desire for goodness and the work of faith with power; in order that the name of our Lord Jesus may be glorified in you and you in him, according to the grace of our God and the Lord Jesus Christ.' As we can see from these verses, the focus is definitely on the individual saints doing the works that make an impact. Looking into the hearts of these called-out people we find that there exists a powerful river called desire moving them to good work. Specifically we find there a wellspring named 'desire for goodness'. This phrase about individual desire is placed right at the centre of a very impressive list of events and persons. In this passage the saints' 'calling' is in view. God intends that his purpose for our lives will move through our good desire to ultimately arrive in (and be expressed through) all of our 'works'. This work is characterised by a living and active 'faith' and is backed up by the Spirit's 'power'. It is these works, breathed into by a desire for goodness, which reveal the name and glory of Christ 'in you' and 'you in' Christ. This work, 'glorifying' the Son, in turn reveals the Father of heaven above. Such verses, and others like them, speak clearly of the powerful place the inner or personal desires and dreams of the saints have in the divine strategy.

☞ God intends that the good works of the saints come not so much from without: rather they are to be inspired and drawn from the deep of good desire. It is these heart desires for good that God intends to fuel and ignite all of the works of the saints.

God did not come to empower his Word or his precious Spirit; they are already exalted, along with his name, above the heavens. Nor did he come primarily to validate the role of church leadership and the organisations they build. All these only serve their God-given purpose in equipping, releasing and empowering the life and work of the saints. Morality only defines the proper borders of our activity. It is only by our going into the good in all our work that we can unearth the treasures in the land of promise those moral borders define and safeguard. Men and women's immense capacity to explore and build was given by God for just such a purpose as this.

A healthy testimony

I've got a new position working with a large local government authority promoting health and developing services throughout the community. God put me there and I can't wait to discover what he wants me to find. There's a whole bunch of new people and new challenges and they are all mine. A few years ago this would have terrified me, but now it excites me. I'm going in to find my treasure and I'm going to make it mine.

God's sovereign choice

I am aware that the human heart is a dangerous and untrustworthy base for the divine strategy. If God had not chosen it to be the focus I may not have picked it myself. However, God has made his choice and it is the image bearer he created in the beginning for just such a purpose. The answer is not to move the focus away from a frail heart to an organisation. Such is no guarantee whatsoever against the foibles of the human heart. In fact, sin cloaked in organisational garb is often much harder to detect. The answer is not to run from an untrustworthy heart and hand over the initiative to an external something or someone else we think is safe and sound. There is a time and a place for dependence and submission, but these are not the goal of life. They are a start, but they are not the culmination of God's purposes for the saint's life. The divine purpose works to redeem, restore and see the river of God flow through the heart to the extent that it becomes trustworthy and useful.

☞ The surest sign of Christian maturity is when an
individual is moved by their inner heart's desire to do
the will of God and go into 'the good' as a way of life.
The heart's desires will always out. That is what they
are created to do. It is only when we move them in
line with the divine purpose in all of life in creation
that they will no longer need to find strange and
convoluted ways to their God-given sea.

If we are to bring in the restoration, come to maturity, see the
full harvest reaped and usher in the age to come, we need to
'good work' the earth. If we are to unlock the treasures of
darkness then all of our works in every place must be good.
These works are moved not so much from without; they are
moved from within by the good desires that God first
created, then redeemed and now works to restore. With this
revelation in heart, let's go into our work to see how we as
individuals can work to bring in the restoration of all things.

A story in verse before we proceed . . .

'You will find me, if you search for me'
He came so close and spoke.
He breathed, quickened and moved me and then,
just when I was beginning to live,
so wrapped in grace and comfort,
he went into the quiet and hid himself.

And I am left in open fields with wind at my back telling
  me I am forgotten,
telling me to return and forget the love that held me
  close.
I demand that God show himself to be strong – right
  now.
He makes no sound except,
here a memory with love

and there a truth with distance,
calling.

The accuser, rising up over this apparently abandoned
  life, makes his answer known.
What must you have done to lose your hold on God?
What must they have done to you to make you feel so
  alone?
I take this guilt with anger and it drives me from the
  accusation to the ceremony;
there to secure my rights,
my hold on God.
But the songs falter and the words they fall.
And no familiar elements come to name my soul.
So I give way and head out to find some place
  to help define my failure.

Then comes the desire, deep flame of heat with some
  small light –
so untrusted,
fallible,
spotted,
frail against the power of words spoken by the sound of
  heaven
in those days that came and left me here.
The wind stirs as I remember and moves on heart's
  flickered desire
and silence leaves as God now speaks:

What do you want?
I tell him I cannot want.
He asks me again,
Tell me what you want.
I say to him,
I want to feel strong, secure, loved and powerful.

A third time he says
Tell me what you want.

And, from within, the desire stirred breaks open, saying
I want my fruit to taste satisfied,
I want my good to change things,
I want my difference to touch the life.
God smiles and asks no more and leaves me with myself.

The accuser comes swiftly now to eclipse the smile
  with anger and noise,
telling me to be quiet like God is quiet,
to hide like God hides.
In my shame at wanting to want I demand that heaven
  hate the adversary.
The silent heaven seems unconcerned with noise;
it only waits for my sound to tell the fallen angel what I
  want and who I am.

But I cannot use these unused desires,
so muddy and convulsed,
old pipes pumping brown the useless water.
How can I trust the deceitfully wicked?
Here the law at least affirms my stand
but God seems unconcerned with law.

I, alone among the swelled ranks of the victim,
have one more ploy to take me away.
I step out boldly and do my own failure.
And, in my sin, with the hurt it gave, I tell God to
  rescue me from law and guilt and shame and falling.

He comes, like I knew he would,
with blood and grace and love;

picks me up and places me back in open field of earth
   and sky
and walks away,
telling me he is my Father, waiting.

And I lie down,
dust in the wind,
with nothing left but to listen.
The eagle soars above,
the sea roars in that distance,
a nation calls my name,
my child is watching.

Now my wanting from within has no choice but to fly.
So – through the condemnation by the blood,
through the law by that love,
through the elemental things with the substance that
   belongs,
through the principalities with given power,
the waters from innermost move over earth to sky from
   the choice I make to send them on the wings of good
   desire.
Trusted to fly on winds that rest in heaven's sky,
visions now of all the land fill my heart's desire.

And from the quiet he comes,
sounding celebration song to wrap me round and over,
moving dance with and in the Son.
Word-filled desire sent gifted
   to magnify the pleasured Father of heaven's earth.
His song sweet telling the land that waits,
now come.

And the woven families of earth,
the wounded ones of time,

listen for the strangest reasons as you live to prophesy the
    day to the day things.
And your deep struggle down resonating close moves out
    to travail those with no way through but you.

And all the years that separation brings
the tears of songs begin to end.
The new creation visible,
known,
belongs,
moves the waters once again as canopy over land in sky
    like sea.

And when the Father's face draws into the quiet,
hiding his way into the Son,
so deep into creation,
I know,
I know my good desire's eye looking can find him,
everywhere.

Chapter 19

Restoring The Creation Spheres Engaged by Work

Your work, paid or unpaid, is before you every day of your life. How do we go into that work to find the fullness and gather the inheritance? How might we transform it from a responsibility to a discovery zone? Let's go into work to go through, to go up into the fullness. As mentioned, God created the 'unseen' systems engaged by work so that humanity could accomplish the eternal purpose. We see these administrations of God throughout the record of Scripture and we witness their power today in determining the culture and destiny of every person. As mentioned, the names we have generally given to these systems are government, education, health, business and recreation. I would not want to give the impression that these are fixed categories with firewalls between them. They are dynamic and interacting spheres of human life, defined partially in themselves and mostly in relationship to each other. In the heart of God they are no doubt grouped together and named differently. Business might have much more to do with poetry than we could ever have imagined! However, this is the way we presently name them and hence this is the usual way we presently identify ourselves with them.

In working life these systems will overlap. In particular the business dimension will be found in one way or another in all of the other spheres. A medical centre will have a healing, educational and business dimension. A school will have an educational and business dimension. A small goods firm will have a business dimension and perhaps a training component. What of media? This world of print and electronic communication is drawn from the systems of recreation, education and business. It is not a separate system of itself. There is also work done in the setting of the home, something not measured in monetary terms, but which is essential to the good of our society. To look into the nature of work we need to make the complex mosaic simple, knowing that the principles that apply to the above-mentioned facets of life engaged by work relate to all activity/work in life.

Every man or woman will live and die under the influence of these administrations. These make for the heavens that people's souls breathe each day. These orders (powers), along with the geographical settings in which they are placed (principalities), make up much of the world into which Jesus has sent us. The angelic hosts, both fallen and holy, oversee and stand in line with this created order. They are the principalities and powers placed there to do their own master's will for evil or for the good of humanity. As we have seen, God did not intend the church to be separate from all of this: rather he determined the church to be the fullness. The saints working day by day represent, and hence stand in, the authority of one or several of these spheres. They are called to work in such a way that they bring restoration to them, gain their inheritance through them and along the way shine light into the lives of those living and working within them.

Working among the thorns

'My job, you say. Do you know what I do? I move money around the planet.'

'Well, at least your job is fast moving. I just sell fruit buns, cake and coffee.'

'You think you've got a problem – I have to process claims all day every day for an insurance firm.'

'You've got it made – let me tell you about the pressure I work under. I run my own firm, or should I say it runs me. But with the downturn in Asia it looks like our profits this year will be way down south.'

'At least you can think about Asia. I've waited for a promotion for five years and nothing came except a redundancy package.'

'Well, I should be so lucky; you've got a package. All I've got is a bad back. I have to hang off a building most days doing extensions and most every night I spend haggling with contractors to make sure they turn up as promised.'

'In my firm they're moving towards smart young consultants and they seem to think that I'm neither anymore.'

'That must be hard to handle Dave. I'm 10 years younger than you are and I'm in sales and every time I reach my quota they increase it. Their plan is to burn me out and then bring in the next "young un" to feed his soul to the machine.'

On goes the list of challenges faced by saints in a fallen world, wrestling with the powerful forces of sin, futility and the suffering they bring. Is it any wonder that they look forward to the sound and lights of the Sunday event and that many who turn up do seem a little preoccupied during the proceedings? However, the inheritance God has for these struggling saints is, as we have seen, not found in the support act. The everlasting fruit can only be grown, tasted and eaten in the very world they are struggling to survive in.

From the time of creation we were given the right and the responsibility to name all things. This means that the definition or descriptions we accept or give to any thing, person or event will determine our relationship to them, our ability to see and go into them and ultimately the reality we will build in and from them.

☞ So, if saints call their work secular, boring, carnal, cursed, second fiddle, then this will be exactly what their work will be for them and they will be for it. The names and the descriptions that so many saints give their work bear testimony to the fact that we are presently losing the battle for this third major sphere of the created order.

How desperately we need to rename the spheres of creation engaged by work, breathe life into the saints' work and win it back for the church as fullness. How then do we go into the daily grind and gain the inheritance?

The madness in the method

At this point in a book one usually begins to look for and expect a section on methodology and outcomes. We want to know what practices can be put in place to ensure results. There is much that could be said about what saints at this time are discovering in different fields of endeavour. At the end of this chapter there is a brief mention of a model for ministry that is centred on the working life of the saints. Also there is much more that could be written here in relation to the role of ministry gifts working with the saints to equip them in their work. Space is one of the reasons why this has not been pursued. But more importantly, the reason why we are not considering methodology at this point relates to that very human tendency to grasp the form and lose the content.

We hear or read about something that is new and we immediately try to apply its rules or imitate its practice, hoping of course to duplicate its outcome. What tends to happen is that, because we don't take hold of the relational and qualitative dimensions of what is being presented, we fail to achieve the advertised outcome. This results in our jettisoning that particular method (along with the wisdom that may be inherent in it) and taking up the search once again for the right 'thing' that will bring in that elusive success. The body of Christ is too often tossed to and fro by winds of methodology that come with the dust and are soon gone with the wind. For these reasons in this chapter and the next I want to look more at the underlying principles of our going into work. What is in view here relates to the perspectives we carry to our work and the relational and qualitative realities we discover and establish through that work. These things produce outcomes first in us and then in creation.

We have looked at the nature of the creation existing in the Son of God. In and through the Garden and the incarnation we have seen:

- the 'hiddenness' of God in the all things of creation;
- the glory of God concealed so that humanity might reach for and discover its own 'glory';
- the judgements of God after the Fall that overlaid the full creation inheritance with thorns, sweat and travail;
- the coming of the Son of God as man to suffer his way through all of the divine judgements placed on cre-

ation, making the way open once again to our eternal inheritance in, through and over all things;

- the Son of God standing through the created order as God made man; his body, the fullness of all things, existing in him right through the spheres of marriage, family and work;
- the eternal purpose of God who 'works all things together into the good', seeing there the strategic relationship between our work, the good and the all things of creation.

It is in this creation reality and eternal purpose that we must place our daily work. Our starting point is to decide on the primary name we will give to our work. Knowing that work existed as a creation mandate before the Fall, we can and we must name our work with the name God gave it in the beginning, that being – 'good'. Paul looked into the tyranny of Roman government and said it was 'a minister of God to you for good' (Rom. 13:4). He knew the power of such a sight and such a name. He knew how important it was to orientate the saints to the goodness of this creation sphere in order that they might draw from it the maximum measure of God's good into their lives. If Paul did this for an organisation led by the likes of Nero, then you will surely be able to do the same for the work you are presently engaged in!

Go for Good

So then, what is 'the good'? The good is the qualitative difference and contribution something makes to the glory of God and the life of all. This is a good start, but as the Colossians' truth says, the knowledge of truth is only the starting point. We must press in much further if we are to gain the inheritance and come to the knowledge of God himself. Going into the good is more like mining along a seam of gold, drawing out more and more as you move in. There is no static definition for good. There is, however, the good life that keeps on going into the inheritance in Christ.

In line with the teaching in Romans 1:20, our work involves us in a search for God's 'invisible attributes, his eternal power and divine nature'. We are called to search out the *attributes* of God in the people, place and events in our work. We draw these out and 'work them' to establish the *nature* of God in our work. As we do this we make manifest the *power* of the good. As Romans 8:28 indicates, we work all things in such a way that the good arises and is established. This good is the tangible effect (eternal power) the invisible attributes and divine nature have as they are outworked in relational life.

☞ There are so many attributes in the different facets of a working relationship that we can draw out. They speak to, resonate with and call out to each other. 'What is right' speaks to 'what is pure', what is 'lovely' resonates with what 'is of good repute' and what partakes of 'excellence' calls out to all things 'worthy of praise'. We need to learn to hear them and respond. For they are the very cry of creation calling our name, longing for fulfilment (see Phil. 4:8–9).

The power tools of honour and thanks

The two major instruments God gave to us that we might go in, through and up into all things are the ability to give honour and the privilege of giving thanks. It is these two attitudes or responses in particular that are essential to an ongoing vision of the goodness of God in all of creation. I mention here again the verse from Romans that speaks of people becoming darkened in their heart and futile in their speculations because they did not 'honour . . . God or give thanks' (Rom. 1:21). They looked at the creature and did not honour and thank the creator. They would not go through the things that were made: rather they stopped and used them only for self-glory and self-indulgence. The result was that they ended up serving the very elemental things that were given by God to serve them.

To this day, if we are to come out from under the bondage of idolatry, narrow names and elemental things, we must learn to honour God and give him thanks in and through the entire creation. It is only as we honour and give thanks to God in and through all things, events and persons that we can come to directly encounter all of his good in them. The quotes above from Philippians 4 amplify the different ways we can bestow this honour and give these thanks. Paul said in that passage that as you do those things 'the God of peace will be with you' (Phil. 4:9). God was there all along of course, but he was ever waiting and wanting to be seen, welcomed and discovered by you. The strategic place of giving thanks is brought out by Paul in 2 Corinthians 4:15. He says that as grace spreads out from the lives of those who have come through the dying of Jesus it causes 'the giving of thanks to abound to the glory of God'. Thanksgiving prophesies the goodness of God into the relational atmosphere, causing the nature of God to become manifest between people and things. Is it any wonder that 'God's will for you in Christ Jesus' is that 'in everything (you) give thanks' (1 Thess. 4:18)?

This is why we are called to honour our mother and father, to reverence and hold in awe who they are and what they represent, to respond to them and restore what needs to be restored, knowing that they stand as image bearers through which the eternal Father comes. Only as we do well with them will it be well with us in life. If we want to see the providence of God arrive on, say, Tuesday afternoon then we must work for our employer as to Christ the Lord. For if that way is blocked, then we will surely miss out on many of the sovereign choices God has already made and desires to send to us, packaged in the decisions of the 'thorny' boss we serve.

☞ The *giving of honour* enables us to see the divine nature and the *giving of thanks* enables us to draw out the divine attributes and together they manifest on the earth as a divinely powerful mix.

It is not a matter of declaring the government's latest tax hike, implemented to fund a wage rise for politicians, to be wonderful. Going 'into the good' by giving honour and thanks does not eclipse wisdom. It gives us more insight into reality, not less. That is, I am not advocating a 'think to myself what a wonderful yellow brick road' kind of life. It is not a good thing to pretend something is good when it manifestly is not. Such may be a positive confession, but it is not a wise one. Going into the good enables us to discern what is good. Going into the complaint, the envy, the frustration does not give you insight, it gives you ulcers. Giving thanks for and honour to those in authority will enable you to draw out from them the God-given nature and power of the spheres you engage through them. It will also carry you into and through them into greater and greater reaches of relationship and levels of glory.

Financial consultant listens to the sound

America comes and goes (he has an offer by a large firm to join in a business venture). I know God is doing this on purpose and I am beginning to see his wisdom in this. I am seeing something quite new in my work now. It's always been there but now it's speaking out more plainly. There is so much more of a creation element in it. I come into situations all the time and build on what God gives me – insight, new vision and enthusiasm – without staying there. I think God wants me on the move – in and out of situations so I am not controlled by them. I see a lot of freedom and excitement in this that I haven't been able to take hold of before. I know I'll be going to the US late this month – to bring something forth over there. I cannot be drawn by the money – only by what God wants me to do, otherwise I would be discontented in my heart and spirit. So we go on . . . It's so good to live a life of faith.

What do you want?

Morality defines the borders. The attributes, nature and power of God are the treasure. The good is the impact of these as they are outworked in our relationships through work. What connects our heart to this life-encompassing process is our 'desire for goodness'. It is our desire to do the good for people through our work that unites us to them. In many situations it will be a matter of doing what is right because that is what you should do. However, such a way of life of itself is only 'elemental' religion – a good start, but far from a fulsome finish! God wants us to move from what we 'should do' into all of the goodness our heart desires in the land, the work and the people that make for our territory.

The questions you need to ask to draw out the good at work and the God-given passion in yourself are many. It is your good desires that should ask them. These desires were created in you by God to move, inspire and make you answer them. Let good creation desire ask the land out there and the heart in here: 'What do you want to do to make a difference here? What good must be established here to change and restore this place? Where and whom can I serve to ensure the good is powerfully released? What wisdom from above must I employ to build this house? What is in this place for my heart, my future and my passion? What are the gifts God gave me that I can employ to change this place? Where is the Son of God hidden here? Where is the divine image borne by that woman? What is redemptive promise and creation purpose for this sphere of creation? What are the gifts in that fallen man wanting to fly in heaven's sky?' On and on these good questions can go, stretching out and down into the years of life, uncovering more that can be won, more that can be gained, more that can be given and multiplied away. It is the sight given by the desire for good that will see you through the thorns of travail, pace you through the desert of futility and bring you through to the land promised. There your desire for good will be fed, satisfied by the goodness of the Lord in the land now living before you.

Good work resonates with and joins the attributes, nature and power of God in us to the attributes, nature and power of God in others. As we draw these qualities from the people we serve or work alongside, we ourselves are drawn out and discovered in the process. It is this relational reality we establish that is the major return or fruit from our good work. The monetary return is a part of this, but it is not the measure of the good we have done. As we know there are some highly paid evil works around! Good work unites us to and answers the cry of those trapped under the elemental things. Good work also unites us as the body of Christ, enabling us to stand as one in and through creation. It is the network made by good work that weaves us together as the body of Christ and joins us to the created order. The relationships we forge (within the body and outside), some close, some closer and some more distant, increasingly become the composite of our reality and thus our inheritance.

These 'friends' (recalling Jesus' words to make friends via work and money), and all that they encompass, serve to increase our vision of God the Father in the Son in the creation. Each person we know extends the reach of our experience and the breadth of our opportunities. Each one we welcome into our heart, to whatever degree providence and choice establish, enlarges our capacity for God and for life. Through this way of life we find that the distance that once existed between ourselves and others, a distance (space) created in the beginning by God, is now filled with the creation good we have established between us. In this way good work brings in the creation purpose to fill up all things with the manifest nature – the glory – of God. Through this work the new creation answers the cry of a creation waiting and still wanting to be 'good worked' towards the fullness. In this way the fruit of good work carries us towards the fullest finite knowing and taste of God this side of the ages to come.

Gathering the inheritance

The qualities within all things, people and events are the potential waiting for the fullness, the treasure waiting to be discovered. They are not a dim reflection of the real and removed God of elsewhere. They are not concepts and feelings pointing away to a Platonic realm of perfect forms and ideals. They are the manifestation of God – the expression, the fragrance, the language, the water and the breath emerging from the 'hiddenness' to be found by you and to find you. We have been so restrained in our going into this life by our otherworldly orientation and misconstrued fear of idolatry or materialism. However, once we know the essence within the form of things we can begin to sense the very nature, person and presence of God drawing us strongly in, moving us powerfully through and welcoming us up into our inheritance in the Son. Again, it is only when we stop at the form that idolatry meets and keeps us there. We must breathe much more deeply the life around us, not holding out till the next. As we do we will breathe out so much more of the life he has given us and thereby sound to the age to come the sound that says 'come'.

☞ In and through our work in the unseen orders of the creation we are called and privileged to find the justice and holiness of God in government; the beauty, suffering and playful delight of God in art, literature and leisure; the power and supply of God in business; the wisdom and knowledge of his Spirit in education; the wholeness of God in the wonder of our physical life and in the healing disciplines.

This justice, this beauty, this wholeness and wisdom are found in the relationships we engage as we discover and uncover the attributes, nature and power of God in others. The eternal creator God, no longer safely removed by rationalism or mysticism from our life in creation, no longer hidden behind the thorns and the travail, is in this way made manifest and enjoyed in all things, through all things and over all things. We have the right to name, we have the call to occupy – we were made for this! Is it any wonder that God prepared all those good works before all time for us to walk in?

Nutritionist engages creation medicine

Well, what can I say, but I have just spent one of the most awesome weekends of my life. I had the honour and privilege of being part of a two-day conference on nutritional influences in neurological disease. It was presented by a prominent neurologist/ surgeon in health care in the States. He was the main speaker and the conference was attended by several hundred neurologists and medical doctors and a few fringe-dwelling nutritionists/ naturopaths. Ah ha, I hear you say, what's so great about that? The opening session was called 'The Flaws of Modern Medicine'. His first words were that we are on the frontiers of modern medicine where we will see that the heavens and the earth are not separated as was first presented by Descartes and perpetuated by Newtonian physics. He spoke boldly about what we would call the Nicolation spirit in health care. In amongst the incredible biochemical science, amassing empirical evidence and changing philosophy of medicine (I would rather say a return to the acknowledgement of the power of creation and how we are to seek God's power out in that), I was hit with revelation after revelation. The presence of God was so strong. One of the biochemists spoke of how the seemingly weak things are in fact the most powerful. The final statement of the day was, 'I thank all of you for being here and challenging your paradigms. Please follow your heart and good work.'

Needless to say I was paralysed in my chair, my eyes welled up with tears and I praised my awesome God. My life's work is his work. I spoke to the gathering last Sunday of my heart's desire to see Creation Medicine as the medicine of the future and that I want to stand in front of Jesus and say I took his Spirit into the heart of humanity and spoke the truth in regard to the power of healing that comes from his *creation. My passion and desire for God to be glorified and trusted in regards to his plan for health care is burning into a bit of a bonfire, but I secretly know it is a towering inferno in my spirit. I weep and groan for the unveiling of his power through all of his creation. Not just through humanity, but also through his herbs, his seed-bearing plants and his fundamental laws of physics and chemistry; after all he is, as we know, in, through and over all things.*

Good Rewards

This way of life, as you may well imagine, is very rewarding! The apostle Paul knew well what sowing into the spirit and reaping eternal life was all about. To the Galatians he described it this way: 'Let us not lose heart in doing good, for in due season we shall reap if we don't grow weary. So then while we have opportunity, let us do good to all men and especially to those who are of the household of the faith' (Gal. 6:9, 10).

What are some of the signs that this reaping has begun? What does the abundant life Jesus promised look like when it arrives? The effects of restoring and filling a sphere of the creation by going 'into the good' are, to say the least, immense! To name a few . . .

As a saint you come into the blessing of your inheritance because you are no longer subject to the 'elemental things' of the earth. That is, you are not under the bondage of the name given by fallen humanity and the prince of the air over the spheres of your life. It no longer names you: rather you are now in a place where you have begun to name it. You have begun to live as subject to no one thing because now you are able to possess, enjoy and release all things. You establish the rule of the government of God over your life and work and are no longer overwhelmed by the storms of attack. You now stand on the rock, overcoming wickedness in high places because of your righteousness or right living in and through the creation. In this standing you release angelic hosts, the guardians of the created order, who minister to you as an heir of salvation. They work with you to further establish that good for yourself and for others.

Unstopping the wells

The earth begins to release to you your reward. This is now possible because your good work has resonated with, joined you to and drawn out the attributes, nature and power of God in all things. You begin to draw from the depths of the many wells within creation. Here you enter in to the blessing of Abraham: blessed in the field and blessed in the home. In relationship with others, growing in stature and maturity, your heart is able progressively to attract and encompass more of the inheritance. That multiplication factor in God, which ensures that to those who have more will be given, comes on line to accelerate your occupation of the heavens.

As you live you declare and establish the wisdom of God in the creation spheres right through into the heavenly places. Through the deeds of light you reprove and expose the deception and darkness of the present world system. Your good works shine that great light Jesus spoke about, thus enabling fallen people living in darkness to see how life and work were made to be by a good God. Even in the suffering and the travail of life they see the compassion of God resonating from your life to sound the healing, declare the forgiveness and proclaim the salvation. They now know that God is good, that the creation was never meant to be defined by the father of lies and used to deceive, destroy and steal. They can see that God made all things good, created them rich, declared them powerful, wanted them full of life and filled them with divine abundance. Here through good work your 'quiet life in all godliness' begins to arrive on the street.

By occupying through good work you have shone such light that the invisible God can now be seen and 'understood by that which is made'. The kingdom now begins to make sense to people because they see it in your life, your relationships and your work. The lost cannot see God in the abstract and the conceptual; even when you are saved you have a hard enough time doing so! God begins to be seen and he is the God of the earth, the God of family and marriage, the God of reality and work. The light is now shining strongly in a dark place and those in the land of the shadow of death are drawing close to its brightness. As you grow in this relationship with others you increasingly occupy the unseen spheres of creation. In the restoration that comes with this occupation the age to come draws closer. Heaven within your reach, glory called forth, ready to complete what has been substantially restored. The fullness of the stature of the man Christ Jesus now belongs to the body standing strong in marriage, family and work. Soon his prepared heaven will emerge from within everything and through everything to become the eternal crown over everything.

So, if you still think your job or work is outside the purposes of God, or if you consider your work as mostly a place to practise virtue and earn money, then I strongly urge you to think again! Before we visit 'the restaurant of God' in the land of the living, let's indulge in a little methodology.

Brief snapshot – redemptive structures

Right now there are hundreds of thousands of businesses established by saints in the spheres of the created order engaged by work. Many of the saints who work in these businesses desire to see them built on kingdom principles. In a post-modern world, where society relates mostly to what is useful, tangible and workable, there is a tremendous opportunity for these work-places to become the front line of our engagement of creation as the church. Once leaders take hold of the truth that the church can exist in every sphere of life, they can with confidence and wisdom begin to serve those who are that church.

Increasingly we are seeing what might be called 'redemptive structures' coming into being. These businesses seek out the purposes of God in the sphere of creation they engage, with a view to bringing substantial restoration to that sphere. In these settings, a relationship (either paid or unpaid) is established with an individual who is a ministry gift of Christ. He or she works (serves) to see the believers involved in the business encouraged, equipped and resourced for more effective ministry. The people who operate and work in these businesses seek to establish powerful relational networks that radiate from their place of work. All of this is done with a view to shining light and bringing salvation to the lives of those who engage the services and/or purchase the products of that business. Missions, particularly in places within the 10/40 window, are increasingly using such an approach in an endeavour to penetrate and reach societies with the gospel.

If it's good enough for the field, then it surely must be good enough for our own increasingly unreached society.

Field books and Internet web pages, produced by saints working in spheres such as counselling and health (both orthodox and complementary medicine), business,

education, the arts and others, are coming on line. (Information concerning one such website can be found at the end of this book.)

These serve as an encouragement and forum for those in the body of Christ seeking to work with impact beyond the congregation in a postmodern time.

Enough of that – let's eat . . .

Chapter 20

Good Food Served on The Best Tables

'I'm employed in a restaurant on the corner down the road, a very long way from your book. Tell me about the good to be found in my serving meals to people every Friday night. I know it satisfies their hunger, gives them time out to be with their friends and pays my bills, but is there more?'

God at Work

We could stop right there with a workable definition of what goes on at a shift in a restaurant. However, it is right there, at just such a crucial juncture, that we need to go much, much further. We need to search out all of the good God has placed in this restaurant waiting to be found in the giving of that meal. We need to locate God in just that kind of place and time, for workplaces like this one combine to make for creation. And saints just like this one can only become creation's fullness in places like these. What follows here is intended to draw together more of the truths we have looked at. It may seem a little strange at first, but take courage in knowing that it is not as strange as many of the other things we find ourselves doing in life!

You arrive, look into the kitchen and smile at the chef. You say hello to the shift manager and get the briefing.

There's a party of 37 coming, 22 others are booked, plus some of the regulars are bound to turn up unannounced. It's Friday night and it's going to be pretty well full up. The food is good (we will presume this as a fact; if it were bad then it would be a good thing to improve it). The hunger is God-given. It is a creation reality that causes us to head out daily into the world of people to work, relate and mature. In the act of giving this meal and in the act of receiving there is good. And finally in the response to that meal, in return for that good, there is the financial (I will call it) gift (rather than payment) made, which also is good.

The goodness of God *is* in, through and over all things that are happening here. His attributes, nature and power are within things like food, appetite, music, people and the surrounds. God is there in the relationships that are formed in the giving and receiving of these things. God is present in the working together of these things as they move towards their fulfilment and our inheritance. The goodness inherent in all of this is not an abstract quality separate from God. This goodness is the very goodness of God himself. It

> By wisdom a house is built, and by understanding it is established; and by knowledge the rooms are filled with all precious and pleasant riches. (Prov. 24:4)

is his presence expressed through his attributes, his nature and his power. He is there to be felt, heard, seen and known on that Friday night. It is good work that serves to draw out this hidden God that we might know the goodness of God in the restaurant of the living.

All well and good but what about . . .

'But what if things go wrong and it is not good? What if evil comes instead of good? And what about the 210 diffi-

culties in my life that I have to carry to work each day? The
bills, the mishaps, the tiredness, the worry about the future
of my children and the bad decisions I have made that
follow me around?'

The finite creation reality means that if we and others
can go into the good then we and others can also go into
the 'not good'. Thus evil can and evil does come our way.
In this it is important to realise that our experience of fallen
reality is, in so many ways, the measure of where we are in
life and who we are in our life. After a given period of time
in marriage, family, friendships or work the relational
reality set up is generally a direct reflection of who we
really are. The difficulties may feel like the enemy, but in
many ways they are our truth encounter with fallen reality.
They are the thorns pressed against, now evident and ready
to be overcome. This is not to say that if your company is
taken over by another and you are given a redundancy
package, then it's your fault. Things like that are more a
measure of the broader reality. What I am referring to here
is the immediate relational reality we engage each day.
Here we are looking more at the microcosm, rather than
the macrocosm. They are ultimately related, but we will
not go into that matter here. The way we deal with struggle
and failure in the 210 anomalies of life is essential to the
whole process whereby we journey through these thorns,
resonate with those who suffer in the same way, see our
own strongholds torn down and thus emerge to gain the
inheritance.

Most people know about being and doing good. However, it is the saints who are distinguished by their ability to
go through suffering and death into life. We must go
through at just such a crucial place as this. Remember the
bread we enjoy is behind the sweat and the baby only
arrives in our lap through the travail. God has made it all
good. Even the evil that people might bring cannot over-

come the ultimate goodness of God to be found in every facet of life and experience. In fact it only accentuates our need, not to rejoice in the evil, but to press in more decidedly to gain the good.

Filling work with creation content

When we see God as being in, through and over all things, our fellowship with him during our shift at the restaurant deepens, the result being that our life and relationships impact so much more strongly on the environment we work within. This changes us, this changes those we work with and this ultimately changes the sphere of creation we engage through our work. Once we know that the goodness here is God himself, then we can draw the essence of that work and all that radiates from it into the words we speak to others and the worship we release to God. It is at this restaurant that goodness fills up words like food, serving, smile, response, patience, kindness, taste, supply, cook, friends. From our meal we turn to taste and see that the Lord is good. We stop for a moment to touch the kindness of his heart in giving his life for his friends. We smile in response to his patience and look forward to the marriage feast when he will serve and we will sit. Then these words, dripping with divine content, speak back again and resonate deeper into our work to give us greater sight and bring us greater good.

This richness stirs up our inner wells of good desire. The creation-filled words and works begin to unstop these wells and what we want in and through all of our work comes on line and into view. We begin to release these deep rivers of living water, one with the indwelling Spirit, over the dry ground we work upon. From here the many seeds hidden in the earth beneath and around our feet burst open and multiply the life and the fruit we enjoy. In all, as we savour the person and presence of God, communing with him in the creation reality he has established, a very different encounter with life and with God becomes our own. We begin to detect the providence of God arriving through the people we meet, our words fill with creation content and we prophesy. We find ourselves changing the nature of situations and we joy in the discoveries of every opportunity. In this way we build a life with the attributes, nature and power of God in, through and over all things. We are those who know the blood and grace that answers sin and failure. We now know that our God is at work to work all things, events and people in this place towards good. We are those able to suffer our way through any obstacle to gain the reward. It's no wonder the Jews will be made jealous by such living grace so evidently shown to the Gentiles!

> Through the sweat of your travail
> you'll eat the bread I've broken.
> And through the thorns of blood and tears
> you'll taste the fruit I've opened.

Putting it in this way might seem a little overdone. I mean after all, it's only food! Not to mention that 'there are around 50 other people in the restaurant that need attention and if I did this kind of thing in relation to everyone the meals would get cold and I would get fired and that wouldn't be good! Also the chef is barking and those customers in the corner are whining and the clock is ticking. If you theologians don't want anything else to eat, then thanks for your patronage, here's the bill.' Yes, the struggle against the pressures and the futility you face is great. But the greater struggle relates to your bringing that futility into a perspective, into a theology, into a strategy that will enable you to get through more than an 8-hour shift. You have to transform your struggle to survive into a travail that gives birth. Your work is hard because God has made it hard. Satan stirs, sin compounds, but God has decreed and named the suffering. He has stamped it with his purpose. It can become your ally if you name it as he does.

This is your land, given to you that you might uncover your own God-given inheritance. The people here, the other workers and the clientele need to see the light that shines from the attributes, nature and power that you have the privilege of making manifest. Your response to them and your response to the creation reality around you sounds the sound of the Father into that place. Your work, no matter how mundane it appears when compared to powerful ministries that come to town, is the key to the divine strategy. As you do this work, do it for the good. Go in to the good for its own sake. Do not work primarily for the effect. If you do you will miss the reward. Go in to get the goods, find the glory and give them both away. In this work you will have both your reward and great affect at once.

The presence of God found in everyday work (and our relating to reality in the way we have spoken of here) does not impose on every moment of our space and time. We saw in the Garden the nature of this 'hiddenness' that enables us to relate to life and to God and thus to grow and move in relationship to both. When you first try to see into your work, the things I have spoken of will not jump on line and arrive as a ready-made, shall we say, takeaway. It is something that you need to go into over time, using wisdom, pacing yourself and trying not to stress out with what you are or are not seeing. Remember that we are talking about a change in the way that we see and engage everyday things, people and events. For those not accustomed to looking for or seeing God in such a way, for those who see work mostly in terms of moral responsibility and financial returns, this will be a challenge. I am not saying that under the present paradigm we do not already see and appreciate God in the midst of day-to-day life. The challenge before us, however, is to go much deeper into the strategic nature and power of every facet of life and work to gain the inheritance.

Simple serve?

Are all the outcomes above just a matter of course once we know and work in line with the eternal purpose? The answer is no. It is not simply a matter of choosing and doing the good and all of this will fall in line. No doubt you have already guessed and experienced that hard fact of fallen existence! The reality is that we are engaged in real and strategic warfare against principalities and powers that hold humankind down in deception through the very spheres of creation we are endeavouring to bring restoration to. The strongman holds the goods. Christ has bound him. We are the ones called to go in past our own strongholds and get those goods.

The restoration of all things must begin with ourselves. We each have the calling on our lives to restore and fulfil to ourselves the immediate environment in which we live and work. We will wait forever if we wait for some ideal one or some ideal thing to come and do it for us. Certainly we will accomplish this in relationship with others. But the emphasis in such a statement must be on the words *we* and *others*, not just others. Individually we must take the initiative here; no other, no mantle and no one else's anointing will make it happen for you.

That being said, what is going to make a world-impacting difference to the body of Christ's present state of defeat in the creation sphere of work?

☞ Right now millions of saints are interacting with the systems of the earth in the most decisive engagement of all time. Meanwhile, on the other side of town, most of the ministry gifts of Christ are involved in running meetings and attending to the primary pastoral care needs of many who, in terms of their local church life, have never graduated from the information age and the nurture phase.

It must surely be time we released these ministry gifts from the nest to fly with the church as fullness. There are many good restaurants to be built, many good meals to be served, many good times to be savoured, many good lives to be won – there is much good work to be done.

GEORGE THE ELDER (7)
Back to work

George stepped out of his car, shutting the door behind him in a manner that reflected his new-found confidence. He began to sing to himself the words 'I want to work, I want to work it through' to the tune of some long-forgotten chorus.

He was in full stride, heading towards the elevator, ready to push the button. It was then that another voice broke in, demanding to be heard.

'So George, what are you going to say to Pastor Steve? And are you just going to cave in in front of all the other managers, make it sound like you never meant what you said? What about Rob? Where are your convictions George? Soft option, easy street, when the going gets tough where do you go George?'

George knew who this was and was well programmed to answer its concerns.

'Justification!' said George, like a battle cry. 'I need a reason to tell these guys why I'm staying. I have to tell Steve why I can't be as on-board in the next few months. I have to

tell Rebecca about how brave I was, standing for God in the lion's den. I can't let Rob think I'm a pushover. I can't just say "I want to". I mean, what's that mean?'

Again the face of Winston swam into view. 'What do you want to do George?'

'I want to do what I do best,' George responded.

'What's that?' asked Winston.

'My work,' said George.

It was then that George remembered why he had taken the job in the first place. One morning at church, a long time ago, he was moved to ask God to put him where he wanted him.

'Within days I was offered this job, with this company and these people.'

'So that's what you were trying to tell me,' George said to Winston. 'This is where I work. It's where God put me, and it's what I want.'

'So, it's what you want, is it?' the other voice said, still trying to stitch up the justification side of things. 'What about Steve, Rebecca, your reputation with these guys and with Rob? You need a deal that will save face, not make you sound so self-possessed, so self-centred.'

'OK,' said George, 'tell me what you've got.'

'You will say yes to Rob, yes, with righteous indignation. Yes, Rob, I will do the extra work – again. But only because I have a family that I can't support if I lose the job. I will do it even though you guys don't get it when it comes to life outside this place.' George looked at it, it sounded good. He could imagine repeating it to Steve and Rebecca.

'Steve is next,' said the justifier.

'You will tell Steve that for at least a period of time (you don't have to mention how long) you have to spend more time helping your CEO put the company back on solid ground. You will tell him about the ultimatum and your decision to support your family and, because of all of that,

*you just won't be able to give as much time to church. But
your extra work will come with a bonus, and you will give
some, no, half, of it towards supporting that youth pastor.'*

*'That's for you, Lord,' George added, already a little
unsure of himself.*

*But the justifier in him, the one that had been making
deals like this with conscience, with people and with God
for years, kept on going. 'And you will take Rebecca out to
dinner once every other week and take the children once a
month while she does her own thing.'*

'That's it,' said George.

*For George this contract had all the marks of a great deal.
It was no longer what he wanted to do, it was, like it had
been for most of his life, what he had to do and should do.*

*George congratulated himself by saying, 'So I keep my
job and justify my stand as well.'*

*There was a hollow ring to the statement, but George
didn't have time to listen. He was on his way to the 8th
floor. Standing in the lift, straightening his tie and checking
his hair in the discreet smoked-glass mirrors, he searched
inside himself for some feelings. He felt moral – resolute.
The bell rang, the doors opened, it was Monday.*

*The ever-smiling receptionist greeted him with charming
efficiency. 'Good morning George.' He raised his eyebrows
in silent inquiry as to where he was to go. 'They're all in
Rob's office.'*

'Already?' responded George.

*'Well, yes,' returned the secretary, as if no other option
were possible.*

*George surmised that there must have been a 'ring
around' to get them here early. 'They've been talking, Rob's
been positioning things.'*

Because he expected that, George didn't really mind.

*'That's the way things are,' he said as he moved towards
the double red cedar doors of the CEO's office. For a*

moment he hesitated. 'Be strong now George,' he said to himself. The next phrase that popped into his head was 'roar like a moral lion', but George didn't quite know what to make of that one.

The operator in George took over. 'Knock, firm but polite, sensitive but direct. Don't wait for a sound from the other side.' George turned the huge brass doorknob, stepped in and surveyed the scene. 'OK, now move in George, move! Not too quickly. That's it. Now George, radiate quiet confidence. Smile, not too much now. Let go of your hair! OK, move across the carpet, don't fall over.'

George looked around for Rob. He wasn't there. It threw him a little, because he didn't know who to focus on. He walked up to the group of five men, plus Helen. 'Left me alone with the boys and girls have you Rob? Want to cook me a little longer? Smart move, CEO.'

'George,' said his internal operator, 'say something. Be careful now, not just anything.' Fear came down on him. George swallowed it whole. The justifier, fuelled by conscience, arose. George reached down into his convictions, ready to launch the moral attack. He needed to be first, beat them to the punch. The words were armed and ready, beating in his chest. All systems were about to go when someone got in the way.

'Hey George, didn't you recognise me on the way in? On the freeway? The green car? I thought you were trying to tell me something was wrong, but I couldn't hear what you said and then you just shot past. I caught up with you once more, signalled to you, but . . .'

George cut in, stunned. 'Jim Parsons! That was you, in the car – what happened to your moustache?'

'Shaved it off,' said Jim, rubbing his upper lip.

The next moment was seized by Jim who jumped in with, 'So, tell us, how are you going, George? Did you have a good weekend?'

George looked at Jim's round face and entreating grin –
Winston began to wave. Justification was trying to get hold
of the next sentence. But George knew what he wanted to
say.

'Yeah Jim, it was good, very good. I did some real hard
thinking.' He looked around the room, seeing the strain of
not knowing what he was going to say in the faces around
him. 'Look, I want to work with you guys. I want to work
to see this through, like, like really give it my best shot.
So . . . ,' he looked around at each of them, 'so let's do it.'

There it was. George was on the team. No justifications.
Touchdown.

The response was not one that you would normally see in
a city firm on a Monday. It was a little like church. All the
managers moved towards George, some just a step, some
just leaned forward a little. Helen clapped twice, a few
slapped his back and most of them got round to shaking his
hand. The message got through to Rob, waiting it out in the
next room. He came in, in control, smiling. He shook
George's hand and then cleared his throat, looked round
the room and said, 'So, gentlemen, Helen, let's do it.'

One hour later George was sitting down in his chair,
behind his desk, in his office. He had not felt like this for
years. It was his job, he wanted it, and he knew he wanted it.
God was in the place and he knew that as well. He had won
the war.

On impulse he picked up the phone and hit an automatic
dial number. After a few moments Rebecca answered.
'Hello?'

'Hi honey, it's me, George. Can't talk now, just wanted
to let you know I'll be a little late, Rob wants a quick six
o'clock debriefing. Hey, Beck, know something? I love
you.'

'Love you too,' Rebecca responded, and added, 'Hey
George . . . when it's over, come straight home. I'll be here.'

George smiled, kissed, laughed and hung up.

Straight away the phone rang; there was some trouble on one of the big jobs in the city. 'I'll be there – first thing tomorrow.'

George put down the phone, breathed deep and said thanks. George the elder was back at work.

Chapter 21

Bringing It All Back Home

The challenges before us are great; many of us are uncertain, we appear almost as novices in such a diverse and changing situation. Will our insecurity cause us to cling ever more strongly to the past? I pray not. Strangely enough, our learning and orientation for this time might to a large degree come from the very people we now call lost and uninformed. Could we bear such condescension? If we realise that the cry of creation they sound is given by God to help define our purpose and call forth our sonship we might tend to listen more closely to what they are trying to resonate our way. The sound we need to hear is to be found in the entirety of creation. It will also be the new generation of saints emerging fast from under our feet who will show us how to take the rubble and fractured timbers and build for this time. As old men dream wisdom's dreams, as our generation tries to see into the vision, the children will prophesy, calling the bones to live and the body to rise. We can only be ever humble, trembling like a leaf, listening to the sound of the eternal coming from the creation and the children.

The Contours of the Gospel

It was invigorating to read the conclusions drawn by Stanley Grenz in his book on postmodernism. In it he details 'the contours of the gospel' and the opportunities for the church to relate and impact in a postmodern time. Briefly here we look at some of his conclusions and their relationship to the themes of this book.

Grenz says that 'members of the next generation are often unimpressed by our verbal presentations of the gospel. What they want to see are a people who live out the gospel in wholesome, authentic and healing relationships' (p. 169). Truth was given that 'we might attain wisdom for living' (p. 173). In this postmodern age 'propositions . . . have a second-order importance'. To be valid in this era the truth has to live and work. As the Colossians' truth says, the knowledge of God must journey through wisdom into life, to work, to fruit if we are ever to arrive at that full finite knowing of God himself. The purpose of our knowing and our preaching, Grenz says, is that others 'might encounter God in Christ and then join with us on the grand journey of understanding the meaning of that encounter in all of life' (p. 171).

The postmodernists have rejected the divisions that the Enlightenment/modern mind has made in the nature of humanity. Their tolerance for those who would fracture people into body, soul and, in some streams, spirit, is thin and getting thinner. In regard to this, Grenz says, 'The gospel we proclaim must speak to human beings in their entirety.' To do so 'involves integrating the emotional-affective, as well as the bodily-sensual, with the intellectual-rational within the one human person' (p. 171f.).

Many saints trained in the old mindset are very unsettled with the current generation's preoccupation with the realm of nature. There is much New Age idolatry afoot. However, we need to realise what God intended when he made us to see and experience spiritual reality in the things he has made. The fact is that the Platonic worldview that first overtook the church and then captured the West is two steps away from God's ordained way of revelation.

We have reacted strongly to the philosophical overlay that fallen humanity has used to define (and somewhat distort) the intrinsic creation reality. But rather than running away from the creation, let us move towards the divine attributes, nature and power so many people are trying and stumbling to reach. Many have seen, named and felt something in the created order that we could have known and experienced long ago had we not been captives of reason and the other realm.

Grenz says that, 'Our anthropology must take seriously the biblical truth that our identity includes being in relationship to nature, being in relationship with others, being in relationship with God and, as a consequence, being in true relationship with ourselves' (p. 172).

Postmodernists see the creation as one, ridding their world of the old Platonic dualism between the spiritual realm and the physical and relational realm. In this they do not see transcendence because they know they can never know transcendence. They are not aware that they can be known by the transcendent God in the immanence of the Son. Grenz says that we of course need to reject the postmodern belief that there is no overarching and universal truth to be discovered. As saints we hold to, and proclaim the reality of, the person and work of Christ the Son of God of whom the Scriptures speak. Such a revelation Grenz calls the metanarrative 'encompassing all peoples at all times' (p. 164). I believe that even though the postmodernists' assertions concerning our inability to know about or actually encounter the eternal God are wrong, the premises they use to develop these conclusions are in fact quite biblical.

Postmodern philosophers are in effect saying that we cannot know truth objectively or ultimately. This is because we are inside the creation, living behind our senses and within our feelings, looking out from our worldviews and describing what we see with our languages. From these and through these things we construct our reality and decide on our truth. In many ways this philosophy aligns with the way of revelation we have looked at.

☞ From Romans we know that the infinite God made finite humankind, placed them in creation and then called them to come to know that same God through the things he had made. I believe the premise of the postmodernists, that truth is known in relationships, in community, in language/naming and through the spheres of creation, is correct. What they lack is an understanding that there does exist a divine revelation able to light up this truth. There is a word able to give their world the meaning and value they still seek and live in hope of.

What time is this season?

What is striking about the postmodern paradigm are the many parallels between its world and that of the Hebrews. It resembles the Hebrew worldview far more than the Greek mindset that gave rise to the Enlightenment/modern mind. Is this just an unusual coincidence of history or is there more to the plot? As we know, God alone is sovereign over history and providence. Our theology says that he ushers in the times and the seasons, setting the boundaries in which even Satan is free for a time to act. We may or may not literally be at the end of human history, but we have 'done' most of the worldviews that can be done. Of course the prior times all partook of the same providence and both the Father of lights and the father of lies enacted and unfolded their mysteries in each of them. This time, however, is the climax of so much of what they were, containing the best and worst of many of their worlds.

More people live without restraint than at any time since Noah. Theirs is, however, a desperate kind of freedom, at once manipulated and controlled by the market and its media outlets and then stirred to purchasing frenzy by the same. This generation expects so much and gets so little; it knows not what it wants but wants it now. The new orthodoxy says that there is now no orthodoxy. People welcome this heady conclusion but do not seem to drink of its tasteless contradiction. The stakes are very high. A strange and great power is loose on the earth; its flux is twisting everything and everyone so fast.

Might it not be reasonable to assume that God has had some hand in the overthrow of the 2,500-year-old ploy of the enemy to dislocate us from reality? It matters not if he used a Pharaoh or a donkey to do the postmodern job, for, as history shows, no one resists his purpose to sum up all things in Christ. I believe that the Lord of the harvest is bringing into being a season in which both society and the body of Christ can see down the storylines with Hebrew sight.

We might feel uncomfortable with many of the arguments relating postmodernism to providence. But the questions remain even apart from their apparent strengths or weaknesses. The first question is whether or not God is sovereign over history, and secondly, how can the church speak so as to be heard, let alone understood, in this extremely fast-changing and complex world?

☞ The options are few. Some say we should return to the safety of solid Sunday preaching like the Reformers of old. I don't believe a retreat to the drawing board will attract any attention from our society. It may help us feel defined and safe again, but sooner or later we will have to emerge to do business with the creation. I fear that another ten years of getting our bearings from the Reformation (yet again) will leave us culturally stranded on a kind of semi-tropical island.

This small terrain of ours will end up a novelty. People will look, but no one, excepting a few anthropologists, will be able to fathom the language we speak and the moves we make. Reformation providence was good and, like most things, looks even better from a nostalgic distance. However, the today providence is working until now and now is the day we must engage.

Again, I am not saying that we should embrace all that the fast-emerging postmodern philosophy has to say. However, our other historical alternatives (for example the Enlightenment or the modern) are going, going, gone. I believe that the postmodern worldview delivers the clearest vision of reality and the best opportunity for insight into the divine strategy of all the other paradigms since the Fall. With the modern edifice crumbling we need to decide whether we will remain in the rubble, lamenting the death of the deification of human reason, or rise and take hold of the opportunities this postmodern world of flux presents to us. I believe that the new creation in Christ can rise with Hebrew sight to speak into and form the emerging postmodern world for God. In this unique time we can answer the longings, the broken promises and unmet desires scattered across the postmodern landscape with a tongue that speaks a language now able to be heard. The fabric of the created order torn through history is on the mend! The mystery of iniquity may cloud many lives but the mystery of godliness is still blazing through into a postmodern day.

The future is here

Postmodernism is not just a new way of doing art. It is a world shooting up with vines and branches, large leaves and exotic fruit, tangling its way into and over every old building and worn-out idea history has had. It is occupying much of the soil of the earth, taking the knowledge of the territory, declaring its love for the land. It weaves in with the character of community, grasping the power of language, story and song, and is taking the creation on a ride into the unknown.

This glorious creation was meant to be taken somewhere, it was meant to journey into the fullness of Christ who is its creator. Within our life right now are the sound and the knowing to move the creation towards that fullness. It's our call to unwrap, to live, to work, to restore and to sound into the lives of those whose travail still knows no birth. Never has there been a more strategic time to hear the cry of creation and to call out to our Father – a time to live the sound he answers through us, resonating deep, gathering to thunder into the age God's providence has given the sons.

After all of these millennia the three spheres of the created order have not been shaken – people in marriage, people in family, people engaging the world through work. These are the realities in which the people wait; these are the way of revelation God has made. Our moving out into creation as the body of Christ is no longer an option. God, through his use of history, is forcing our hand. Much of the water, the grain, the oil and the old but good wine in our store is running out. If the goodness of the earth, the occupation of the heavens and the inheritance of the sons are to come, then we need to get out, right out, and live to fulfil these spheres of the created order.

Stitch up the universe

The dead end we have reached at the end of the 20th century in our understanding of transcendence and immanence is nothing less than the dead end of modernism. All along our problem was that we sought to contain these truths in some rational definition. We tried to categorically separate them so as to know them. Further to this we tried to make the revelation of God found in Scripture a categorically distinct document, housing and hence containing all revelation. For conservative Evangelicals the Bible became a transcendent document in itself. For Barth it spoke of the transcendent Christ coming from outside into the finite. Both defined their stance by positing it against the creation. Both used the clumsy instruments of Descartes in their attempt to cut the tissue away from the blood of life in creation. Yes they wanted to guard against liberalism, pantheism and panentheism. But their reaction did not serve us or them very well. That powerful Greek tendency to separate the pure and eternal from the profane of life and that Enlightenment culture that believes that the concept can actually hold the substance of truth could not and did not deliver to us a clear way through to the revelation of God.

Of course the Bible travelled a good distance through this time. It reached the concept, it took its place in ethics, it even changed some social policies. The Word was released to help our families, inform our work and establish our ecclesiastical patterns. There were great acts of compassion and many powerful missions to unreached nations. Again almost all of this was the church operating in the first phase and the initial stages of the second phase of the divine strategy. Beyond this, however, the wall closed in and the truth was not permitted to reach and ignite much of the inner and personal desire of the saints in life and work. But the Word became flesh for more, much more than the above-stated gains, as great as many of them have been. The Son of God became the Son of Man to show man how to search out the Son of God in, through and over all things.

Certainly not all language now speaks of him, not all humanity proclaims him; much suffering and death happen apart from fellowship with him. Reacting against this tragedy, are we to rush away to the 'otherness' of the rational concept and the undefiled spirit realm? What are we hoping to find by this strange Greek obsession? Is God really contained in the proposition? Is God found in a realm that is nothing less than a loose collection of emotions and concepts extrapolated off into who knows what or where? No, he is not. The eternal God is revealed in the immanence of the Son who is to be found right throughout the finite creation – a creation that contains people, nature, history, language, and yes, reason and emotion. And when the immanence of God became a man he did not do so to take us away from all of this. All that he did was to carry us deep into life in creation, bringing us through the attributes, nature and power into the life eternal.

☞ Christ himself spoke of the importance of his going away so that again we might turn to face each other in the relationship, in the temptation, in the suffering and even the death – that we might turn to face the cosmos with its beauty and its terror and, as in the beginning, enter in to find the Son who cries out as the counterpoint to the Son who speaks.

As we lose our life to find it anew in him in creation we will meet the language of Babel and speak with a new tongue, we will meet the suffering and the death and resonate the love that came to touch the people of that place. We will engage every story of every created tribe and bring each one home to its fulfilment in the Son – that Son who is the only begotten of the Father; that Son who is the essence and fullness of the creation; that Son who will speak forever into his creation from the divine and eternal story. We can and we must heal the heavens and the earth by welcoming the Son of God in, through and over the all things that exist in him.

The Hope of Glory

It is only when we see the church as the fullness of the created order and see the gathering as its pillar and support that we will see the end of our containment in the building, the meeting and the programmes. We must give the name 'church' back to the saints in marriage, family and work. Only then will they prevail against the gates of hell that these spheres of creation directly engage. We must connect the church as pillar and support to the church as fullness and know which expression is the servant of the other. We must release the divine resources presently held within the church as pillar, moving them out to empower the church that lives in marriage, family and work.

Again it needs to be stated: If the Son of God stands in, through and over the all things of creation; if he is head over his body, the church – a body called to be and become the fullness of him who fills all in all – then it follows that the ministry gifts must give saints a knowledge of that Son and live to build that body. It is here that I believe church leaders and teachers have fallen short. Yes, we have preached from the Bible of Jesus Christ the Son of God made man, now in heaven, who will come again. We have told the saints about the historical Jesus who came, died and rose again, ascending into that heaven. We have told of the personal indwelling Christ who loves, forgives and empowers their life and service for God by his Spirit. All of this is tremendous. However, under the influence of our Greek heritage, we have located the Son of God in a far-removed, indefinable and transcendent heaven that has little to do with this age and most to do with an afterlife. Added to this, we have said that when he comes he arrives in and through another version of that Neoplatonic spiritual realm, a realm distinct and detached from the 'natural' things we relate to in our daily life.

We have not given the saints the knowledge of the Son of God standing throughout the created order in which they live, move and have their being. For this reason they are not able to rightly place themselves in the creation scheme of things.

☞ The result is that believers are left with a narrow and obscured vision of the Son of God in their marriage, in their family, in their relationships and in particular in their work. Thus their ability to correlate the personal Christ preached on Sunday with the creation they encounter every day of the week is, compared to what it should be, very limited in its scope.

We challenge them to turn their eyes upon Jesus so that the things of earth will grow strangely dim. But if we gave them the knowledge of the Son of God standing through the seen and unseen spheres of creation then, rather than facing a dim-lit earth, they would see the creation light up with the knowledge of him.

Leaders of local churches need to give more permission to the saints, trusting them to find their ministry and thus their inheritance in their own life and work; not restraining them via the Greek tensions set up between their life and church life: rather teaching them to discover for themselves more and more of the undiscovered Son (and in the process find themselves) in, through and over all things – giving them strong incentive to head down the track where their treasure is to be found. It is time for the ministry gifts of Christ, with the Word of God and the power of agreement, to equip the church now standing through the creation for *the* works of ministry: like John the Baptist and Jesus the Christ, predominantly ministering the Word out there in the field, rather than perpetually educating believers for church life in the fold.

The creation must set the scope and context for the life and ministry of the sons and daughters. Look at the way in which the Second World War creates and calls for Churchill and South Africa makes Mandela. If these large contexts bring forth and propel individuals by drawing out their gifting with the power of agreement operating on that scale, imagine the kind of people who will be drawn forth and fashioned by the immensity of the creation. The saints must stand through the creation and the ministry gifts of Christ must stand with them, right through every place and every level of glory they were created and redeemed to occupy.

Buying back the family home

It is when the corporate gatecrasher that enclosed the church in an 'organisation' is gone that we will again be able to face each other across the family table and look directly into the eyes of the church. Between the saints will exist the attributes, nature and power of God and no interloper. In this fellowship the unseen within all things will become the seen in relationship between us. It is here that work, diverse and moved by good desire, will again come into focus as the key that makes a difference in answer to the cry. In these lives and through this work the seed of the kingdom planted in the people of God will grow. We will rise to the Father, strong in our identity as sons and daughters; we will journey in the Son, close and intimate as his beloved; we will live through the Spirit, empowered and passionate for the work

– the love between us alive with the good that pulses with attributes, nature and power divine.

From our local expressions the household of God will become a clan and then a tribe. A culture will be established across vast tracts of land as a people emerge to work the earth. This people will gather in events large and small to celebrate the harvest life returns into their lap. Once our dying is done we will rise into something that the Hebrews of old knew and many indigenous people still know well. We will still need to roster the singers, nurture the young and organise the meals. Our buildings will not necessarily be abandoned. I believe they will finally be understood by many in a generation that wonders what on earth they presently stand for. Many things we do will look the same. But the whole ethos, culture and impact will be radically different. It will not matter if we have large or small gatherings, meetings of 10 or 10,000 in homes, buildings or barns. These will be known as the servants of the house and no longer the strange mono-measure of most all things church.

The chaos at which many leaders currently wag their heads will make sense because they will be able to see it and name it very differently. Many thousands of saints currently wandering outside our local church buildings will again be able to belong to a relational matrix that can cope with interdependence. The relational values we establish will build up the environment of accountability the corporate grid has so narrowly defined. Elders will stand in their servant authority across the city and in the gatherings. Ministry gifts will stand with saints, equipping them to go for it in life and work. The unity that we seek, a unity that currently sees congregations coming together for prayer, celebration and outreach, will accelerate as saints join hands across the city through networks that work the spheres of creation towards the good.

Multitudes, currently standing outside of the kingdom,

wary of surrendering their lives to the church subculture, will enter into the freedom and strength of the relational and redemptive reality that emerges. And the nations of the third world, many of which are now exploding in the first phase of evangelism and hurrying into the corporate patterns we in the West have prescribed, will return to the land and the creation and build in line with their own culture and its unique creation purpose. It is only then that his body the church will really live as having nothing but possessing all things. Only such a relational reality will see the body stand right through all of the spheres of creation to become the fullness of him who fills all in all. It is that church that will bring home the restoration harvest to our Father God.

In establishing this relational reality with each other and the creation we will need the assistance of our indigenous brethren, or in certain cases the indigenous treasure now only held on pages of history. The sound of the Spirit is calling us to restore the land by establishing peace with the original people of that land. How long will we continue in our disconnection from each other and from the land? To touch creation we will need to submit and respond to our indigenous brethren in Christ. We will need to answer the cry of many of the sons of Ham: those raised up by God as the greatest servants of the earth. These are the gatekeepers of so many lands, the ones whose very form and character was genetically selected to fit the contours and colours of the land they first occupied. If we are to join with the earth and journey to the heavens, we will have to join heart and hand with them. There needs to be peace between the sons and daughters if we are ever to be named and welcomed as peacemakers of the earth. If the land is to release to us its fullness, if we are ever to marry it, then we will have to covenant with the ancient keepers of its ancient heart.

The sound meets the desire

Where does that sound from the Father for his creation arrive on the earth? It is too deep for words to encompass, so it is more than understanding. It is far greater than the law of physical requirement, so it will not primarily impact our conscience and demand our obedience. It cannot arrive in one person's vision telling us where our life energies and resources should go. No, it must journey into every redeemed heart – that being the Hebrew sense of heart – the core of our being in its thinking, feeling, deciding and gifting. It must come to be one with the wellsprings of our heart's desire: a desire that wraps up truth, sonship and power and moves strong, emerging through good work to deliver the good that is predestined to change all things. It is this good desire, searched out by the one who searches the hearts, which God gave to ignite our created purpose. Its power stirs the passion of dreams to travel down the life-lines of wisdom, character and providence. What pleasure this new creation's rising brings to the Father's heart! Imagine his joy when the image bearer that he spoke into existence and made in innocence returns through the creation to be like him – mature, replete with his inheritance, ready to rule forever.

At this time it is the apostolic gift God placed first in the church that must set the character for all other ministry gifts. Apostolic pastors, prophets, evangelists and teachers must at this time release apostolic saints to break ground and lay hold of their own unique, diverse and rich land. Where is that land for them? Is it in the concept told them again and again? Is it in the ideal forever out of reach, keeping them hungry and dependent on leaders? Can it be in the meeting that sings of it? Is it in the revival that initiates it?

This land is in the work, this work is in the earth
and the earth, the creation, is in their desire.
It is gathered in and emerges from the desire of hearts
– heart sounding and moving with sound from the deep
   of the eternal Father
as he comes into, through and over all that good desire
   wants.
It moves towards all of creation's own wanting,
waiting in that fruit our heart sees and our desire hungers
   us for.
This land, our land, will take the seed,
it will welcome the plough that suffers its way through
   the hardness
into the soft waiting of the under earth
and it will spring up resonating with the cry of those
still breathing for release from the elements.
And we will become the fruit that others taste
as they become the fruit we joy,
gathered to each other's inheritance,
growing, reaching in vines and leaves, branches and fruit,
diverse and colour up towards the fullness.
And there – a full and wild heaven,
welcomed fires out of every atom,
rushing through every moment,
descending fire of sword in shout,
colliding in all of us,
all at once,
forever.

Bibliography

Barna, George, *Today's Pastors* (Regal Books, Gospel Light, 1993)

Bavinck, Herman, *The Doctrine of God* (Edinburgh: Banner of Truth Trust/Grand Rapids: Wm. B. Eerdmans, 1979)

Beckham, William A., *The Second Reformation: Reshaping the Church for the 21st Century* (Houston: Touch Publications, 1995)

Berkouwer, G. C., *Studies In Dogmatics: General Revelation* (Grand Rapids: Wm. B. Eerdmans, 1983)

Blaiklock, E. M., 'Ephesus' in M. C. Tenney (Gen. ed.), *The Zondervan Pictorial Encyclopedia of the Bible in Five Volumes*, Vol. 2 (Grand Rapids: Zondervan, 1978)

Brown, Colin, *The New International Dictionary of New Testament Theology*, Vol. 2 (Carlisle: Paternoster/Grand Rapids: Zondervan, 1986)

——, *Philosophy and the Christian Faith: A Historical Sketch from the Middle Ages to the Present Day* (Downers Grove: InterVarsity Press, 1968)

Bruce, F. F., *New Testament History* (New York: Doubleday, 1985)

Cranfield, C. E .B., *The International Critical Commentary: A Critical and Exegetical Commentary on The Epistle to the Romans*, Vol. II (Edinburgh: Edinburgh University Press, 1983)

Dallimore, Arnold, *George Whitefield: The Life and Times of the Great Evangelist of the Eighteenth-Century Revival*, Vols. 1

& 2 (Edinburgh/Carlisle, Pennsylvania: The Banner of Truth Trust, 1980)

Dawson, John, *Taking Our Cities for God* (Lake Mary, Florida: Creation House, 1989)

Edwards, Jonathan, *The Works of Jonathan Edwards*, Vols. 1 & 2, revised and corrected by Edward Hickman (Edinburgh/Carlisle, Pennsylvania: The Banner of Truth Trust, 1984)

Erickson, Millard J., *Christian Theology* (Grand Rapids: Baker Book House, 1985)

Geisler, Norman L., 'Panentheism' in Geisler, N. L. (ed.), *The Baker Encyclopedia of Christian Apologetics* (Grand Rapids: Baker Book House, 1998)

Grenz, J. Stanley, *A Primer on Postmodernism* (Grand Rapids: Wm. B. Eerdmans, 1996)

Grenz, J. Stanley & Olson, E. Roger, *20th Century Theology: God and the World in a Transitional Age* (Carlisle: Paternoster/Downers Grove: InterVarsity Press, 1992)

Hughes, Philip E., *2 Corinthians*, NICNT (Grand Rapids: Wm. B. Eerdmans, 1982)

Peel, William C., *Living in the Lions' Den Without Being Eaten* (Colorado: NavPress, 1994)

Regele, Mike, *Death of the Church* (Grand Rapids: Zondervan, 1997)

Ringma, Charles, *Catch the Wind: The Shape of the Church to Come – and Our Place In It* (Sutherland, Sydney: Albatross Books, 1994)

Sayers, Dorothy L., *Creed or Chaos?* (Harcourt & Brace, 1949)

Silvoso, E., *That None Should Perish* (Regal, Ventura, no date given)

Wright, N. T., *The New Testament and the People of God: Christian Origins and the Question of God* (London: SPCK/Fortress Press, Minneapolis, 1992)

* * *

Website information: www.beyondtc.com.au